LUIS *de* CAMOËNS
AND THE
Epic of the Lusiads

LUIS *de* CAMOËNS

AND THE

Epic of the Lusiads

By HENRY H. HART

Norman

UNIVERSITY OF OKLAHOMA PRESS

By HENRY H. HART

A Chinese Market
The Hundred Names
The West Chamber
Seven Hundred Chinese Proverbs
A Garden of Peonies
Venetian Adventurer
Sea Road to the Indies
Poems of the Hundred Names
Luis de Camoëns and the Epic of the Lusiads

THE PUBLICATION OF THIS VOLUME HAS BEEN AIDED
BY A GRANT FROM THE FORD FOUNDATION

Library of Congress Catalog Card Number: 62-11276

COPYRIGHT 1962 BY THE UNIVERSITY OF OKLAHOMA PRESS,
PUBLISHING DIVISION OF THE UNIVERSITY.
COMPOSED AND PRINTED AT NORMAN, OKLAHOMA, U.S.A.,
BY THE UNIVERSITY OF OKLAHOMA PRESS.
FIRST EDITION.

In memoriam patris et matris

Preface

WHILE PREPARING *Sea Road to the Indies,* a volume on the discoveries of the Portuguese in the Eastern seas, I had frequent occasion to consult *The Lusiads* of Luis de Camoëns. As I delved further into his work, my curiosity was aroused. Who might this distant relative of Vasco da Gama be? What kind of a man was he? What contribution did he make to Portuguese and world literature? To my astonishment, I discovered that no detailed account of his life or times was available in English. In fact, I found only three biographies of book length, one of them being the long-outdated two-volume *Memoirs* brought out by John Adamson in 1820, which does little more than repeat the garbled, inaccurate accounts of earlier foreign writers, with the addition of translations of some of Camoëns' lyrics, many of them spurious. The second "Life" was written by Sir Richard Burton of *The Thousand Nights and a Night* fame. This work, in two small volumes, was written in 1881, and though it contains many interesting notes and throws light on the lore of the Camoëns era, it adds but little to our knowledge, especially since Burton, along with Adamson, accepts much misinformation about the poet and uses as evidence many poems

vii

once ascribed to Camoëns but now rejected by the best authorities. Other than a very small—but valuable—volume of 105 pages (exclusive of notes) by the profound scholar of Iberian literature and historic personalities the late Aubrey F. G. Bell, published in 1923, there is little offered for the English-speaking reader seeking information about Camoëns, who is unanimously held by the Portuguese to be the greatest of their poets.

That there is a real revival of interest in the man and his works is evidenced by several recent biographies in Portuguese, Dutch, French, Spanish, and Swedish, by the publication of a sumptuous English metrical translation of *The Lusiads* by Leonard Bacon, and by an excellent prose translation of the epic by William C. Atkinson. Of the large body of Camoëns' lyrics, no adequate or complete translation exists in English, or in any language but German (by Wilhelm Storck, Paderborn, 1880–89), and many of the German renderings are only paraphrases. Burton tried his hand at translating a portion of them, but in an English so archaic that it is well-nigh incomprehensible, his work appearing in 1884. Like the German translator, he admitted hundreds of lyrics now known to be by a hand other than that of Camoëns.

I believe that a life so fascinating and adventurous that it borders on the unbelievable should be made available and its high drama presented to the modern reader.

The material used in this volume, from its very nature, ranges over half the world, much of it being buried in government archives or sixteenth-century chronicles. Histories and biographies of Camoëns' contemporaries, letters, chance remarks, and marginalia in books of the era have been drawn upon where they might throw light on the extraordinary adventures and mind of this remarkable genius.

In this work of research I have been aided immeasurably by Mr. Robert H. Haynes, assistant librarian of the Harvard College Library. I have also been given valuable assistance by Mr. S. J.

Riccardi of the New York Public Library; by Mr. Donald Coney, librarian of the University of California, and his staff; by Dr. César Pegado, librarian of the University of Coimbra; by the library staff of the Hispanic Society of America; and by Dr. Sá da Costa, one of Lisbon's learned and genial publishers.

Francis M. Rogers, professor of Romance languages and literature at Harvard University, has given encouragement and wise scholarly advice and has patiently listened to readings of the script. He has also most generously compiled for Appendix III a list of the books which were available to Camoëns in the preparation of his *Lusiads*.

To Elsa Campbell McFadden of San Francisco go my profound thanks and gratitude for her aid in the translation of the verses that appear in the book (all of which, except where noted, are mine) and for her painstaking examination of the manuscript.

To Helen Corliss Babson of Los Angeles I am indebted for a number of acute criticisms and suggestions.

My late daughter, Virginia Hart Page, was of great assistance in preparing the manuscript for the printer.

The Bibliography lists only the books actually used in the preparation of the present work.

HENRY H. HART

San Francisco
January 18, 1962

Foreword

MANY OF THE FACTS in the life of Luis de Camoëns are admittedly obscure. Even his earliest biographers—who tell the tale only by way of introduction to their editions of his work—are contradictory, or their stories are a farrago of truth and fancy, legend and invention. One must search out many of the facts in the poet's own letters, his lyrics, and his epic. Even here one is obliged to walk most circumspectly, for the sifting of the authentic events of his life from the imaginary leads one along a path beset with many gins and pitfalls.

The searcher after truth finds that legends often become facts in the hands of the early biographers and that these legends have been perpetuated—often elaborated—by later writers. Hundreds of spurious poems have been drawn upon to prove events; there is often a confusion of names and references to documents which have vanished—if they ever existed.

The residue, however, brings to us a life more adventuresome by far than that of François Villon, as chivalrous as the *Cyrano de Bergerac* of Edmond Rostand, and as replete with excitement, love, and tragedy as *The Three Musketeers* of Alexandre Dumas.

Though I may have differed at various points from the conclusions of some other writers, I have tried to eliminate doubtful episodes, as well as poems whose authorship is dubious.

To arrange most of Camoëns' lyrics chronologically has taxed the scholarship and ingenuity of many students, Portuguese and foreign. I have, as closely as the genius of the two languages permits, endeavored to give an accurate translation of the lyrics and the passages cited from *The Lusiads*. Whenever possible, I have placed these translations where, to me at least, they appear to belong or to make the best sense in point of time.

With few exceptions, Camoëns' poems bear no titles, and since no two editors admit all of the same verses to the canon of his works, the poems translated have been referred to in the notes by their first lines to facilitate identification.

If in this volume, with all its imperfections, I have been able to bring Luis de Camoëns to the attention of English-speaking readers and to have him relive for them and if by so doing I have in addition stimulated a desire to learn more of the brave little Portuguese nation and the exploits of her valiant, venturesome sons in the age of discovery, I will have been adequately rewarded.

H. H. H.

Contents

xiii

Illustrations

LUIS *de* CAMOËNS
AND THE
Epic of the Lusiads

Come hither, faithful confidant
Of the discontents whereof my life is full,
Paper, whereon I pour all my griefs.
With no reason clear,
A contrary and unbending Fate,
Deaf to all my prayers and tears,
Has dealt these blows.

       .   .   .

Let us recount this tale
To God, to men, and even to the wind,
A tale more strange
Than aught to mankind's mem'ry known.

                 —CAMOËNS, Canção "Vinde cá"

Prologue

A goode Booke is the precious life-blood of a master spirit, imbalmed and treasured up on purpose to a life beyond life.
—Milton, *Areopagitica*

Who would understand the poet, must go to the poet's land.
—Goethe

I

Once there stood in Galicia of Spain a noble castle whose lord went forth to the wars, leaving his young wife within its walls. The fighting over, the knight rode back to his castle, where he was received with joy by his lady. When he questioned his seneschal about what had taken place during his long absence, the old man hesitatingly told his suspicions of the relationship between the lady and her page. Outraged, the lord of the castle laid the accusation before his wife. Tearfully, she protested her innocence, but in silence he strode to the cage where perched his *camão*,[1]

[1] Legend, preserved for us by Greek Aristophanes and Roman Pliny, tells of a bird called by them *porphyrio* (and by the Portuguese *camão*). It was a gentle creature, of tender heart, and could not survive infidelity by the wife of its lord.

3

opened it, laid the bird in his wife's arms, and leaving the room, locked the door behind him. All through the long night the woman sat motionless, holding the bird as her lord had left it. In the morning, he came to her—and found the bird alive and well. So, goes the tale, he vaunted her pure innocence, dismissed the seneschal, and resolved that the name of the bird should be forever preserved as that of the family.

Thus runs the legend of the *camão*. The tradition persists that the family name of Luis de Camoëns was derived from this circumstance, for the plural of *camão* is *camões*. And Camoëns recounts the tale in one of his verses. So who is to deny the claim?

II

CoIMBRA, the ancient Conimbrica, lies beautiful on its hilltop on the northern bank of the river Mondego where it leaves the mountain fastnesses and hastens in a broad, peaceful stream to meet the sea.

Straggling from the shore up the slope to the University, the ancient part of the city, with its narrow, twisting lanes, its cobbled squares and arched gateways, has not greatly changed since Camoëns dwelt there more than four hundred years ago. The Old Cathedral, in which the poet so often prayed, is just as it was when he entered it from the upland square, and from the summit the same magnificent vista of hill and forest and stream still meets the eye, and the same craft shaped in the ancient Phoenician fashion still ply up and down the river.

Little is changed in the older part of the city, and near the waterside one can even now be lost in the maze of narrow streets and tiny courts, whose stone and brick houses have stood for centuries. Who would know the Portugal of the age of her great kings and discoverers and viceroys will find it in Coimbra at dusk and in the moonlight, when all that is modern fades into the background. Then one easily imagines the clank of armor, the glint of steel

4

helmet and halberd, the passing of knight and villein in doublet and hose and sweeping feathers, and there, too, one seems to hear the night watch call and to see the smoky flame of torches as they wend their way through the shadowed streets and gloomy lanes.

I

~ Eden ~

Joy is a water
Flowing limpid and clear,
But life, alas, proffers no cup!
    .   .   .
The water slips away through our fingers;
We drink but the tears
That fall from our eyes.
                    —ALBERTO DE SERPA, "Fábula"

Rejoice, O young man, in thy youth, and let thy heart cheer thee
in the days of thy youth, and walk in the ways of thine heart, and
in the sight of thine eyes; but know that for all these things God
will bring thee into judgment.
                    —Ecclesiastes 11:9

CHAPTER I

Coimbra

After crossing the Douro, Lusitania begins, and we have the town
of Coimbra.
—Pliny, *Natural History*, IV, 35

Here once were cool shade and blossoms fair,
Here water and living springs, and all things green,
And here did birds carol their songs of love.
—Sá de Miranda (1490–1558)

The year 1521 marked the zenith of the brief glory of the kingdom
of Portugal. That glory was the result of the work of Prince Henry
the Navigator, who died in 1460, the discovery of the Cape of Good
Hope by Bartholomeu Diaz in 1488, the first years following the
opening of the sea road to the Indies by Vasco da Gama in 1497,
and the conquests of Affonso de Albuquerque.

The reign of Manuel the Fortunate, who succeeded his cousin
and brother-in-law John II in 1495, had witnessed the heyday of
Portuguese power and expansion, when Lisbon was for a time the
richest city in Europe and the envy of all her neighbors. Manuel's
dominions reached from the mountains of Alemtejo to Goa in
India and even to the seas beyond, and he assumed the boastful—

9

and not too accurate—title of "King of Portugal and of the Algarves on this side of and beyond the sea, in Africa, Lord of Guinea and of the Conquests, Navigation and Commerce of Ethiopia, Arabia, Persia and India."

Now Manuel was gone, and lay in his kingly sepulcher in the Monastery of the Jeronymos in Belem, outside Lisbon, in the church erected by him to commemorate the departure of Vasco da Gama from that spot on his successful voyage of discovery.

To the casual observer, the Lusitanian kingdom was still the cynosure of all Europe, and its prosperity and eminence appeared enduring and unassailable. But all was not well beneath the surface. The great captains who had secured the empire were no longer alive. Dom Francisco de Almeida, the first viceroy of India, had died in battle with the savages in South Africa, and Affonso de Albuquerque, the real founder of Portugal's Indian empire, the warrior who had extended Portuguese conquests from Malacca to the Persian Gulf, had died embittered and disappointed in the city he had seized for his sovereign and made the capital of Portugal's Eastern possessions. With his death, decay and corruption had set in; even before Manuel had laid aside the scepter the empire was weakening, and no efforts seemed able to arrest the swift disintegration of Portugal's vast power.

After Manuel's death, John III, his son, unfit by temperament and training for the throne and greatly under the influence of his narrow-minded, bigoted Spanish queen, Catharine, was unable to cope with or even to grasp adequately the tremendous problem that imperial government presented: the expansion of a tiny agricultural kingdom of probably no more than one and one-half million souls into a world power wielding dominion over vast territories and populations in the East. Portugal's ascent to the position of a great world power had been swift, in the lifetime of a single generation, but the ineptness of her rulers, the exiguity of her population, and the greed, corruption, and cruelty of those entrusted with power overseas and at home weakened her long before she fell into the rapacious hands of Philip II of Spain in 1580. It was into this parlous state of affairs in the kingdom that Luis de Camoëns was born in the city of Lisbon at some undetermined date in the year 1524.

The Camoëns family, which was originally Gallego, had lived for generations in Camonens (now Camos) in the valley of the river Minor in Galicia, not far from Finisterre. In the civil wars which raged in Spain after the death of Alfonso XI, Vasco Perez de Camoëns, a knight, had been a partisan of Pedro the Cruel, but when Pedro was assassinated by his half-brother in 1369, Vasco was forced to flee his ancestral home and seek refuge across the Portuguese border. A poet and polished courtier, as well as a valiant soldier, he was welcomed in the little kingdom, and from him, in the passing of time, sprang several branches of the Camoëns family. Antão Vaz, the paternal grandfather of Luis, married one Dona Guiomar Vaz da Gama, and thus the poet, Luis de Camoëns, was a distant blood cousin of the famous discoverer of the sea road to the Indies, who died in the year of the poet's birth. Luis' father, Simon Vaz de Camoëns, was a *cavaleiro fidalgo* (a gentleman knight) who had married Anna de Sá e Macedo, a native of Santarem.

When Luis was three years old, the dread plague that had swept over Europe again and again, carrying off tens of thousands, reached the Portuguese capital, where it found easy victims among the dwellers in the narrow, filthy streets and dark alleys. All who could do so left the city, among them King D. John III and his court, who traveled to the ancient capital of Coimbra, where a royal palace was situated, a city which had been but lightly touched by the scourge.

The boy Luis and his parents also fled to Coimbra to seek refuge with his grandparents. It is in Coimbra, then, that we have our first real glimpse of Camoëns, just as he was passing from boyhood to adolescence.

Genius is most often unknown and unobserved until it flowers and reveals itself, and no stories or anecdotes of the young Camoëns have been preserved. We know nothing of his boyhood friends, and none of their names have been recorded. All we can glean of his youth must come from his poems, for no other documents survive.

His father returned to Lisbon after the subsidence of the plague and occupied a position as an officer of the King in the warehouse of the Casa da Guiné e India, while the boy, an only child, remained in Coimbra with his mother, living in the home of her relatives, who ocupied a prominent place in the life of the city.

That the lad grew to love the old town with a deep, intense affection which remained with him all his life is not to be wondered at by those who have sojourned there. The waters of the Mondego, flowing swiftly down from the hills of the Serra da Estrella, are so sunny and cheerful that they have been described as a "cry of joy of the river at nearing the ocean." Dark valleys, with all the mystery of the unexplored, reach like long fingers from the foothills into the mountains whence the river hurries. But the Mondego could be so turbulent at times that dikes were built to prevent the flooding of the fertile fields extending to the water's edge, leaving but a strip of clear, bright sand, where the women of the town came (as they still do) to wash their linens, spreading them to dry and bleach in the sun.

A stone bridge built by the Moors centuries earlier united Coimbra to the southern bank, where stood the great Convent of Santa Clara and, amid groves of laurel, cedar, and pine, the monasteries of Santa Anna of the Bentos and Santa Anna of the Marianas. Beyond could be seen the heights of the Louza and, to the north, the Serra de Bussaco and the far-famed Convent of the Carmelites.

Higher on the southern shore stood the grove of cedars and

orange trees where once dwelt—and was murdered—Ines de Castro, the Spanish mistress of Prince Dom Pedro, heir to the Portuguese throne, later known as Pedro the Cruel. The story of this, the most famous tragedy in Portuguese history, was woven by Camoëns into the fabric of his epic, *The Lusiads,* written long afterwards when he was living half a world and many years distant from the city where he had spent his childhood and youth.

The streets of the lower town—often flooded by winter rains—were always full of movement, as they are today. Sturdy, barefoot fisherwomen, resplendent in brightly colored skirts and embroidered kerchiefs, peddled from house to house, carrying broad, flat trays of glittering fish upon their heads, while others sold fruits, vegetables, and chickens along the cobbled lanes. There was always activity on the river, too, where rafts of pine and oak and chestnut were floated down to build the growing city and barges carried cut granite from the near-by hills and loads of red clay to the brick and tile kilns.

When approached from the south, Coimbra, with its white houses and red tile roofs, gleamed like a fairy city. It was full of gardens, whose flowers seemed to cascade down the slopes, the somber trees of the monastery of Santa Cruz accentuating the colors of the surrounding landscape, while on the steep hillsides were market squares and the Sá Velha (Old Cathedral) with its cloisters, their lower walls covered with ancient blue, orange, and dull-red tiles. In the old church in the lower town, Dom Henriquez, founder of the kingdom, and others of the royal line lay in their gloomy stone sepulchers, for the kings dwelt in Coimbra in the far-off days when the Moors still held Lisbon and the south.

The Portuguese have ever loved music, and the boy Luis must have rejoiced in the popular songs of the day and in the folk tales and romances of old Portugal recited by the washerwomen who gathered around the fountains and wells of the city and on Mondego's banks. Most often these tales were sung in sad verse and soft cadence, rude poems handed down for centuries by word of mouth, poems full of the *saudade* of the Portuguese, of which we shall hear much in the life story of Camoëns. For *saudade,* a word that defies translation, is the "sweet sadness"—*Weltschmerz* or *Sehnsucht* (here we have the German words nearest in meaning) —the wistful melancholy which Vergil called the *lacrimae rerum:* the tears that flow for the woes of the world. *Saudade* has been a strong and ever present characteristic of the Portuguese people, even when they are happiest,[1] and in one of his songs, written when life had brought him one bitter disappointment after another, Camoëns cried out with that same *saudade* in his heart, looking back to the carefree days of his youth in Coimbra:

> Que, se possivel fosse que tornasse
> O tempo para tras, como a memoria
> Por os vestigios da primeira idade![2]

The Renaissance had come late to Portugal, but under Manuel the Fortunate and his successor, John III, the wealth of the country and a newborn interest in learning attracted scholars and their books from all over Europe. The desire for a higher culture seized upon both sovereign and people. King Diniz had founded a university at Coimbra in the year 1290. Twice transferred to Lisbon, it was at last permanently established by John III at Coimbra, where it was first housed in the Monastery of Santa Cruz. There, two separate colleges were organized, one for the rich nobles, the other for the less wealthy nobility and the bourgeoisie, the two groups

[1] One has but to hear the *fados*, songs still sung in hundreds throughout Portugal today, to find *saudade* in every line, every note. *Fado* means "fate" or "fated" and perhaps is best translated "sad melancholy resignation to all the untoward in life."

[2] Canção "Vinde cá, meu tão certo secretário." The lines quoted here are translated thus:

> Oh, that it were possible to turn
> Time backward, and in memory to trace
> The footsteps of my early youth!

having separate classes and dormitories. Teachers were brought from France, Spain, Germany, England, and even from far-off Scotland,[3] a library of more than one hundred thousand books from suppressed monasteries was assembled, and the University was opened under the directorship of Diego Gouveia. In 1537, John III ordered a full program in the teaching of the humanities, and ere many years had passed, Coimbra became known in all Portugal as "the second Athens."

At the age of twelve, Luis attended the College of Arts. Two years later (the University was not returned to Coimbra until 1537), he took up his studies at the University.

Now life changed for the boy. Gone were the freedom of the streets and games in the courts and squares. He had to settle down and apply himself, for the life of a student was no easy one. Latin must be learned, not as a dead language, but as one to be written and spoken. He read widely in Ovid, Cicero, Lucan, Horace, and Vergil—in fact he appears to have covered the whole range of Latin literature. Though nowhere has he given evidence of a first-hand acquaintance with Greek, he acquired an encyclopedic knowledge of both Greek and Roman mythology (probably in Latin), and Spanish he learned so well that he wrote poems in that language as fluently and as idiomatically as though it were his mother tongue. Italian was familiar to him also, many of his poems containing either direct quotations or paraphrases of the Italian poets of the Renaissance. To all this he added history, geography, and the other humanities in the curriculum. His memory was remarkable, for his work, much of it written in India and China, where he surely had no access to more than a few books, is saturated with the results of his studies in every field. Moreover, he was fortunate in that his uncle, D. Bento de Camoëns, prior of the Monastery of Santa Cruz de Coimbra and chancellor of the

---

[3] The famous Scottish scholar George Buchanan (1506–1582) was a member of the faculty at the University of Coimbra.

University, was able to guide him in his studies, advise him in many ways, and control his temper, which early gave indications of being a violent one.

The great square of the college was surrounded on three sides by classrooms and dormitories. The fourth side was open (as it still is), with a magnificent view of the city far below, the river winding its way to the sea, the hills toward Batalha to the south, and the hazy blue mountains all about.

The discipline of the University was severe and the courses demanded much concentration, but it was traditional, when the day's work was over, for the students to wander down through the narrow, winding streets, past the tiled houses, with their projecting waterspouts and balconies overhanging the roadways, to the taverns and shops of the lower town. There they would drink and sing and play on their guitars until it was time to go back up the hill—and the curfew hour was an early one.

In thus mingling with his fellow students, Camoëns made friends of many young sons of Portugal's aristocracy. From them he acquired the ways and manners of the court, while imperceptibly, but surely, were formed in him the humanist and man of letters, the student of both action and thought. His eye and ear were sharp, the scholar within him awake and avid to learn, though experience had not yet aroused his genius.

There is no existing record of Camoëns' graduation. Gossip of the time had it that he quarreled with his uncle, the Chancellor, while others claimed that he received his degree of *Bacharel Latino* —but nowhere has the poet himself left any indication as to why he terminated his studies. There is a persistent tradition that at college he was a turbulent, rebellious, quarrelsome student, which may explain his silence concerning any possible academic reason for his leaving Coimbra for Lisbon and the great world beyond.

Not all of Luis' time was given to his books. Boys grow to maturity early in the lands of Europe's south, and four centuries ago

From Hernani Cidade, *Luís de Camões: O Lírico*, Lisboa, 1952

Luis Vaz de Camoëns, painted from life by Fernando Gomez

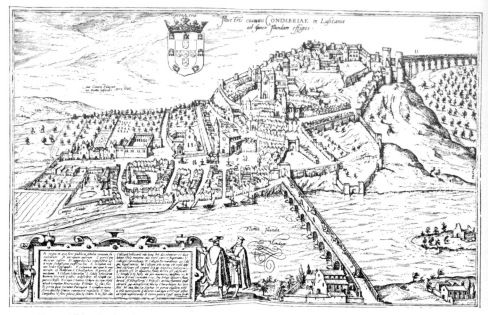

From Albino Forjaz de Sampaio (ed.), *Historia da Literatura Portuguesa,* Vol. I, Lisboa, n.d.

Coimbra in the sixteenth century

one was considered an adult sooner than he is today. Luis handsome (and probably perfectly conscious of his physical attractions), sensitive, enthusiastic, intense, undoubtedly attracted the young women about him and in turn was drawn to them. His lyrics breathe of his being always in love with love itself. And that love was the peculiarly Portuguese combination of sentimentality and a morbid outlook, an age-old cult that ever seemed to produce in the Lusitanian an intense passion combined with unhappiness and even tragedy. For the Portuguese (as witness so much of their literature) could not separate love from suffering and death, and Camoëns, a true son of his people, while often attracted by sensuous, even sensual beauty, was at the same time quixotically filled with an intense longing, a desire to be loved for love's sake, a love most often unfulfilled and by its very nature incapable of fulfillment. So, possessing, as he did, in full measure the all-pervading Portuguese *saudade,* few of his lyrics reflect a dream or even an expectation of triumphant or simple happiness to be found in love.

There lived in Coimbra John de Camoëns, a distant cousin of Luis, with his wife Branca Tavares and their daughter Isabel, and the student often visited in their home. He must have fallen in love with the young girl when she was fourteen or fifteen years of age, for his earliest verses appear to have been written in her praise—praise of her beauty, especially of her translucent green eyes. The poems seem to have made little impression on Isabel, for when an eligible young man named Alvara began to court her, she soon turned from her cousin and his suit.

Young as he was, Luis de Camoëns learned what it meant to love and not be loved. Although a man's first infatuation is not often the great love and ruling passion of his life, he usually recovers in good time. It is believed, however, that Luis' chagrin at Isabel's rejection of him was one of the contributing causes of his leaving Coimbra, although there is no documentary evidence, except that of his early poems, to explain his departure.

Luis could never forget Coimbra, where his happiest and most carefree days had been spent, and the valley of the Mondego ever remained a beautiful, unfading memory to which he could turn in dream and in song when life dealt him one misfortune after another. And Isabel de Tavares,[4] though he probably did not realize it at the time, had unwittingly awakened the muse within him, causing him to crystallize his joys and sorrows, his longings and disillusionments, in verse.[5]

From the girl who had so summarily dismissed him he turned in his verses to the scenes where his early years had been spent, bidding them farewell in the first of those pastorals[6] which are some of his most poignant lyrics:

> Clear sweet waters of Mondego,
> Stream fraught with memories dear,
> Where hopes, all false, alas,
> Did keep me blind too long,
> I leave thee,
> But fond memory clings.
> Though from thy shores I wander far,
> My heart with thee remains.
> If Fortune wills
> That this poor clay, where dwells my soul,
> Be borne by wind and wave
> To lands both new and strange,
> No change can come.
> My spirit will on wings of thought
> Fare back to thee,
> And in thy murmuring waters pure
> Shall I lave my weary soul.[7]

---

[4] Children at this time often took the name of their mother rather than that of their father.

[5] See Appendix I, Poems 5, 6, and 7.

[6] *Ibid.*, Poems 8 and 9.

[7] Soneto "Doces e claras aguas do Mondego."

This was Camoëns' farewell to Coimbra, for there is no indication that he ever returned. He went forth from his home in the university town to seek forgetfulness, and mayhap a brighter day, in Lisbon, the capital of the kingdom, far to the south.

CHAPTER II

The Road to Lisbon

—It is a goodly sight to see
What Heaven hath done for this delicious land!
What fruits of fragrance blush on every tree!
What goodly prospects o'er the hills expand!
—BYRON, *Childe Harold's Pilgrimage*, I, xv

Portugal, Europe's garden, planted by the sea
. . .
Mother-land, daughter of spring-time suns,
Rich mistress of field and orchard fruits.
—THOMAS RIBEIRO, "A Portugal"

THE ROAD from Coimbra to Lisbon led down the narrow, winding cobbled streets of the city through the Arco de Almedina, a city gate surviving from the days of the Moors, passed before the ancient church where slept the first kings of Portugal, thence down to the river's edge, over the old stone bridge thrown across the Mondego by the Moors centuries before, and up the hill on the southern bank past the Convent of Santa Clara to the crest, near the ruins of the ancient Roman city. There one had a magnificent panorama of the University town. It lay lovely in the folds of its hills; gardens and white houses with rose, green, and moss-gray tiled roofs spread like a bright carpet from the University on the heights to the pines and oaks and willows down along the river bank. Fisherfolk climbed the slopes, carrying heaped-up trays of their catch. Peasants came into the city, some riding mules, others slowly driving carts laden with fruits and vegetables. Children played at the waterside, and the washerwomen chattered as they scrubbed and spread their linen in the sun.

A journey down to the capital usually required six days. The first stretch of road was a rough one: over the mountains and through forests of great cork oaks, interspersed with fields of wheat, rye, and barley. Vineyards and orchards lay on the sunny hillsides, tiny villages nestled in the valleys, and great stone piles, castles of kings and nobles, towered on the high peaks where they could control the riverine and road traffic.

On this the main highway of the kingdom moved an ever changing, colorful, and fascinating pageant of Portuguese life. Tonsured monks, often barefoot, traveled alone or in company from shrine to shrine, while prelates rode by on horseback, followed by trains of servants and pack animals. Ragged beggars wandered from monastery to convent and from convent to monastery seeking food or alms. From time to time nobles and gentlefolk came by on gaily caparisoned prancing horses, the men in doublet and hose, the women clad in flowing many-colored robes, and the sun's rays flashed bright from helmet, spear point, and cloth of gold and silver. Workers in the fields, journeymen craftsmen going from town to town, drunken brawlers coming home from the taverns in the early morning, milkmaids carrying their buckets of foaming milk, falconers with hooded birds on their wrists, peasant girls guiding their geese with long sticks, drovers raising great clouds of dust with their cattle on the way to market, shepherds with their dogs herding sheep, woodcutters wielding their axes with ringing strokes in the forest, cutpurses, vagabonds—all of these formed a never ending procession.

The first place of consequence on the journey was Leiria, a market town on the river Liz. Here lay wide expanses of hill and valley, silent save for the thrushes singing in the olive trees and the clear notes of a church bell from the town below. Descending the slope, one could see the town sprawled beyond the river, two hills rising behind it.

On market days the place was full of the hum of voices, the cries of children, the lowing of cattle, and the crowing of fowl. Around the crowded square were displayed the produce and the wares of the countryside, just as is done today. The crowds, selling, buying, and bartering, were well ordered withal, for the Portuguese have ever been a civil, courteous, quiet-spoken folk, with dignity and respect for themselves and their neighbors.

On a hill far above the town, surrounded by groves of pines and poplars whose silence was that of a cathedral, rose the yellow-brown towers of the palace of King Diniz, built in 1324. The palace had its story, still familiar to every Portuguese. In spite of all his kindness to his people, D. Diniz, for some unknown reason, had forbidden his queen, the sainted Elizabeth, to give alms. One day he encountered her as she was on her way to visit a poor family, a great basket of food concealed beneath her cloak. "What have you there?" he demanded suspiciously. "Roses," faltered the Queen. "Let me see them," insisted the King. Terrified, but not daring to disobey, Elizabeth threw back her cloak, and lo! the crusts in the basket had changed to a great mass of fragrant red roses!

After leaving Leiria the road wound for hours through a forest, that forest which supplied much of the timber for the ships of Vasco da Gama, about whom Camoëns was to sing so eloquently in his *Lusiads*. On toward Lisbon, the next important town on the highroad was Batalha, "Battle Abbey."[1]

[1] The abbey was erected by King John I in fulfillment of a vow taken before

Within the church was the royal cloister with its three lacy marble parapets, each decorated with the armillary spheres of the arms of Portugal and the cross of the Order of Christ. Still farther on was the Incomplete Chapel (not unlike that of Henry VII in Westminster Abbey), a florid, roofless structure, where swallows nested in the niches of the arches and on the carved architraves. The heart of the abbey was the octagonal Chapel of the Founders, where in the half-light of tall stained-glass windows stood the sarcophagi of the family of Dom John I, founder of the House of Aviz. In the center of the chapel, where all was silence and peace, stood the double sepulcher of John and Philippa. The King's recumbent effigy was in full armor, his right hand clasping the right hand of his English queen. In niches around the sides of the chapel were buried their four sons, the *inclyta geração, altos Infantes*—the illustrious race, the noble heirs royal—of Camoëns' *Lusiads*. There lay Pedro, John, and Fernando—he who had passed the best years of his life as a hostage of the Moors, among whom he died. With them, in a plain, severe tomb, lay Prince Henry, known to history as the Navigator, who had inspired and guided the overseas discoveries of the Portuguese. The English blood of all four sons was attested by the insignia of the Order of the Garter and the arms of England, quartered with those of Portugal, carved on each tomb. These were the royal dead, the founders of the might of Portugal, whose lives and deeds Camoëns was later to immortalize in the verses of his great epic.

There is a high ridge between Batalha and the narrow vale where the streams of Alcoa and Baça meet, and from the summit could be seen the Cistercian Abbey of Alcobaça, surrounded for miles

going into battle with the Spanish near the village of Aljubarrota. He swore that if he were victorious—a victory which would assure Portugal independence from Spanish rule—he would build and dedicate a church to St. Mary. The battle was fought and (partly with the support of English archers and their famous cloth-yard shafts) won by D. John on August 14, 1385. It is described in Canto IV of *The Lusiads*.

about by its orchards of plums, peaches, and pears, interspersed with vineyards and melon patches. Alongside the road as it wound down into the valley were wells, where blindfolded donkeys plodded endlessly in circles, turning wheels, to the rims of which were attached earthenware jars that scooped up water and emptied it into sluices, whence it was carried off to irrigate the fields and orchards.

Facing the tiny town square stood the abbey itself, founded by Afonso Henriquez in commemoration of the capture of the stronghold of Santarem from the Moors. It was an immense structure housing over a thousand monks, some of whom in turn offered prayers night and day throughout the year, without intermission.

The church was long, high, narrow, and gloomy, its roof supported by massive close-set columns, its floor of varicolored tiles which showed the wear wrought by the tread and shuffling of countless feet through hundreds of years. Set in its walls were scores of stained-glass windows, shedding a soft, suffused light on all within the edifice.[2]

Beyond the peaceful garden of myrtles outside the sacristy and the Hall of the Kings was the Cloister of D. Diniz, also called the Cloister of Silence, a beautiful, arcaded two-story structure. But the central point of interest in the abbey was the Capella dos Tumulos, the Chapel of Tombs, where were buried Dona Ines de Castro and Dom Pedro, her lover.

The two massive sarcophagi were set foot to foot, for it was Dom Pedro's wish that when summoned on the Day of Judgment the first sight of each should be the other. The recumbent crowned figure of Ines was peaceful in her regal garments; that of D.

---

[2] These have vanished, destroyed, it is said, by the French during the Napoleonic Wars. The rare and exquisite stained glass of the great rose window over the entrance portal and the carved wood screen of the choir, famous for its beauty, were demolished at the same time. The sanctuary of the sacristy was ornamented with rows of carved and painted busts of saints, each, curiously enough, having a hollow in the breast containing jeweled relics. These were also despoiled by the invaders.

Pedro, also crowned and with a long beard curled like that of an Assyrian king, lay with stern countenance and closed eyes, his right hand grasping his sword, his favorite dog resting at his feet. At the foot of the tomb were carved two processions, each tiny figure marvelously expressing some emotion. One of the long lines depicted rejoicing souls ascending into Heaven, their arms upraised in praise and song, while the other portrayed dejected, incomparably miserable creatures descending the steep road to Hell. A crowd of spirits in Purgatory filled the remainder of the panel. At the other end, exquisitely carved, were scenes from the life of Jesus. The decoration of both sepulchers was planned and executed under the watchful eyes of Dom Pedro himself.

Some of the most beautiful verses in Camoëns' epic are those which recount the tragic tale of Ines de Castro, culminating in the grim, stately nocturnal procession from Coimbra. For the tomb at Alcobaça was the end of the long journey for the dead Ines. Here, as along the seventeen leagues from the Quinta das Lagrimas, men stood in the night in two lines with flickering torches borne aloft. Here were ranged nobles and *fidalgos* in long black cloaks, and rows of women in white mourning veils, to meet and kneel in obeisance as the solemn cortege bearing the body of Ines entered the chapel, where the corpse was placed in the casket and sarcophagus prepared for it. Here, in the Chapel of Tombs, where Dom Pedro had caused to be inscribed the words *Até a fim do mundo*,[3] his agonized last farewell, the heavy stone lid was lowered on Ines.

The road southward from Alcobaça continued on for seven leagues to Santarem on the Tagus, the birthplace of Camoëns' mother. The river swept in a broad curve at this point, and small flat-bottomed craft with brown or rust-red sails plied between the town and Lisbon, some carrying wheat and olives from the fields

[3] "Until the world comes to its end."

of Salegan, others laden with newly fired pottery for the folk of the capital. High above the town on a rocky point rose the crenelated walls of the old Moorish ramparts of Alcaçova, dominating the traffic in the river below.

Founded by the Romans and later named for Santa Irene, a martyred nun, Santarem was once the residence of kings and within its walls were many historic buildings. Here stood the ancient Church of St. John of Alporão,[4] containing the tomb of D. Duarte de Menezes.[5] Near it was the Convent of Graça, with a beautiful rose window and portal copied from Batalha, and before the altar of one of its chapels was buried Pedro Alvares Cabral, the discoverer of Brazil. In Santarem, too, were the square where the murderers of Ines de Castro had been tortured and executed and the place in the fields down by the river where Afonso, the only legitimate son of King John II, had been killed by a fall from his horse in clearing the way to the throne for Manuel the Fortunate.[6]

By water, it was but a few miles from Santarem to Lisbon. Boats were always available, and it was probably from one of the little vessels sailing down the Tagus that Camoëns first beheld the capital which he had left when a child of three.

---

[4] Now a museum.

[5] He had been killed by the Moors, and his body had never been recovered. He had, however, given his wife one of his teeth that had been extracted (some said it was one recovered from the Moors), and the tooth, in a parchment casket, was the sole occupant of the tomb.

[6] Cf. Henry H. Hart, *Sea Road to the Indies*, p. 81.

26

CHAPTER III

Lisbon

Forward, forward, Lisbon,
Since thy good fortune
Resounds throughout the world.
—Gil Vicente

And thou, noble Lisbon,
Art beyond all others
Princess of the earth,

. . .

Thou, whom the flowing seas obey.
—Camoëns, *Lusiads*, III, 51

A VESSEL APPROACHING the capital from Santarem in the first half of the sixteenth century entered a broad reach of the lower river, whose southern bank receded, while to the north loomed low hills dotted with castles and groups of houses. Then monasteries, convents, and villages lined the shore, seemingly ever closer together, finally merging into one indistinguishable mass. Next to be seen were the masts of fishing boats riding at anchor or drawn up in serried rows on the bank. Here was Lisbon, another Rome, dominating its seven hills and covering the foreshore of the estuary of the Tagus, which is its harbor. The air was ever filled with the cries of fishermen and the chanteys of workmen loading and unloading river boats. On the broad stream, out where the waters were deeper, the high-sterned galleons of the Indian fleet anchored to discharge their cargoes of spices, precious woods, and finely woven fabrics of the East, while with much creaking of ropes and shouting of men casks and bales were lowered into the hatches of other vessels preparing for their long voyage to far-off Goa—or even farther. They would return in a year and a half or two years, if they were fortunate enough to escape the perils of shipwreck, scurvy, and savage enemies, to fill the coffers of the merchants who risked their wealth in these voyages.

The water front of Lisbon was colorfully busy from early morning to sunset when ships came in from the East. Strange merchandise was there. Stacked in large piles like cordwood was sandal from India and the Islands. Ivory tusks lay in bundles on the shore, shortly to be stored in the King's own warehouses. Sacks of fragrant camphorwood, pepper, and nutmegs were carried on the shoulders of barefoot sailors and muscular, half-naked Negroes, while others of their kind unloaded musk, cinnamon, and ginger. Set apart from the heavier merchandise were bales of calicoes from the Malabar coast and silks and porcelains from China and Japan on the other side of the world, together with gold and silver tissues from the looms of Persia and northern India. Soldiers of the King stood guard over sacks of gold dust, bars of silver, and bags of pearls and precious stones, while on the shore where outgoing boats took on their cargoes stood officers enlisting young men as sailors or soldiers to go to India and the Moluccas.

Camoëns had been fortunate in securing a position in Lisbon as tutor to Antonio, son of Dom Francisco de Noronha, Count of Linares, who, having served for three years as ambassador of King John III at the court of Francis I of France, had returned to

Portugal in 1543 and was now occupying his palace in the suburb of Xabregas, on the bank of the Tagus. Thither Luis made his way.

The streets were very narrow—so narrow that a carriage could barely pass through—and people of wealth or importance rode horses or were carried in litters. Near the water front it was almost impossible to make one's way without being crushed against the walls of the houses by passing horses. In the wider roads and in the squares, little Spanish conveyances (florões) were used, and here the crowds were as motley as those along the quays: prosperous fat citizens, artisans, nobles, and fidalgos in their fine raiment, arrogantly pushing through the throng, scarred and crippled soldiers back from the wars in North Africa, bronzed sailors, slaves,[1] muleteers, fishwives, children—and everywhere beggars.[2]

The main business thoroughfare was the Via Nova, in whose arcades all things were sold. Here were found weavers, glovemakers, shoemakers, booksellers, furniture dealers, apothecaries, and a variety of shops exhibiting all sorts of wares—silks, jewelry, and Oriental importations. Here were groups of women shopping, wrapped in bright-colored cloaks, on gilded chopins, clogs of cork with soles half a palm thick, to make their wearers appear taller than they were. In the words of a French visitor: "Portuguese women are small and clean; those of high rank go without the veils worn by those of the lower class, the people of which know well how to lift them when it is to their advantage to show themselves."

In the bazaars near by were the slave blocks, where more than

[1] At the time of Camoëns' arrival in Lisbon, a great part of the population consisted of slaves.

[2] Strange as it may appear to the modern mind, the beggars of Portugal were treated as a recognized social class. They were considered necessary, that charity might have objects for its pious generosity! Beggary was a profession followed by many—the greater the number, the greater would be the glory that would redound to religion and the greater would be the honor for the monks who fed them from the great cauldrons of food daily dispensed in the monasteries.

two thousand of the poor creatures were auctioned off yearly for the Portuguese market. In Lisbon alone there were an estimated twelve thousand slaves. They were stripped naked and placed high on a block where the prospective purchaser could see them, and were inspected like horses or cattle, pinched and pummeled, their muscles flexed, their eyes and eyelids examined, their mouths forced open and their teeth scrutinized.

From the main streets, others, most of them no more than narrow, winding lanes, led to open spaces surrounded by public buildings and private dwellings. In many of these squares were fountains serving the inhabitants with water for all their domestic needs. Here people of the better classes walked or rode and, mingling with them, idly sauntered the gilded youth of Lisbon, affecting the utter boredom and melancholy which were the fashion of the day.

Arriving at the Count's home, Camoëns was received by the family. Dona Violante de Noronha was the daughter of D. Fernan Alvares de Andreade, Treasurer-General of the Crown. Born in 1522, she had married when she had scarcely reached the age of twelve; she was thus but two years older than Luis.[3] D. Francisco himself was of royal descent, the King always referring to him as *mio amado primo,* "my well-loved cousin." Their young son, Antonio, was drawn immediately to his new teacher; on his part Luis found the boy an apt pupil, and a strong and lasting friendship soon grew up between the two.

The newcomer had rare good fortune from the day of his arrival, for the family was one to whom all doors in Lisbon were open. He himself was most presentable, for his years at the University of Coimbra and his associations there had given him polished manners as well as a fine educational background, and despite some

---

[3] Before her marriage she had been a lady in waiting to Dona Maria, daughter of D. John III, who should not be confused with the Infanta D. Maria, daughter of King D. Manuel.

irregularity of features, his gold-red hair, blue eyes, great charm, and winning ways drew both men and women to him. He acquired more than the social amenities, however, for he was now a member of a household where there were constant gatherings of the most important men of the kingdom, and there the affairs of state were often the topic of conversation. Thus he could not fail to learn much of European and Indian politics and to hear discussions of history, literature, and the arts.

The work with the boy Antonio he probably found most congenial. The shelves of the large, comfortable library were, we may be sure, well stocked with the classics of the time, and during his many hours of leisure he could not only renew his acquaintance with the books of his college years, but read—and read widely and deeply—in the finest literature available. Here he could become familiar with the romances of chivalry and the writers of the Renaissance. History, too, he could study, in addition to the chronicles of the kings of Portugal, tales of war and discoveries in unknown seas and savage lands. All this was stored in his fertile mind, later to find expression in epic and lyric verse. Then, too, he was privileged to have the friendship of D. Francisco's secretary and adviser, Francisco de Moraes,[4] whose life had been an exciting and

[4] While in Paris with Count Noronha, Francisco de Moraes became infatuated with Mlle. Torcy, a lady in waiting to Queen Leonor (the widow of the Portuguese King Manuel). She was much his junior and in no way returned his affection. His folly was unbridled, and though he hardly spoke her language, he fell on his knees and poured out his love to his inamorata in the presence of the Queen and the court, covering Mlle. Torcy (known as La Belle) with embarrassment and himself with ridicule. By the time Camoëns met him in the palace of D. Francisco, he was cured of his passion and was busily writing his *Cronica de Palmeirim de Inglaterra*, a prose romance of chivalry which was to make him famous. He later became treasurer to D. John III, took a Portuguese wife, and returned to France on a royal mission. The last years of his life are hidden in obscurity, but it is known that he was stabbed to death one day as he entered the Rocio (the central square) of the city of Evora. Though the dedication of the *Palmeirim* (to the Infanta D. Maria) is dated 1544, the first known edition is that of 1567.

venturesome one, and from him the poet could learn much of court life in both France and Portugal.

Not all of young Camoëns' time and energy was spent among the leather and vellum tomes and manuscripts of the Noronha library. He was still a youth, and women attracted him mightily. He seems to have lost his susceptible heart even to D. Violante, wife of his employer, but his professed love never went further than the writing of two poems.[5]

One of the favorite amusements of Lisbon society was the composing of verse in imitation of Italian forms and in meters native to Portugal. Often there were contests in the writing of poetry: giving a theme to one of the young gallants and challenging him to write lines interpreting it. In such contests, the development of a given line into a poem, Luis became adept, and he was soon sought after for these light verses, whose forms he mastered early in his studies and in the writing of which he soon surpassed all others at the court of D. John.[6] This facility of poetic expression caused him to turn more and more to the making of verse. Saturated as he was with the classics, he wrote many poems on mythological subjects and on themes other than his loves, though the latter seemed to be foremost in his mind.

His thoughts reverted often to the scenes so vividly impressed on him during the long journey from Coimbra, and from time to time he wrote stanzas in an effort to recapture the beauty of the landscapes. These verses he preserved, and many of them he later wove into longer poems. One was of a sunrise:

> Now early dawn with palest rose endued,
> Draws near to ope the eastern gates,
> And drives from the highest mountain peaks

[5] See Appendix I, Poems 11 and 12.
[6] *Ibid.*, Poems 13, 14, 15, and 16.

Black darkness, enemy of light.
The restless sun, enamored of the morn,
Pursues with fierce and fiery steeds,
Spreading his glory o'er the world
In pure, warmth-giving radiant light,
While birds, new-wakened from their sleep
From branch to branch in joyance dart,
And with sweet and gladsome melody
Herald the coming of the day.[7]

A stanza from the earliest of his philosophic poems, far removed
from his own personal experiences, evidences the profound influence of his favorite Latin poets, Horace and Vergil:

Happy the man whose dreams soar not too high
And who asks not to know the things beyond his ken,
Who leads his flock beside the cooling stream
And accepts with joy the simple fare they yield.
The turns of fortune's wheel affect him not;
He has but one regret—that life is short.
He sees the dawn rise rosy in the east
And the spring's unfailing waters at his feet,
Yet never questions whence the rivers flow,
Nor who guides the sun at eve beneath earth's brim.
He plays his pipes beside the grazing flock,
And to him are all the mountain herbs well known.
He does not seek to learn the secrets of the world,
But accepts his God with simple, quiet faith.[8]

Thus far in Lisbon, Camoëns' life had been fairly calm. His love
for Isabel Tavares had been, after all, a boy-and-girl affair which,
though at the time it seemed to him deeply tragic, had evidently
been quickly healed by his journey and the busy, exciting, and
pleasant life that had awaited him in the capital. Like other young

---

7 Canção "Já a roxa manhã clara."
8 Oitava "Quem pode ser no mundo tão quieto."

men of his class in Lisbon, he appears to have been rather casual in his relations with women, moving from one not-too-serious an affair to another, but his heart had not been deeply touched. Now, through an unforeseen incident, the whole course of his life was to be changed.

CHAPTER IV

Catherine

My lady,
If some jealous god should snatch thee from my sight
In all thy loveliness of snow and rose,
And no longer might I see those eyes
Whose splendor is the sun's despair,
Never could he tear thy image from my heart,
So sealed and dedicate to thee.
There it is and there it stands,
Impregnable 'gainst all assaults of fate.
            —CAMOËNS, Soneto "Senhora minha"

Oh, would that one knew
Whence love doth spring,
Or what seeds that same love doth sow!
            —Old Portuguese Folk Song

ON GOOD FRIDAY, April 13, 1544, Camoëns attended Mass at the
newly built Church of the Chagas.[1] Taking his place in the

---

[1] It received its name from the confraternity which founded it: a group of mari-
ners who sailed in the fleets to the Indies and Brazil. They had taken for their group
the name of *Chagas de Jesus*, "The Wounds of Jesus," and the church was called
"The Church of the Wounds."

crowded section reserved for the nobility and gentlefolk, he looked about him, and suddenly his eyes encountered those of a young, golden-haired girl. The first glance made such a profound and stirring impression that (as he wrote in his earliest poem in her praise) she appeared "an angel fair" in the half-light, the glow of the candles, and the drifting wisps of incense smoke. He was so fascinated, so oblivious to all else about him, so full of the vision that his thoughts formed themselves into impassioned lines of poetry.[2] That day he wrote the first sonnet for the woman his love for whom was to move him so deeply that throughout the vicissitudes of his life he would never forget her:

> All heads were bowed in reverence
> In humble worship of our Lord,
> And before His holy presence
> Lips moved in silent prayer.
> Until that hour was my heart my own
> And straight and open was my path,
> When of a sudden two eyes met mine,
> Eyes, alas, too high for me to look upon.
> Before me knelt an angel fair,
> All radiance, charm and grace.
> The vision struck me wholly blind,
> And reason fled my brain.
> Ah, Nature, mother of mankind,
> Why are some born of high degree
> And some of low estate?
> Will there never in this wide world be
> A righting of this wrong?[3]

[2] The striking resemblance of these verses to Petrarch's third sonnet to Laura indicates that Camoës had an intimate acquaintance with Petrarch's poetry. Not only the ideas but even some of the phraseology closely follow those of the Italian, who saw Laura for the first time in church on Good Friday, 1327: "Era il giorno ch'al sol si scoloraro . . . ." (It was the day when the sun's rays paled in pity for their Lord, when I was made captive—and drew not back—by your beautiful eyes, my lady.)

Saudade! Even in the enthusiasm of his sudden infatuation there seems to have crept into the last lines of the sonnet a shadow, a premonition that this love would not end in happiness. And his entire life answered the question in those last lines. For him there was to be no righting of the wrong.

During the days that followed, there appears to have come to Camoëns a spiritual awareness and fervor—a mystical inspiration not unlike that which had moved Dante to write as he did of Beatrice. And though, like Dante, he was to know earthly love for other women, so, too, like Dante, the vision of the young girl was to remain the guiding influence in his life, for in her he was convinced that he had found the perfect flower of spiritual love.

He again saw the unknown girl at Mass and was able to learn her name. She was Catherine de Ataide—daughter of D. Antonio de Lima, *mordomo-mór* of the Infante D. Duarte, and D. Maria Bocanegra, a gentlewoman of Spanish birth and lady in waiting to the Queen—and she was just fourteen years old.[4]

She so occupied Camoëns' thoughts that he composed poem after poem[5] for her; indeed, she seems to have taken complete possession of his being. Finally, we know not how, he received a formal introduction to her. The attraction was evidently mutual, and it would appear that he presented her with some of his verses. In this fashion began the romance of Luis de Camoëns and Catherine de Ataide, a romance that was to bring lasting happiness to neither.

The court of John III of Portugal was a strange one for an empire which was seemingly at the peak of its power and wealth. Instead of the brilliant social life and the galaxy of talent and wit that

---

[3] Soneto "Todas as almas tristes se mostravam."

[4] Women married young in sixteenth-century Portugal. We must remember that D. Violante had married at twelve, and "Aonia," the beloved of the romantic writer Bernardim Ribeiro (1482–1552), was but thirteen.

[5] See Appendix I, Poems 17 and 22.

might have been expected around the throne, the atmosphere was chill and gloomy: an atmosphere that seemed to emanate from the sovereigns themselves, an outlook that definitely stamped them as opposed to light or cheerful thought or, indeed, to too much interest in the affairs of this world, for both King and Queen were an unnatural, abnormal combination of smug pietism, bigotry, and moroseness. This attitude was communicated to those around them, and but increased the Portuguese tendency to excessive sentimentality and *saudade*. In fact, it influenced the literature of the era to such an extent that few happy, light-hearted verses were written, and most of what we have (save the folk songs) are lugubrious, despondent, pessimistic, even tragic.

D. John himself, called the Pious, had no taste for magnificence or display. His Spanish queen, Catharine, was the daughter of Juana la Loca (Joan the Mad) and granddaughter of Ferdinand and Isabela the Catholic, her father being Philip the Fair of Burgundy. She was a posthumous child, born on that weird funeral journey during which Juana was conveying her husband's body to Granada for interment. The strange melancholy and idiosyncracies of her mother and the somber and oppressive environment of Catharine's childhood had contributed much to the shaping of her austerity and religious intolerance, and moreover, she brought to her adopted country all the bitter fanaticism of the court of Spain. This, together with her powerful influence over an incompetent husband, had much to do with the molding of D. John's policy of religious intolerance and his encouragement of the dread Inquisition.

The rigid rules of conduct imposed upon his court by D. John III cast a sickly pallor over the young lives caught up in it. One feared the consequences of the slightest misstep, for dire punishment had already been visited on those who violated their dictates.[6]

[6] D. John was even inclined to introduce into his kingdom the traditional Moorish seclusion of women. A friend of Camoëns (to whom he had addressed verses),

John and Catharine had surrounded themselves with a dreary, severe, solemn majesty, frowning on all that seemed to them to savor, even in the slightest, of frivolity, for a ruler who favored and encouraged the Inquisition found it easy to adjudge love a

John Lopes Leitão, a royal lance-bearer, was imprisoned for imprudently looking at women through a palace keyhole. The poet Falcão (an illegitimate son), who became a *moço fidalgo* (page) and whom Camoëns met shortly after entering D. Francisco's service, became enamored of one D. Maria Brandão, though she was but eleven and he not even fourteen. They married clandestinely, but the secret could not long be concealed. Maria's parents immediately had her confined in the austere Cistercian Convent of Lorvão as punishment, an annulment of the marriage was obtained by her father, and shortly thereafter she was married off to a more eligible person, to whom she bore three sons. The luckless Falcão was imprisoned for five years, during which time he wrote his celebrated eclogue, the "Trovas de Crisfal," in which he sang of his sad amour. At the end of the five years he was shipped off to India, where he died, unmarried, but leaving in his turn an illegitimate son. These are but two of many tales of the difficulties encountered by young lovers in the court of D. John III.

Times had changed since King D. Manuel was wont to be rowed, in a barge draped with rich tapestries, on the river to the sound of sweet music. No longer were the courtiers and foreigners of high degree sumptuously entertained at the palace, but even the long-faced pietism of King John and his queen could not entirely suppress the customary feasts and celebrations of the *terreiro* (now the Praça de Comercio). However, at times a far grimmer and more portentous display crowded the place. At frequent intervals an altar was erected and an awning stretched over part of the area, for since D. John favored the Inquisition and gave it both protection and encouragement in its nefarious work, here were held the solemn processions of the autos-da-fé.

The chronicles of the period throw scant light on the arrangement or furnishings of the palace, but a description of a royal dinner of the times has come down to us (see Elkan Nathan Adler's *Jewish Travelers*). In 1525 there appeared at court a swarthy impostor, Reubeni by name, a dwarf in Oriental costume, who claimed to be the ambassador from a (non-existent) kingdom in Arabia, while in Egypt he claimed to be a descendant of Mohammed. Reubeni (or his secretary) kept a diary, which is preserved in the Bodleian Library at Oxford, and in it is given a fascinating picture of a royal dinner at which he was present:

> I went to the palace and saw how they prepared the table for him [the king] and all things too numerous to mention. I saw on the table great and small bowls of silver . . . and the large vessel from which he drinks water is of gold . . . all the lords stood before the king, each one with his cap in his hand.

39

crime. The women of the court were virtually cloistered, the sovereigns even arrogating to themselves the choice of husbands for them—and there was no appeal from these decisions. Luis surely

---

And the boys of ten years of age and upwards and some of the lords were before the king round his table, each on his knee, bowing. The king has four officers, each of whom has a rod in his hand with which they strike and keep off the crowd before the king, for the fear of the king is over all the people. . . . They were blowing with trumpets and playing all kinds of musical instruments, and the king sat at the head of the table, and his three brothers behind him, and they gave him a great basin of silver for him to wash his hands, and the ewer in which the water was contained was of gold. Two of his brothers stood up and bowed before the king, and they kissed the silver basin before the king washed his hands in it. The third brother of the king, who was the Cardinal, bowed before him and kissed the basin after he had washed. And there was a lamb killed, but not by the knife. They removed its stomach, but the lamb was entire from head to feet and had golden horns. They also placed on the table four pigs, entire from head to feet, and many birds, and they removed the former from the table and put on the latter. They cut for the king all kinds of meat and he ate a little from each kind. And so they did for his brothers, for each of them had servants by the table— Afterwards they gave whole fruits to him by himself and to his brothers by themselves, and gave them sweets and many things. Then they removed the cloths from the table, and the king stood up near it, and the priests blessed him, while all the people bowed low.

As the years passed, John turned more and more toward religion, finally becoming a fanatic, taking a far greater interest in ecclesiastical matters than affairs of state. Strangely enough, combined with his fanaticism was an unbridled desire for women, by several of whom he had children. His conduct as a young man became so notorious that his family decided that he must marry, selecting as his bride Catharine, sister of Charles V of Spain (1525).

While both the King and the people appeared on the surface deeply religious, the state of morality in Portugal was deplorable. Justice was bought and sold in both secular and ecclesiastical courts, and the country swarmed with rascals who lived—and lived well—by their wits alone. Robbery and violence were common. Extravagance increased beyond belief; the palaces of nobles and courtiers were crowded with innumerable unnecessary servants, to such an extent that there was a scarcity of labor both in the cities and on the farms. Portugal's greatest historian (Alexandre Herculano) plainly states that "any journey made by the king was a genuine scourge for the people through whose district he travelled. His immense retinue of parasites . . . devoured the substance of landowners and farmers. Pro-

knew of this attitude of King John and Queen Catharine, but he evidently ignored it, for he dared to write and circulate a sonnet in answer to a trifling gift from Catherine:

Fair woven fillet that I hold
As pledge for that love which is my due,
If now, in seeing thee, I lose my mind,
What destruction would those tresses wreak,
—Which might the sun disdain?
I know not if thou art answer to my prayer
Or with design to break my heart
Thou wert thus given me.

Fair woven fillet in my hand,
I hold thee close, so dear to me,
A solace in my loneliness.
And if no further healing comes,
Tell her in code to lovers known
This part of her I now accept,
Who mayhap can win no more.[7]

Meanwhile he continued to write graceful "society verses" with astonishing adroitness and felicity, and was becoming known for his poetry even in the inner court circle around Dona Maria, daughter of the late King Manuel. The court had an intense interest in the writing and reading of poetry, and some of what he wrote must have fallen into the hands of men and women who recog-

---

visions, horses, carriages—everything was seized—the robbers either not paying at all, or else giving worthless promissory notes! Members of the royal entourage often found their amusement in wantonly burning or otherwise destroying crops, estates and forests. But if in secular matters the kingdom was in such dire straits, things were no better on the ecclesiastical side. The higher clergy for the most part, cared only for the enjoyment of their revenues, and through their neglect the people were often forced to forgo the services of the churches and the administering of the sacraments. Even the Order of Christ was scandal-ridden and a hotbed of corruption."

7 Soneto "Lindo e subtil trançado que ficaste."

nized in this unknown young gentleman-scholar from Coimbra, a poet, a writer far above the poetasters who frequented the circles of the rich and mighty of the kingdom. And Luis, flattered by the increasing attention paid him, was nothing loath to exhibit his talents in influential quarters. So he wrote *redondilha* after *redondilha*, sonnet after sonnet, together with *sextinas, oitavas,* and all the other forms of verse that were currently the favorites at court.[8] But his talent and charm won him many enemies as well, for there were gossips—small, mean men who were jealous of one who gave so much promise, one who might threaten their own positions—and even this early in his career Camoëns began to feel their antagonism. Moreover, his facile success in verse and the ease with which he had found a place in Lisbon society increased the self-assurance and assertiveness that were his. He was quick with tongue and sword; men were wary of both, and loved him none the more for it—and his strutting and easy conquests of young women with his verses and physical charm were to cost him dearly.

There were some bright spots in the picture, however, and Luis, not interested in politics, nor seeking any part in them, turned to the literary groups, whose activities seemed propitious for his advancement.

For some time after meeting Catherine de Ataide the poet was content to send her verses declaring his love, without confiding in anyone. But his impulsive nature could not long be restrained, and, becoming bolder, he turned to his employer[9] for assistance in his suit. He did this in a long, rambling eclogue full of flowery devices—classical references and strained effects, all of which betrayed his youth and inexperience—but with all its faults, it was far superior to much of the work of his contemporaries. It was in this poem that he gave the first intimation, though vague, of his determination to write the saga of Portugal's heroes.

[8] See Appendix I, Poems 23, 24, 25, and 26.
[9] *Ibid.*, Poem 27—only partially quoted.

When the stanzas were circulated (together with others of his poems), they aroused interest and curiosity in the salons of the court and soon brought invitations to social gatherings. Even though he was poor, his talents were a key to the doors of King John's courtiers—as long as he did not appear to them to be ambitious or seeking royal favors. At these assemblies the poet often met young women, many of them charming, sophisticated, and well versed in flirting and in flattering susceptible, simple young men. In the phrase of one writer, "their most dangerous weapons were always the veil, the fan and the rosary—and they used all three with devastating effect." His head was turned: he fluttered around the young beauties of the court like a moth around a flame —and, it is to be feared, his wings were sometimes singed, as he himself confesses in one of his poems.[10]

He was enamored of this new life, its luxurious surroundings, its atmosphere of perfume and silks, of music and dancing, of brilliant conversation and congenial companions. Here, too, he met famous writers, among them Bernardim Ribeiro, secretary to King John, a *cavaleiro fidalgo* like himself and a man whose romances he had read. Two others were Sá de Miranda[11] and Jorge de Montemôr. The latter, however, wrote, for the most part, in Castilian and later departed for Spain, where he became a musician and singer in the royal chapel.[12] Another welcomed at court for his contribution was Pero de Andrade Caminha of Oporto, though his poetry, when analyzed, was cold, artificial, and devoid of music or lofty thought. He had read some of Camoëns' work, was envious of what were (he must have acknowledged to himself) far better lines than he himself could write, and took a violent

---

[10] *Ibid.*, Poem 28.

[11] One of the three most famous Portuguese poets (1465–1536).

[12] Many of these men, some of them Portugal's sweetest singers, suffered tragic fates. Ribeiro lost his reason because of an unfortunate love affair, and Montemôr, after serving as a soldier in Holland, was killed in a duel in Turin, Italy.

43

aversion to the younger man—a hatred which endured throughout Luis' lifetime. Caminha wielded a sharp and acid pen, assailed Camoëns in various epigrams, and in later years lampooned stanzas of *The Lusiads*. In fact, he never missed an opportunity of attacking both Luis and his work, either openly or by innuendo, finally succeeding in alienating many of the poet's acquaintances. However, despite this and other antagonisms, Camoëns continued to write and to be read with admiration and approval, until, as a contemporary declared, he was "Apollo among the Muses."

Finally the reputation of Luis' verse reached the ears of the most famous Portuguese intellectual of the day, the Infanta Dona Maria, daughter of the late King Manuel, who became interested in his work and invited him to her salon. It was in reality a command, one which he obeyed with alacrity.[13]

D. Maria had received an education far above that which was customary for the women of her generation, for not only was she well versed in Latin, history, and literature, but she was also passionately fond of music, the dance, and the arts. At the time Camoëns met her, she was described by a contemporary as "white as a lily, her hair blonde with coppery reflections, her figure tall and majestic as the divine Juno between her peacocks, her head Olympian, her mouth fine, with no sign of the underlip of the Hapsburgs. Her eyes were of a limpid blue, sad, intelligent, keen. Their expression [was] at the same time proud and gentle." She was the despair of all who came to Portugal to paint her portrait,

---

[13] Manuel the Fortunate married three times. By his first wife he had a son who died in infancy. By his second wife he had ten children, one of whom became D. John III. By his third he had two children, the younger of whom was the Infanta D. Maria. She was born on June 8, 1521, six months before the death of her father. When D. Maria was but two years old, her mother, D. Leonor, left her children in Portugal and proceeded to France, where she became the wife of Francis I. Mother and daughter did not meet again for thirty-five years, when they were together for a short time before D. Leonor's death.

for it was the custom, when royal matches were negotiated, to send a picture of the woman to her prospective husband.[14]

The princess had surrounded herself with brilliant women, and her salon inspired, encouraged, and criticized. By its praise or condemnation it could make or destroy the reputations of the writers, musicians, and poets of the kingdom.

The interview with Luis was short; it appears to have consisted merely of a few words of commendation on his work. It was enough, however, to inspire several poems.[15]

Although its inner circle was probably barred to the poet, the court permitted its womenfolk to submit subjects to various writers, asking them to compose verses demonstrating their talent and versatility, and it is to this practice that we owe a large number of Camoëns' *redondilhas,* sonnets, and other poems. After the lines were submitted and the stanzas written, they were passed from person to person, from the *camareira-mór* (chief lady of the bedchamber) to the *mordomo* (lord steward of the royal household), who conveyed them to the lady for whom they were written.

---

[14] D. Maria was finally known as *sempre noiva,* "always betrothed," for though several royal marriages were arranged for her, they failed to materialize and she died a spinster. In existing portraits she appears as a pale, rather cold blonde, with a long, thin face and sad eyes, her hair caught up in a net of pearls and her throat adorned with a pearl necklace. The strict etiquette and gallantry of the court at Lisbon and D. Maria's exalted and isolated position as half-sister of King John shut her off from much of the life about her. She was a pawn in the game of princes, and her hand was often offered and sought because of her wealth—she was the richest princess in Europe—and her value in creating or strengthening alliances with foreign potentates. History has accented her wisdom more than her beauty and gentleness of character. Contemporary Portuguese chroniclers showered her with flattering epithets. "Flower and honor of princesses," "splendor of purity," "first of Portuguese women," "untouched flower of virginity," "model of chastity," "Minerva of her century," "beautiful Minerva," "a phoenix in her prudence and singular understanding of all facts," "most erudite"—these were but some of the expressions used in writing of her.

[15] See Appendix I, Poem 29.

45

She, in turn, placed them unopened in the hands of the Queen, who broke the seals, read, censored, or commented on them. If they passed her severe scrutiny, the one to whom they were addressed finally received them. From the very nature of their contents, however, a number of Luis' verses were surely never subjected to this scrutiny, since he, like other writers, could contrive to convey his lines in divers ways directly to the persons for whom they were intended. Moreover, probably many such verses were addressed, in the manner of Horace, to fictitious women, and never left the poet's hands, being in some way preserved until after his death. However, such as reached the ladies of the court were read and passed around, that others might enjoy and discuss them, thus making Camoëns, young as he was, better known in literary circles in Lisbon than he could otherwise have been.

In spite of his devotion to Catherine de Ataide,[16] Camoëns could not control his nature, that nature which seems ever to have craved physical nearness to a woman. Conquests of those who were flattered by his verses or won by his impetuous, impassioned charm were undoubtedly his, but, contradictory as it might appear, he still sought an ideal love that could be a reality. When perchance there came to him a sense of guilt in this taking to himself these light-o'-loves, he shrugged it off, pitifully, with the old proverb *Asno que tem fome, cardos come.*[17]

One day, a request for a poem was delivered to Luis by a servant of the palace. It was from Dona Francisca de Aragon, daughter of Nuno Rodrigues Barreto and Leonor de Nilan and favorite lady in waiting of Queen Catharine. Blonde, beautiful, and clever, D. Francisca was the envy of all the women of the court, whom she outshone in charm and intellectual alertness. Though she could have been the most sought-after young woman[18] in the pal-

---

[16] *Ibid.*, Poem 30.

[17] "A donkey who is hungry will eat thistles."

[18] She was just fifteen years old when Camoëns met her. Twenty years after

46

ace, the queen guarded her from those who desired to form close friendships. The poets of Lisbon strove to outdo each other in praising her, and D. Manuel de Portugal, Montemôr, and others wrote tributes to her beauty in both Portuguese and Spanish. Caminha, too, wrote an ode of twenty-four strophes, calling her "Francisca of the pure blood and lineage of the famous kings of Aragon—one whose smile stirs all souls and conquers all spirits." This was the young woman who from her exalted station had requested verses from Camoëns.

No offense was taken at the extravagant lines, with their protestations of love, that Luis sent her.[19] Such poems were current at court and were accepted only at their face value, judged for rhyme, rhythm, and the clever turn of a phrase. And D. Francisca, not for a moment believing that the poet was serious in his verses, sent other requests, with the approval of the queen. Luis, however, forgetting Catherine for the moment, believed that he had found in D. Francisca the youth, beauty, and spirit of all women. In the words of a Portuguese essayist, "he, a bee, dazed and drunken with perfume, kissed all flowers in a single blossom," and sent her poem after poem.

Camoëns had left the court, D. John de Borja, the Lisbon agent of the Spanish king, wrote a letter concerning her, the only description known to us:

> D. Francisca de Aragon . . . has been in the house of the queen of Portugal since her early youth. She is the lady most valued by Her Majesty, and is even more highly esteemed for her knowledge, vivacity and beauty. She is the person for whom the queen shows the greatest affection. Each time the *camareira mór* goes to lunch or dinner she goes alone to attend the queen, for the latter enjoys her conversation, since she is clever at it, and has a quick tongue. She is held the woman best versed in the duties of lady-in-waiting of our time in Portugal, and we are assured that she could conduct a school for training ladies-in-waiting because of the way she serves the queen.

In 1576, reasons of state caused Queen Catharine, sister of Charles V, to marry D. Francisca to D. John de Borja.

[19] See Appendix I, Poems 30, 31, and 35.

47

To the gallantry in all these verses D. Francisca was anything but responsive. Though young in years, she was a sophisticated woman, and Luis, hardly out of his teens, stirred her heart in no way. One of his poems was a sonnet such as no woman had probably ever received. It was a strange poem—geological, as it were—for most of the metaphors were of the mineral world:

> With stone, hard stone, and metal
> Hast thou encased thy soul.
> Thy tresses are of purest gold,
> And marble is thy brow of stainless white.
> Thine eyes are emeralds, pools of shadows,
> And garnet are thy cheeks.
> Thy lips of rubies without price are carven;
> Thy teeth are strands of faultless pearls.
> Thy hands are from the smoothest ivory fashioned,
> And translucent alabaster is thy throat,
> Where one may trace, like ivy-tendrils,
> The polished deep-blue lapis of thy veins.
> But what holds me most in awe and adoration
> Is to know that, though all else be stone,
> The heart within thy breast, my own beloved,
> Is as a diamond, flawless, chaste and pure.[20]

Although his verses were most graciously accepted, D. Francisca herself decided that Luis was going rather far, though she probably saw him as he really was: a sensitive, high-strung young man, whose poetry came from his heart, inspired by a woman far above him socially. She summoned him, explaining matters as best she could, and proffered her sincere friendship.[21] This Camoëns accepted gratefully, although, unfortunately even this rejection

[20] Soneto "De piedra, de metal, de cosa dura."

[21] The friendship pledged by D. Francisca, who lived to be more than eighty, was Camoëns' treasured possession through life.

From Visconde de Juromenha (ed.), *Obras de Luiz de Camões*, Vol. II, Lisboa, 1861

The signature of Catherine de Ataide

From Jaime Cortesão (ed.), *História da Colonização Portuguesa do Brasil,* Vol. I, Porto, 1921

Lisbon in the sixteenth century

as a lover was not sufficient to awaken him fully to mature thinking, for he still retained the assurance, even the brashness, of youth.

The months passed, and Camoëns had been in Lisbon more than
three years. His relations with the family of D. Francisco de
Noronha seem to have been uniformly happy. He had gained an
entry into the aristocratic circles of Lisbon society and had established his reputation by sheer genius. As he later proudly declared
in his *Lusiads,* he had achieved this

> Not leaning on ancestral lineage
> Or noble pedigree

but through his own efforts—he who had come to the capital an
unknown lad from provincial Coimbra. But it was not enough
to have mastered the meters and modes of Italy and of his own
Portugal. He was now attracted to the drama, which had not yet
taken a significant place in his country's cultural life. Few Portuguese had written for the stage before the time of the great Gil
Vicente, and none of importance had followed him. Seeking a
new medium in which to exercise his talents, Camoëns resolved
that he, too, would essay the writing of dramas and become known
as a playwright as well as a poet. Entirely inexperienced, except
for some youthful efforts, he selected a classic drama, adapting
its plot and dialogue to meet the ideas and fashions of his own day.
He had read Plautus (251?–184 B.C.) in the original Latin (or perhaps in the Spanish version of Villalobos or the Italian of Ludovico
Dace), and he now turned to that Roman writer of comedies,
whose works were no doubt easily obtained in one of the book-
shops of the capital,[22] for inspiration in his new venture.

[22] Portugal had not only been importing books but had set up its own printing
presses as early as 1489. At least the first dated book, a Hebrew commentary on the
Pentateuch, appeared in that year. Thereafter many books were published, both in

49

The play was finished at last. He had written a sketch of the comedy during his college days at Coimbra and had acted in it with some of his fellow students. This, however, was a revised version containing many timely references. Entitled *Enfatriões* or *Amphytrion,* it was written in *redondilha* form, the dialogue partly in Portuguese, partly in Castilian, the latter, of course, being understood by all educated men and women.[23] When the comedy was produced, it met with immediate popularity, adding to the reputation which Luis was acquiring in the capital.

After the successful performance of *Amphytrion,* he was besieged more than ever for verses, until he found difficulty in refusing innumerable requests.[24] Meanwhile, his courting of Catherine with verses[25] continued. Once more she managed to send him a token of her affection—a crystal phial. He acknowledged it in impassioned lines that have been preserved:

> This crystal phial enwrapped in silk,
> Rose-adorned
> And bound with tress of fine-spun gold
> Is to me a gift divine,
> Wrought by the hand of fairest nymph,

Lisbon and in other Portuguese cities, in Portuguese, Hebrew, Latin, and Spanish, thus supplying abundant material to those who were able to read.

It must be remembered that, especially after the expulsion of the Jews from Spain in 1492, Portugal had a large, cultured Hebrew population, at least until orders of expulsion were issued by Manuel I.

An examination of the monumental *Livros Antigos Portuguezes* (three magnificently illustrated quartos) of the late exiled King Manuel II or of Américo Cortez Pinto's *Da Famosa Arte da Imprimissão* will throw much light on this little-studied subject.

[23] The plot was farcical—the story of Amphytrio and his wife, Alemena. While Amphytrio was away fighting in a war, Jupiter, disguising himself as her husband, seduced Alemena, that she might give birth to Hercules. The play, in which much of the comedy is based on mistaken identities, is in no way a plagiarism of Plautus.

[24] See Appendix I, Poems 44 and 45.

[25] *Ibid.,* Poems 39 and 43.

More gracious than the ruby blush of dawn
This slender phial is a symbol of your finely
    moulded form,
The silk is like unto the texture of your skin,
The tress, light fetter
That with ease
My freedom does enchain.[26]

So he lived on in his fool's paradise, and during these happy
days he wrote some of his light-hearted songs.[27] In one of them he
avowed his undying affection for Catherine in an acrostic, the initial letters forming the words, in Portuguese, "yours as a captive":

Myself have I yielded unto love;
My life as well I give,
Eager to serve, a willing slave,
Content with this great good,
Wounded, despairing a thousand times,
To attain your heart, to win your love,
So cherished, so sublime.
Praised be the day! praised be the hour
When your love was granted me!
I forswear all else,
Vowed to this single love,
In constancy to live and die,
To be worthy of your hand.[28]

Another of his charming lyrics summons the whole world to
witness his love:

My song of love I shall so sweetly sing,
In such phrase and sentence softly harmonized,
That e'en the heart that never passion stirred

---

[26] Soneto "El vaso reluziente y cristalino."

[27] See Appendix I, Poem 37.

[28] Soneto "Vencido está de Amor meu pensamento." In the original Portuguese
acrostic, the initial letters form the words *vos[s]o como cativo.*

Will waken and beat faster when it hears.
I shall recite love's gladness and its griefs,
Its thousand raptures and its deepest pangs,
Its foolish quarrels and its heaving sighs,
Its reckless daring and its groundless fears.
All this shall I sing in such entrancing wise,
That the world will know and envy those in love.
But of your dear face and your bewitching smile,
I must content myself to tell the minor part,
For tongue falters, pen and genius fail
To paint the wonders of your simple grace.[29]

His head in the clouds, reveling in his popularity and rejoicing in his love for Catherine, Luis was blind to the realities of the world about him and to the fact, patent to others, of D. Antonio de Lima's financial straits and his desire to repair his fortunes by an advantageous marriage for his daughter. Moreover, Camoëns failed utterly to recognize the increasing antagonism that his very success had aroused against him—a failure that was to destroy all of his most cherished hopes and dreams.

[29] Soneto "Eu cantarei de amor tão docemente."

CHAPTER V

Exile

Thus was life changed against my will
By decree of cruel, unloving Fate,
An exile from my fatherland
. . .
Driven ever forth by Destiny,
Who devours man's years before his time.

—Camoëns, Canção "Vinde cá"

SHORTLY AFTER THE PERFORMANCE of the *Amphytrion,* a marriage
was to be celebrated at the home of one Estacio da Fonseca, and
Luis was commissioned to write a drama for the occasion. Since
there was no theater in the capital, the play was to be presented
in the courtyard of the Fonseca palace; the King, the Queen, and
the court were to be in the audience.

When the day arrived, the courtyard was crowded, except for
the space reserved for the impromptu stage. From the windows
were hung silken flags and costly tapestries, and gaily dressed men
and women filled the balconies. A flourish of trumpets heralded
the arrival of the King and Queen, whereupon all present arose,
the men doffing their plumed velvet caps, the women bowing low,

until Their Majesties were seated. Another flourish of trumpets announced that the play was about to begin; three taps of the rod of the master of ceremonies, and Camoëns strode onto the little stage to deliver the prologue.

With bad judgment he had chosen for the plot of the play the historical tale of King Seleucus of Syria and his son Antiochus.[1] Luis had read the story in his Plutarch and had noted the reference to it in the *Trionfi* of his beloved Petrarch. It was an interesting tale and made good drama, but to present it in Lisbon before the court was a ghastly error, and might have cost the poet his life.

As the play progressed and the plot unfolded, it became clear that the story of Seleucus and his son was dangerously parallel to that of the late D. Manuel, King John's father, who had taken as his third wife D. Leonor, sister of Charles V and the affianced bride of his son.[2]

And now, in addition to this great indiscretion of Luis was added another: those in the audience who were aware of his illy concealed love for Catherine could find in the lines double meanings and references to her that could not be mistaken. Moreover, he represented D. Sancho, the second king of Portugal (1185–1211) as dancing the *machatin,* a grotesque dance imitating an attack by soldiers. And there followed a line announcing "then enters Royal Catharine, carrying a sieve full of idiots." Lines that might well be interpreted as holding up a past—and more particularly a present—sovereign of Portugal to ridicule constituted a grave and flagrant case of lese majesty, especially when pronounced publicly in

---

[1] Stratonice, Seleucus' second wife, was but a few years older than Antiochus, who fell deeply in love with her. When Antiochus realized the impossibility of ever having her for his own, he grieved until he became desperately ill. Warned by his physician that Antiochus was at death's door because of this secret love, the King magnanimously renounced her and gave her as bride to Antiochus.

[2] She was D. Manuel's niece, and a dispensation from the Pope, readily granted, was necessary before the marriage could be performed. Queen Leonor was the mother of D. Maria.

the presence of King John and his censorious queen. Even if the brash young dramatist had now realized his mistake, it was too late to repair the damage. As the curtain fell on the last lines of *King Seleucus,* so was it lowered on the youth, prospects, and joy of living for Luis de Camoëns.

He had not long to wait for the inevitable blow. It was decreed that he leave Lisbon at once, and, though the place of his exile was not specified, he was ordered not to attempt to plead his cause.

The Portuguese word for exile, *desterrado,* is a terrible one. Literally, it means "torn from the earth." He was banished from the capital, with its exciting, stimulating life—the life that had awakened and developed his poetic talent—just on the threshold of his career. He chose as his destination Santarem, his mother's birthplace, where still dwelt his maternal aunt (married to one Barreto) and others of his relatives. He was probably received civilly enough, for he was not of sufficient importance to be the subject of gossip for the boatmen and wayfarers from Lisbon, and the good people of Santarem had interests closer to their hearts than small events in the faraway court of King John.

Santarem could have offered little attraction to the poet. There were none of the scholastic inducements of Coimbra nor the heady, stimulating color and life of Lisbon. The conversation of the towns-folk about cattle, weather, crops, and families unknown to him could have had no interest for him. He appears to have continued to write verse, but poems that were often very different from those he had produced in Lisbon. Still, in them he found the expression and relief denied him in the sharing of his life with the erstwhile companions. Naturally, some of the poems were to Catherine.[3]

As time passed, the natural beauty of Santarem and the countryside about must have influenced Luis, for in the verses written at this time are similes and metaphors drawn from his surroundings, and more and more often they took the place of the con-

[3] See Appendix I, Poems 46 through 48 and 49 through 53.

ventional classical references which had rendered some of his earlier verses turgid and artificial:

> All the beauties that on earth abound
> —The folded velvet shadows of the hills,
> The verdure of the ancient forest trees,
> The gentle curves and windings of the stream
> (Where sadness should never long abide),
> The sullen roar that echoes from the sea,
> The dying sunset glow behind the serried peaks,
> The stragglers of the herd returning homeward,
> The clouds in mimic warfare in the sky,
> —All these wondrous gifts that nature grants
> Bring naught but weariness of heart.
> Without the warmth and radiance of thy smile
> My world is desolate and cold.[4]

Another passage from one of his eclogues, modeled on Vergil (who was the master standing by his side in the writing of much of his poetry), reflects his deep feeling for nature and his kinship with its moods:

> The wind sighs in the branches of the trees
> In harmony with the sobbing of the stream;
> The chattering bird in yonder leafy shade
> Pours out her grief upon the chilling wind.
> Pluck soft and low thy lyre's strings,
> For from her bower in the green-clad poplar tree
> The gentle nightingale in mournful note
> Bids thee sing thy saddest dirge.[5]

Some months after Camoëns banishment, one of the little wars which were constantly waged between the Portuguese[6] and the

[4] Soneto "A formosura desta fresca serra."

[5] Ecloga "Que grande variedade vão fazendo."

[6] The wars in Morocco constituted one of the vain, quixotic, and wasteful enterprises of the kingdom. Not content with driving the Moors from the peninsula, the

Moors broke out, and the Moslems laid siege to Ceuta and Maza-
gan. King John called for volunteers, and Luis joined the forces
that were about to sail.[7] Thus, overnight, the exile became a common soldier and sailed for the seat of trouble.

Portuguese of the fifteenth century sought additional laurels. King John I had five
sons, among them Prince Henry the Navigator. Seeking to win their spurs as
knights, one of them suggested an expedition against the Moors, who were engaging
in piracy on the southern coast of Portugal. Though no war was declared, an expedition was fitted out to capture Ceuta, the ancient Roman Septa. Taken by surprise, the citadel fell into the hands of John and his three older sons, remaining a
Portuguese possession until it fell, with the mother country, under Spanish rule in
1580. (It may be noted that the voyage to and from Morocco constituted all of the
seafaring experience of Prince Henry.) Ceuta was not held by the Portuguese without frequent efforts on the part of the Moors to regain it. Situated, as it was, in a
most strategic position, it stood just opposite Gibraltar at the entrance to the Mediterranean. But, though costly in blood and money throughout its occupation, the
Portuguese were determined to cling to it, their hope being that in some way the
trade of the Indies might be brought overland from the Red Sea through the territories of the legendary Prester John (when, if ever, he was found), a hope stimulated by the fact that caravans had from time to time crossed the Sahara to the
Moroccan coast. Added to this were the spirit of crusading and a desire to convert
the Moslems to Christianity; thus religion and self-interest both motivated the
Portuguese in their North African adventure. The practical result was that when
Ceuta came under Portuguese control, the Moslems transferred the terminus of
their desert caravan routes to Tunis. Moreover, the kingdom of Prester John was
not found on the North African coast. Though the Portuguese effort to hold the
cities wrested from the Moroccans was profitless, it took its toll of thousands of
young men who died in battle, of disease, or as captives in the noisome dungeons
of the Moors. But in spite of their precarious hold on their Moroccan citadels and
the dangers that beset them on every side, the youth of Portugal eagerly sought
(1505–1509), once described Morocco as "their school of fencing and the milk of
their babyhood."

[7] Commutation of penal sentences—even for capital crimes—to foreign military
service was common during the reign of John III.

CHAPTER VI

Ceuta

Now the heartache for the past,
Pure torment, bitter-sweet.
—Camoëns, Canção "Vinde cá"

AT LONG LAST Ceuta hove into sight, and the wearisome voyage was over. The town, with its whitewashed houses, lay like a streak of sunlight against the background of the somber Atlas Mountains, the minarets of the mosques on the hills pointing like long slender fingers toward the hot blue sky.[1]

---

[1] Ceuta had first been settled as a Phoenician colony eighteen hundred years before, with a citadel on the acropolis of Mount Acho, the second of the "Pillars of Hercules" of the Romans, and faced Gibraltar across the strait. When the Romans conquered Mauretania, as they called Morocco, they gave the town a new name, *Septem Fratres* (Seven Brothers), because of the seven hills within the fortifications. Its ships controlled the movement of vessels passing in or out of the Mediterranean, and, after the Romans had wrested it from the Carthaginians, it had known many masters. The Vandals occupied it when the Roman grip on North Africa was relaxed; after the wars of Justinian, when Belisarius brought North Africa under the scepter of the Byzantine Empire, it was ruled by Count Julian and later by the Arabs, who called it "Sebta," a corruption of the Latin *Septem*— whence the European name. Ceuta then fell into the hands of the Idrisid kingdom of Morocco, only to be torn from it by the Omayyads of Cordoba in Spain. Still

Here was to be Camoëns' home—if he survived the attacks of Moors and disease—for two years, a place far different from the cities of Portugal. Even the cathedral was an ancient mosque, con-

later it was a bone of contention and fiercely fought over by various ruling families of Arab Spain and Morocco, but in spite of these vicissitudes, it carried on a regular trade in the Mediterranean, and coral from its reefs was shipped all over Europe. It was also a regular port of call for vessels of Genoa, Pisa, and Marseilles.

The saddest tale of Morocco and the Portuguese was that of Fernando, brother of Prince Henry the Navigator. One of the most pathetic episodes in Portugal's colorful history, it presents Henry, not as the chaste prince devoting a lonely ascetic life to encouraging and inspiring attempts to find a sea road to the Indies, but as a cold-blooded, ambitious, stubborn man, a poor commander of troops, and one who sacrificed his own brother to his insensate ambition and callous inhumanity.

Immediately after the death of his father, King John I, Fernando, backed by Henry, demanded of his gentle and meek brother, King Duarte, that an expedition be launched against the infidels at Tangier. He could not be dissuaded from his purpose, and finally, with much misgiving, Duarte yielded. A fleet, with an army (entirely too small for an attack on the flower of the Moorish troops) commanded by Prince Henry, sailed from Lisbon for Tangier. His self-confidence blinded him to the threat of the overwhelming forces that faced him, and misfortune dogged his footsteps from the first; his men suffered hunger and thirst; the Moslem forces defeated him at every turn and, finally, surrounding him, forced his surrender.

The terms imposed by the victors were humiliating; among them was the demand that young Prince Fernando (he was only thirty-two) be surrendered as a hostage until Ceuta was returned to them. Although Henry agreed to these terms, he had no intention of keeping his word. Fernando knew this, but nevertheless went, a willing sacrifice, to his imprisonment. The terms of the surrender once settled, Henry sailed away to Ceuta, whence after five months of illness, he returned to Portugal. The ill-fated Fernando was first taken to the Moorish court at Fez; then, when the Moslems realized that Ceuta was not to be returned to them, they treated him with every indignity and cruelty. Laden with heavy iron fetters, he was compelled to work in the Sultan's stables and orchards as a slave. Finally, four years later, he was thrown into a gloomy, filthy cell, too small for him even to lie down in comfort, and in another fifteen months he was dead. The Sultan had his body eviscerated, filled with preservatives, and hung naked on the city wall, exposed to the abuse of the mob, who had good reason to hate the Portuguese for their perfidy. Later the corpse was placed in a lead coffin and buried in the wall. In 1469, when King Afonso V captured Tangier, the remains of the martyred prince were recovered and reburied in Batalha Abbey near his parents and brothers. This story impressed Camoëns profoundly and he retold it in his *Lusiads* (IV, 52ff.).

59

verted to a church. The native section (Almina), with its foreign dress and customs, always fascinated new arrivals; moreover, many of the Moors, together with Jews (who lived apart in the Mellah, their own quarter), frequented the lower town to trade—and some of them to act as spies as well.

All sorts of strange foods were sold and eaten in the market. Besides fish (tuna, bonito, sardines) brought in from the harbor, in pots at outdoor restaurants bubbled *couscous* (the national dish: mutton mixed with carrots and balls of barley flour with parsley), filling the air with its appetizing aroma. Behind heaps of fruits and vegetables, eggs, and chickens squatted chattering peddlers, while in a corner of the market place barbers plied their trade in the open, cutting hair, trimming their customers' beards, dyeing them with henna or shaving them with crude razors, using no soap or lather. Self-styled "doctors" hawked dried leaves, roots and barks, and weird powders of various colors, all offered as panaceas. Under tiny awnings sat public stenographers, composing letters, drawing up documents, or listening gravely to the dictation of their clients. Here a little crowd was gathered about a snake-charmer playing on his reedy pipe, there a group watched a juggler with his tricks, while others were entertained by a teller of tales. A constant file of people, donkeys, and horses, and an occasional camel, streamed through the closely guarded gate, bearing loads of charcoal and wood, fruits and vegetables, while in the shade along the walls of the houses veiled women sold bread, sweetmeats, and crude ironware hammered out in native forges. At the shops—mere holes in the wall or little elevated rooms, open to the street—passers-by were importuned to buy leatherwork, pottery, and inlaid metalwork, as well as jewelry and cloth. The market place was crowded; townsmen wearing white mingled with tribesmen in bright-colored *djellabs* with hooded *soulham* (resembling monks' gowns), many carrying daggers at their belts—some of them priceless weapons with gold, silver, or jeweled handles. And through the crowd swaggered Portuguese soldiers, off duty, for, masters of the town, there was little for them to do but idle away their time with cards, dice, wine, or the native women. Their service was dangerous enough, for when not on guard in the citadel they were called upon almost daily to quell native rioting within the city or to sally forth from the gates to drive back the Moslems, who were ceaselessly engaged in *razzias* (marauding and plundering expeditions) on the neighboring villages, which the Portuguese endeavored to protect. They were constantly on watch, too, to prevent the enemy from gathering under the very town walls to attack.

Camoëns' reading of the chroniclers and the annals of the Portuguese kings, together with his own observations, must soon have convinced him (though as a soldier of the King he dared not speak his mind) that the Moroccan adventure of the Portuguese could never succeed.[2] Failure was inevitable. Morocco was not like the Brazilian and East African territories, peopled by easily subjugated barbarians, for here the Portuguese had come into conflict with a civilization and culture in no way inferior to their own. Arts and letters had flourished in the country for centuries; the land had a political system of many generations' duration and possessed a religion productive of moral virtues and disciplinary practices. Each humiliation inflicted by a Portuguese victory only served to stiffen Moroccan religious hatred against the Christians, for the Moslems believed that the conflict was for a holy cause:

[2] Begun as a crusade to satisfy the sons of D. John I, neither the conversion of the Moors nor the hope of profitable trade had materialized.

The expeditions to India and Brazil had seriously drained the men and resources of the land—expeditions against which the wisest among the counselors of D. Manuel had strongly advised again and again (see Hart, *Sea Road to the Indies,* p. 85). These expeditions, though they temporarily brought wealth in gold, spices, and slaves, gradually exhausted the manpower of the little kingdom. Indeed, at the time of the Indian discovery the population of Portugal was no greater than one and one-half million souls. To seek to conquer a great overseas country like Morocco necessitated a fleet, large armies, and tremendous material resources, none of them available to the Portuguese kings.

amujahide.[3] Morocco was thus the seat of permanent warfare, a vain crusade transferred to African soil, and Ceuta was often in a state of siege, wherein raids, surprises, and ambushes were common occurrences by day and by night. It was a conflict in which to kill, capture, or rob was the aim of both sides.

In Ceuta, Camoëns was brought face to face with the realities and horrors of guerrilla warfare—a warfare but little, if any, different from that waged sporadically in Arab lands in Africa and Asia since the Second World War. Death was ever threatening, and the constant sight of men carried in dead or dying from skirmishes outside the walls or of ragged, emaciated, ransomed captives, as well as hearing tale after tale of torture, rape, and plunder, could not have failed to bring vividly home to Luis the cruelties, the callousness, and the indifference of men when once the thin veneer of civilization has been stripped off by the bloody and ruthless hand of war.

A letter to an unknown friend in Lisbon, a farrago of prose passages and poems, reveals the bitterness that exile and exposure to soldiering in Africa had brought into his life. His love of Catherine, his exile, and the months of toil as a soldier in Ceuta had preyed

---

[3] The Moors were in no way inferior to their opponents as warriors, impetuous in attack and tenacious in the struggle, and they had ever before them the assurance of their prophet, Mohammed, that death in battle would immediately transport them to a Paradise of delights. Moreover, they were vastly superior in number to the Portuguese, who had to convey not only troops but all their supplies and munitions over a sea swarming with pirates and hostile vessels. Only an incredible stubbornness and blind fanaticism could maintain such a losing struggle for long. Portugal never succeeded in getting more than a precarious foothold in some of the coastal cities, and a long string of dilapidated, crumbling fortresses is the only sad reminder of the Herculean efforts of six kings to establish Portuguese hegemony in North Africa. Though treaties of peace were signed again and again, they were usually violated by both sides before the ink was dry on the paper. It was the breaking of such a treaty between King John III and the ruler of Fez that renewed hostilities in Ceuta and caused the King to call for volunteers for an unpopular war.

upon his mind, and took shape in this letter, wherein he wrote:

> In this world there is no fortunate destiny except for him who holds as good that which he has. And hence I look upon myself as being content with my sad lot!

Later in the same letter he declares:

> It takes a great effort to seek to put on a happy face when the heart is sad! The canvas never takes on this color willingly; as the moon but reflects the clear light of the sun, so takes on the countenance the hue of the heart.

And he despondently concludes:

> Now one must either live in the world without truth or with truth but without the world.[4]

One of his longer poems, apparently written at this time, reveals the same desperation and despondency.[5]

At last the two years of Camoëns' military service were over, but on the eve of his departure for Portugal he again received a severe blow from what he had come to believe was a malignant fate that had singled him out for repeated assaults, a belief which is expressed very often in his poems. He was severely wounded in the right eye, causing complete blindness in it.[6] The resultant wound and scar must have been very apparent, for we gather as much from those of his poems that make reference to it, either directly or indirectly.[7]

4 Carta "Esta vai com a candeia na mão."

5 See Appendix I, Poem 54.

6 One account states that the wound was received in a sea battle, another during a land attack, and a third that it was the result of an explosion. Although fanciful portraits show a patch over the eye, the only portrait that was apparently sketched from life (in 1570) shows the right eye without a patch, but far smaller and duller than the large, lustrous left eye.

7 The word *olho* (eye) occurs repeatedly in Camoëns' later poems.

And so Camoëns, who had doubtlessly counted himself fortunate to be returning to Portugal to resume his normal life after the ills that had beset him, had, in a brief moment, become a tortured, maimed creature. So, too, with that prescience so often granted the sensitive mind of a poet, he probably envisaged the grim future that lay before him, for he must have known that in the very flower of his youth the road that might once more have led to fame and happiness was closed to him forever. Now he was a penniless, half-blind man with a scarred face.

As the ship that was to take him back to Portugal set sail, the man who watched Mount Acho—the Jebel Musa (Mount of Moses) of the Moors—fade into the distance was no longer the buoyant, handsome figure who had left Lisbon two years before. He set foot on the bank of the Tagus some days later dejected and facing life with but little hope.

CHAPTER VII

Trincafortes

If pity doth sojourn
In mountains, streams or valleys deep,
If love doth dwell
In beasts or birds or plants,
In stones or in the sea,
Let them all now hearken
To the long tale of my griefs;
Let them heal their own fell wounds
In hearing tell of mine,
For nothing but a greater grief
Can lesser sorrows heal.
—Camoëns, Soneto "Pois meus olhos não cansam"

THE LISBON OF 1550 was, in spite of the austerity of the King and Queen, a city where vice and crime were rampant in many quarters. The treatment of the Jews and Moors, together with the acts of the Inquisition,[1] had done much to upset the peace of the capital,

[1] One of the grimmest and most terrifying books ever written is that by Portugal's most famous historian, Alexandre Herculano: *History of the Origin and Establishment of the Inquisition in Portugal*, translated by John C. Branner, former president of Stanford University.

and the all too frequent sight of the horrid processions of the Inquisition, with their burnings and tortures in the palace square, contributed not a little to the brutalization and demoralization of the populace. The number of Negro slaves (and enslaved Moorish captives) imported for labor on the large estates had forced great numbers of indigent farmers and their families into the city. So many unfortunate women were forced by poverty into prostitution that drastic laws were passed in a futile effort to abolish the traffic. The slaves—many of them branded on the face with a red-hot iron—who escaped and sought refuge in the obscurity of Lisbon's squalid rookeries were numerous and added to the lawlessness. Illegitimacy was common, and numbers of children, abandoned by their parents, drifted into vice and crime. Visitations of pestilence, aggravated in the filthy, crowded streets and houses of the Mouraria and the lower city, periodically contributed to the upset of normal life. Though the population of the capital had trebled since the discovery of the sea road to the Indies, little or no effort in housing or sanitation had been made by the government to protect the overcrowded inhabitants. The King and nobles, for all their professed devotion to religion, were disturbed not at all by these frightful conditions, for they had their comfortable dwellings in the city and their estates in the provinces, and since these were largely manned and cultivated by slaves, attention to the citizenry was deemed unimportant. Thus while the upper classes of the country were enervated by luxury and sloth, the lower classes were gradually being reduced to beggary.

The court itself was corrupt in every way, the nobles vying for royal favor and the conferring of unearned pensions. The enforced departure of the Jews and Moors was followed by the confiscation of their property, and both this and the actions of the odious Inquisition encouraged bribery and blackmail.[2] The state of affairs

2 The King himself, for all his pose of piety and devotion to the Church, did not hesitate to employ the assassin's dagger to eliminate those whom he wanted re-

in the capital was worse than elsewhere in Portugal, since, in addition to the existence of all these factors, Lisbon was the principal seaport of the kingdom, always swarming with unemployed seamen and soldiers, scions of noble families gone to seed, and impoverished vagabonds.

Imminent dangers threatened the country, though all appeared normal to the casual observer. Portugal was seemingly rich, but the wealth pouring into her coffers from Asia, Africa, and Europe was being rapidly misused and wasted. The corruption of money and power was spreading, like a cancerous growth, into every corner of the land. The kingdom was small: its people in the days of Vasco da Gama numbered not more than one and one-half million, and nearly half this number had now vanished—gone to the Indies or to the many trading posts on the African and Brazilian shores. Thousands were at the bottom of the seas or in foreign graves. The cost of living was inflated disproportionately. Peasants flocked to the cities; farming was being neglected and industry was flagging, while much land lay untilled or abandoned. Ignorant men, grown rich in India, were preferred to the honest citizenry at home for place and honors, and civic virtue was unable to resist the poison of gold and the scent of spices. The real wealth of the land—the labor of its people—was drying up: bread had tripled in price within a few years, and for the poor, meat was a luxury.

moved from his path. A letter still exists, signed by him, in which he writes to one Francisco Lobo: "Trusting that you will do what is expected of you—in the manner and with so much care that in no way it may be suspected whence it was done . . . and I say that in this ship that has just come from India came Domingos Vaz, Pilot —I order you so to behave—that he be killed, and cost what it may, and with such prudence as should be taken with my great secret." Together with this letter has been preserved the receipt given to Lobo for "one hundred cruzados and one horse saddled and bridled," signed by the assassin, one Fernam de Almeida. The receipt acknowledges the payment, "by virtue of a letter of the king, our master, in which he ordered me to do some things in his service." With such dastardly deeds not only condoned but openly performed by the head of state himself, it is not to be wondered that Portugal was fast approaching the brink of moral and political ruin!

In spite of all the treasure flowing into private hands, the King was living on loans from Flanders and the sale of offices and pensions, and for the first time in her history, Portugal was accumulating a public debt.

This was the land to which Luis had returned, and it was in Lisbon's slums that he was now condemned by circumstances to live.

Camoëns sought to settle down and reshape his shattered life into some sort of pattern, but it must have been far from easy. He was not always able to avoid former friends and acquaintances on the busy streets, and of those whom he met, some probably rejoiced at his misfortune, while others would look upon his military service, not as the beginning of a career, but as expiation for a crime.

The women were the most cruel. One who drew near and recognized him turned aside in disgust, exclaiming "Devil!" loud enough for him to hear. When he smiled at another whom he had known, she looked at him with a cold stare and spat: "Face without eyes!" He struck back, sending them bitter, sarcastic verses. One of these read:

> How can it be, my lady,
> That you an angel fair,
> Have won a devil's love?
> 'Tis passing strange!
> I cannot understand!
> There you have certain proof
> That I am constancy itself,
> For a devil's very nature is
> The angels to despise.[3]

The hatred of the poet Pero de Andrade Caminha was evidently intense, for when he learned of Camoëns' accident he could not resist a cruel jibe, and one of his epigrams is believed to have been aimed at the helpless one-eyed man.

[3] Redondilha "Não posso chegar ao cabo."

A Wager Between Two

One has two eyes, and his vision is clear,
The other but one, his vision scant.
The first unto the other said
"I'll lay a bet with you, my friend,
To see which one the better sees."
Then spoke up the one-eyed man and said
"I win! Behold, I see more than you,
For I see two eyes in you,
And you but one in me!"[4]

On one occasion, in an autographical poem, Camoëns spoke of his accident as "an experience of the strange wrath of Mars, god of war—that my eyes should see and my hands should touch his bitter fruit." This, and a remark in one of his letters from India, wherein he wrote, referring to a certain Manuel Serrão, that "he was, like me, blind in one eye," are his only recorded references to his deformity, which he bore bravely and without complaint.

His exile in Santarem and his two years of military service in Morocco had been in vain. The displeasure of the Queen and the opposition of Catherine de Ataide's father had been very effectual, and all doors were closed to him, for no one would consort with a penniless one-eyed soldier disgraced by his sovereigns. So the lonely man sought the only company left him: returned soldiers and sailors and the wastrels and ne'er-do-wells who skulked along the water front and in the dark slums of Lisbon. But even with the women who haunted the dingy, smoky taverns Luis was gallant, displaying flashes of the old poetic fancy and wit in light lines he scribbled off to them. One of these poems has been preserved in the collection of his lyrics. Although the verses are nonsense, they are framed in the same perfect rhyming stanza form as the roundels which in the sunny hours of his life he had often written for the young women of the court:

4 Caminha, *Poesias*, p. 339: Um tem dois olhos e com vista clara.

Mote: I know not if Helena tricks me,
                 Or if Maria, or e'en Joana;
                 I know not which of these it be.

Voltas: One whispers that she loves me well,
                 Another vows that I am hers,
                 But who accepts a woman's tale,
                 Or can believe she'll not foreswear?
                 I cannot, no, I cannot
                 Believe what Helena says,
                 Nor yet Maria, nor e'en Joana,
                 Or know which tells the greatest lies.

                 One swears great oaths by all that's holy,
                 That I'm the only man she loves,
                 Another, that she pines and sickens;
                 And Joana? She just heaves great sighs.
                 Helena plays me false, forsooth.
                 Joana speaks no word of truth.
                 But lie they one, or lie they all,
                 I'm not deceived—no, not at all.[5]

During this period, of which we have no information other than his own references in letters and poems, Camoëns seems to have assumed a protective coloration contrary to his nature—a hard, defiant exterior—though his verses indicate that he still had hope of regaining a place in his former world. The craving for affection that was his intense inheritance, however, led him to turn to the trulls, the slatterns, and the wenches who were part of the rabble into which life had thrown him. It was at this time that he wrote such verses as that entitled[6] "To a Woman Who Was Beaten By a Man They Call Coresma,"[7] a second called "To John Lopes Leitão, Because of a Piece of Cloth Which He Sent to a Woman

[5] Redondilha "Não sei se me engana Helena."
[6] In the earliest edition of his lyrics.
[7] Redondilha "Não este jais agravada."

Who Palmed Herself Off As a Virgin to Him,"[8] and a third, of
eight quatrains, beginning:

> You are of all women
> The ugliest on earth;
> Of all ill-famed women
> You're the worst, by my faith.[9]

Day by day, apparently, the poem became more truculent, moody,
and quarrelsome. That he had but one good eye[10] had not interfered
with the dextrous twist of his trained wrist and the lightning play
of his steel, as many a rash challenger must have learned to his
cost. In fact, Luis took a perverse—it would seem almost a malicious—pleasure in the reputation he had acquired: a surly, morose,
dangerous person to cross. Born of some peculiarity or outstanding physical or mental trait of the bearer, nicknames are common
to the underworld, and before long Luis was being called *Trincafortes,* or Swashbuckler, a name that soon spread throughout the
slums and dark alleys of the water front.

One of Camoëns' boon companions at this time was the playwright Antonio Ribeira Chiado, a man for whom one of Lisbon's
busiest thoroughfares is named. He had laid aside the habit of
a Franciscan monk in Evora to become a comedian and was living
a merry life among the free drinkers of the capital. Luis had known
him well in the old days and had even referred to him in the
prologue of *King Seleucus.* When Chiado, who was widely known
for his epigrammatic wit, heard of the nickname given Camoëns,
he composed a quatrain with a double meaning:

---

[8] Redondilha "Se vossa Dama vos dá."

[9] Redondilha "Vós sois ũa Dama."

[10] That he was sensitive to his disfigurement at this time we know from an epigram he wrote to a woman who leaned out of her window and called to him, "You,
there, the fellow with the broad-brimmed hat." From this epigram (never printed),
we can infer that she was a woman of the half-world and that Luis was resentful of
her solicitation.

71

Luisa, you'd better take my advice
And don't try to sell such melons twice,
Because that fellow whom you see here
Is Trincafortes, a man to fear.

The poet himself seemed proud of his sinister reputation, for later he boastfully wrote from India to a friend in Lisbon that no one had ever seen the soles of his feet but that he had often seen the soles of others' (i. e., he had laid many a man on his back, but he himself had never had the worst of it in a quarrel or a fray).

Forced to earn a living as best as he could, Luis began to compose poems on commission for people who later posed as their authors. He thus eked out a precarious existence, although he was sometimes forced to accept food or clothing in lieu of coin. One D. Antonio of Cascaes (a town to the west of Lisbon) promised him six stuffed chickens for some copying work, but, after a long wait, only half a chicken was delivered. The poet rebuked his debtor in a quatrain:

The senhor from Cascaes
Owes me six chickens of the best;
Now has come but half of one,
So hungry for the rest![11]

And so for two years, until the middle of June, 1552, Camoëns lived from hand to mouth, neglected and half-blind.

[11] Redondilha "Cinco galhinas e meia."

CHAPTER VIII

Corpus Christi

O grave unbearable unforeseen events
Of fortune and of love,
What penance do you now impose
On hearts all innocent of wrong!
—CAMOËNS, Elégia "Aquela que de amor descomedido"

LUIS WROTE in a letter from Ceuta:[1] "If once a partridge lose but a single plume, there is no ill he can avoid. One brings another; they never singly come." Never were there more prophetic words, for just as a wounded partridge plummets to earth, so, too, was Camoëns to fall suddenly and swiftly into the depths of ignominy and disgrace.

Corpus Christi, a joyful festival, was one of the principal public celebrations of the Catholic church in sixteenth-century Portugal, and it was never observed with more splendor than in Lisbon on June 16, 1552. The desire for luxury, the vain ostentation of the court, the love of the people for a holiday—all made the procession of the Eucharist the excuse for lavish and extravagant display.

[1] Carta "Esta vai com a candeia."

73

After the religious ceremonies there were wild demonstrations throughout the day, the people throwing off their cares and dancing and singing in the streets. By sunset the celebration had quieted down, however, and the dense crowds thinned out.

As night crept on, it cast black shadows, first under archways and in the dingy, narrow streets and lanes of the lower town, then over the towers of the palaces on the hillsides and the high Castle of St. George. The citizens had gone home, and the streets, littered with the faded, crushed flowers and debris of the celebration, were deserted. From time to time the watch tramped by bearing halberds and torches, or a singing, drunken group made its way afoot or on horseback to or from some private feast. A number of the merrymakers were masked, but no one asked questions—if people attended to their own affairs and made no trouble for others.

On this day Camoëns walked the streets, probably not a little intoxicated, drinking cheap tavern wine with his friends. He was in a truculent, dangerous mood, one that boded ill for anyone who might cross him.

Wearing, as ever, his sword and dagger at his belt. Luis was going through the great square of the Rocio toward the Rua São Antonio, near the Monastery of São Domingos, when he saw a richly dressed man on horseback riding toward the house of Pero Vaz. The lone rider was Gonçalo Borges, keeper of the King's harness, a man well known to Luis—and intensely disliked.

Camoëns was about to turn away when he perceived two mounted men, plainly clothed and wearing masks, ride out toward Borges, jesting and jeering as they drew boldly alongside him. By their voices and dress Luis recognized them as members of the band with whom he had often shared wine and lodgings.

Borges seemed in no way frightened, but, annoyed that such rude fellows on their sorry nags should block his way, he drew his sword, intending to push them aside and to clear a way for himself with the flat of the blade. Quick as a flash, the other two unsheathed their weapons and attacked. Borges was no mean swordsman, and held his own with parry and thrust. Seeing him getting the better of the fracas, Luis evidently lost control of himself and, drawing his dagger, ran up behind him. Since he was on foot, he could not easily reach the horseman, but as the latter bent low to thrust at one of his assailants, Luis lunged and wounded him in the neck. Meanwhile, a crowd of late revelers had gathered, and just as the poet struck and Borges slipped from his horse, the night watch came running in from the Rocio. At the sight of them, the two miscreants quickly wheeled their horses and galloped off into the darkness. Luis, caught in the act of stabbing an influential member of the royal household, was helpless. He knew that under the circumstances he would be given short shrift, for a royal ordinance had decreed that "all persons who may be taken into custody by the captains of the watch by night after the ringing of the curfew-bell either unarmed or bearing any sort of arms whatsoever are to be conducted to the Tronco and imprisoned." That the affray had occurred on the night of one of the holy days only aggravated the offense.

Camoëns was taken to the Tronco,[2] one of the most notorious jails in Lisbon. The buildings were old, dark, loathsome, and verminous, with dungeons filthier than slave prisons. Little air or light entered, and the food was vile and insufficient. Camoëns refers to this noisome place in one of his "songs," wherein he movingly describes his plight:

> Human pity failed me,
> And those who might have befriended
> Turned their heads away.
> Space where to set my feet did lack;
> Even air to breathe denied,

---

[2] The name means "the stump of a tree." The prison was so called because in its cells and yards were the tall stumps of trees which had been felled. To these were attached iron collars, manacles, leg irons, and chains, to which the prisoners were fastened like horses tied up for shoeing.

> And I lost all count of time
> And of the world.[3]

For eight months and more Luis lay deserted and neglected. During this time he could learn nothing of the fate of his victim, though he was very sure that if Borges succumbed to his wound, death would be his fate also.

At first it was impossible for Camoëns to reconcile himself to his condition, and bitterness filled his spirit.[4] Later he became somewhat resigned, though he never ceased to reproach himself, and as the long, seemingly endless weeks passed, he composed verses—the only way he had of filling his days:

> Where shall I find a place so far removed
> And so distant from all fortune, good or bad,
> That I may be free from all that live,
> Both man and beast?
> Let it be some dreadful gloomy vale,
> Or solitary forest dark and sad,
> Where no clear spring sparkles in the sun
> And no grass grows;
> I seek a place congenial to my mood.
> There in the shadow of a cave
> Would I entomb myself alive
> And ceaselessly lament.
> There would I be sad in hours of joy,
> And in dismal days would I find my heart's content.[5]

At last he learned what his fate was to be, for during the long months of his imprisonment, a few of his old friends had, unknown to him, rallied to his support, and their efforts to obtain his release were finally successful, though they had to wait on the outcome of Borges' injury. Fortunately for the poet, Borges recovered, and,

[3] Canção "Vinde cá, meu tão certo secretário."
[4] See Appendix I, Poem 55.
[5] Soneto "Onde acharei lugar tão apartado."

evidently influenced by Camoëns' affliction and by the pressure of his friends, generously not only stood aside and offered no objection to the petition for a pardon filed with the King, but even added to the document his own forgiveness in writing.[6]

The pardon was granted, but Luis discovered that it was in reality only a commutation of sentence, for on his release he was to serve abroad for three years as a soldier and to pay a fine of four thousand reis.

Again the poet was to be exiled, but this time no pleasant, sleepy Portuguese town was to be his home, nor even North Africa, a short sail from his native land. He was condemned to leave behind him even the little that made life worth while and to travel halfway around the world to India—a voyage that might easily take from six to nine months—to fight against the enemies of the King in a land which was already the graveyard of countless Portuguese. But it was a royal decree from which there was no appeal. And it was lenient for those harsh, cruel days.

[6] This pardon lay in the Torre do Tombo (the Portuguese National Archives in Lisbon) from the day it was "given in my city of Lisbon on the seventh day of March—The king, our lord, ordered it through D. Gonçalo Pinheiro, Bishop of Viseu and the scholar Joham Monteiro—both of his council and his judges of the palace and of petitions—in the year 1553" until it was discovered in the middle of the nineteenth century by Visconde de Juromenha, who devoted twenty-six years to a search for documents which might throw light on the life of Camoëns. The document itself clears up once and for all the mystery of the reason for Camoëns' imprisonment and why he sailed for India. It notes that a petition had been received from "Luis Vaz de Camoëns, son of Simon Vaz, cavalier" and continues with a recital of the affray in the Rocio (giving the exact location). "And," it continues, "the said Gonçalo Borges is in good health, without any injury or deformity, and has forgiven him, as is shown by the pardon attached to his petition. And he, the petitioner, is a poor young man, and he is going this year to serve in India. And I have listened to his petition with favor, and pardon him his crime— if he was to pay four thousand reis for charity to the Bishop of St. Thomas, of my council, and my almoner." It is likely that Bishop Gonçalo Pinheiro of Viseu, mentioned in the pardon, was himself instrumental in obtaining it, for Camoëns addressed a flattering sonnet to him, punning on the name "Pinheiro," which means "pine tree" (Soneto "Depois que viu Cibele o corpo humano").

The order to proceed by the earliest ship leaving Lisbon[7] was an unusual one, since a man with but one eye would not ordinarily be chosen for military service. Recruits must have been scarce, indeed, for Luis to have been acceptable.

Camoëns' happy life in Coimbra had been brought to an abrupt termination by the unfortunate love affair with his cousin. Hardly had he gained what he imagined was a firm footing in Lisbon than his misguided genius had condemned him to exile in Santarem. And when he sought to purge his boyish error by enlisting for the army in Ceuta his efforts had brought him only half-blindness and abject poverty. Then his despondency and hotheadedness had landed him in prison—and now he was to be cut off from all opportunity of building a new life in his native land.

The years had matured Luis. Those poems written after he emerged from prison reveal a resignation, an ability to face the world's exacting demands, that he had not known before. It is not until one has met with griefs, disappointments, and disillusionments that one can learn to accept and face them, to bow the head and go on with courage, even if one can see little ahead for himself. So through it all, though self-pity often obscured his vision (and appeared in his poetry), Camoëns clung to two ideals that he would never surrender. Even the severe treatment at the hands of his king and the stupidity of administration and waste of lives he had seen in Ceuta could not blot out or dull his conception of Portugal as the fairest land on earth and her history as a pageant of the most sublime chivalry. These treasures—the ideal of womanhood that he held enshrined in his memory and the vision of his beloved country—were to combine with a supreme genius to make of Luis de Camoëns at once the greatest lyric and epic poet of his country and one of the sweetest singers of the ages.

[7] It is not known whether or not Camoëns paid the four thousand reis to charity. He was penniless, and there is no record of any of his friends' coming forward to help him.

One hope, perhaps, remained to him: Fortune might change at last and bring him home rich and independent, as she had so many who had departed, penniless, as soldiers from the shores of the Tagus. Had not Gil Vicente put the common belief in a speech in one of his plays?

"And yet did you return very rich?"
"I assure you that were it not for my captain, I would have had a million as my share!"[8]

It would have been far better for Luis had he given heed to the old song so popular in the reign of King John I:

> Oh, evil night,
> For whom lie you in wait?
> For the poor soldiers
> And the shepherds of flocks
> And the men of the sea,
> What will you grant them?
> They will find their end, too,
> And have more than their fill

Camoëns had few illusions about India, for on every side were heard discussions on conditions in the Portuguese territories, and many of his fellow soldiers in Ceuta had been veterans of the Indian campaigns. Moreover, it was more and more difficult each voyage for the fleets to obtain crews and for the King to secure volunteers for overseas military service. Luis had often heard the recruiting officers on Tagus' bank offering extravagant blandishments to the loiterers and returned soldiers in an effort to persuade them to sign up. There was a continual beating of drums as the King's men marched through the streets of Lisbon, calling on "young men seeking adventure" to enlist in the Casa da India, but on the other hand there were crowds of boys and idlers following the recruits, mocking, jeering, and chanting a quatrain that had come down through a whole generation:

[8] Farsa chamada "Auto da India."

> How many depart
> Who ne'er come back!
> To India more sail
> Than ever return.

And for those who went to fight for the King there was an ironic couplet on the lips of the people:

> With the poor fools of patriots
> Are the hospitals filled.

Luis must have heard his family speak of the struggle that his famous cousin, Vasco da Gama, had had in forcing King Manuel to keep his promises,[9] and he was probably familiar with the similarly disheartening experiences of even the greatest of the founders of Portugal's overseas empire.

There was little time between Camoëns' release from the Tronco and the date of sailing. He presented himself for enlistment and entry for the next voyage. After all his papers had been examined and checked, he was given an advance of three months' pay, as was the custom. He evidently took with him such verses as he had preserved, either originals that no one else had seen or copies of those given his friends.[10]

Palm Sunday arrived and the fleet for the Indies, commanded by Fernando Alvares Cabral, lay at anchor. Flags were flying, pipes playing, and drums beating as the ships made ready to sail. Early Masses were said on ship and shore, and the new recruits, already lined up at the waterside, boarded the vessels. Since it was a church holiday, many were abroad, and the crowd watching the departure pressed down almost to the water's edge.

[9] See Hart, "Sea Road to the Indies," Chapter XX.

[10] Of course no line of his verses had as yet been printed and the reputation he had gained came entirely from the circulation of the written sheets among the different groups in Lisbon. And it should be noted that such groups—people who could read and appreciate the worth of his poems—were comparatively few in number.

One cannot be sure, but there is an intimation in a sonnet found among his papers that Luis saw Catherine before his departure—unless the poem refers to his sailing for Ceuta:

> That dawn, at once so happy and so sad,
> Diffused with sorrow and despair,
> Should hold a place in fame
> As long as there is heartbreak on this earth.
> When it dispelled the dark
> And with dappled light illumed the world
> It saw heart from heart asunder torn
> —A separation never meant to be.
> It alone beheld our blinding tears
> And heard our last sweet words
> —Words to damp the flames of hell,
> And bring peace to damnèd souls.[11]

Her anchor stowed, the ship *São Bento* swung with the tide and moved slowly and majestically down the Tagus like a huge swan. She passed the Monastery of the Jeronymos and the Tower of Belem, then reached the ever widening mouth of the river. Open sea and fresh winds greeted her as she altered course to the south. Ahead of her lay a long, weary voyage.

[11] Soneto "Aquela triste e leda madrugada."

CHAPTER IX

The Voyage to India

Absence has a daughter;
Her name is Saudade.
I keep both mother and daughter
—Alas, 'gainst my will.

—Old Song

I was banished to the Indies,
But 'twas not for theft.
Was it because I hugged and kissed?
Well, they do the same thing there!

—Old Song

THE HARDSHIPS of the Indian voyage were common knowledge, and Luis had experienced a little of the same difficulties on the shorter journeys to and from Morocco.[1] He had probably become

[1] Jan Huygen van Linschoten, a Dutchman who sailed to India in the suite of Vicente da Fonseca, Archbishop of Goa, a few years after Camoëns, has left a fascinating description of sixteenth-century Portuguese vessels and their voyages. In the English translation (made anonymously in 1598), we are informed that all "which sayle in the ship—have for their portion every day in victuals, each man alike, as well the greatest as the least, a pound and three quarters of Biskit, halfe a

reconciled after a fashion, to a long absence abroad, for he knew there was no escape. He was bound to military service in India by the King's pardon and his own signature on the roll of recruits, and there was no turning back.

One poem revealing his courage—perhaps the courage of despair—at leaving Portugal was written just before his departure.

> Heart made firm
> Despite your tear-dimmed eyes,
> I'll cross the unknown waters without fear.
> The time had come to part,
> Though the way was barred
> By yearning and salt tears.
> I rose above all barriers
> With that stubborn pride
> Which foreknowledge of a glorious death

Can of Wine, a Can of water, an arroba which is thirty two pound of salt flesh the moneth, some dryed fish, onyons and garlicke are eaten in the beginning of the voyage, as being of small valew, other provisions, as Sugar, Honny, Reasons, Prunes, Ryse and such like, are kept for those which are sicke: yet they get but little thereof, for that the officers keepe it for themselves, and spend it at their pleasures, not letting much go out of their fingers: as for the dressing of their meate, wood, pots, and pans, every man must make his owne privision: besides all this there is a clarke and steward for the king's souldiers that have their parts by themselves, as the saylers have."

Other writers of the period remark on the same thieving habits of the officers, who held back part of the provisions to sell in Mozambique, on the African coast, and elsewhere. Surgeons were provided for each ship, but they were, for the most part, incompetent, many not having even the rudiments of medical knowledge.

Camoëns was fortunate in that the *São Bento*, the flagship of the fleet, carrying the *capitão-mór*, was also the largest and best outfitted of the five assigned for the voyage and carried one of the most experienced pilots. Fate destined this to be the vessel's last visit to India. Although five caravels had been outfitted, one of them, the *São Antonio*, burned in the roadstead off Lisbon while loading, so only four set sail. Their cargo, like most taken to the East, was not important, consisting, in the main, of barrels of olive oil and pipes of wine; the rest of the hold was filled with provisions and water casks. In fact, the only valuable part of the cargo of any India-bound vessel of the time consisted of the bags of money shipped for the purchase of spices and other Asiatic goods.

Lends to a desperate soul,
For in what untried form
Can angry death e'er strike fear in one
Who lies already bound
At cruel death's feet?[2]

The soldiers, as well as the sailors, were assigned to watches (probably because of the crowded quarters below decks), and in the long hours Luis grew to love the sea, reflecting that love in many of his poems. In days of calm or favoring breezes, when the ship, her timbers creaking, rose and fell lazily with the swells, the men on watch would gather on deck and spin interminable yarns of their adventures in Asia and the lore of the strange peoples they had seen or tell tales of their amorous exploits in foreign lands.

Day after day the *São Bento* proceeded on her course alone, for the other ships of the convoy had become separated shortly after leaving Lisbon. One of them had turned back; another had been swept westward by the winds toward the coast of Brazil and did not arrive in Goa until the change of the monsoon the ensuing year. After some weeks of a favorable following wind, the weather changed, the breezes dropped, and for days the vessel lay becalmed, drifting slowly with the ocean currents. Finally, however, the winds again filled the great sails and the ship got under way, gradually working back to her course. Unfortunately, a large part of the fresh food taken on board had been consumed during the days of calm, and scurvy, the dreaded scourge of sailors on long voyages, made its appearance.[3]

[2] Soneto "Por cima destes aguás forte e firme."

[3] Even the supply of dried onions had either been consumed, spoiled by the damp, or eaten by rats. Although the physicians of the period were ignorant of the fact that the disease was one of vitamin deficiency, they did know that the eating of fresh foods, especially fruits and vegetables, prevented it. However, there was little attention given to providing these for the crew, since it meant extra expense; moreover, there was no method available for keeping such fresh food on hand. Dried

As the vessel neared the southernmost tip of Africa, the winds veered. The old hands, watching the sky and horizon, prophesied tempests and grumbled that the name given the cape by its discoverer, Bartholomeu Diaz, who called it *Cabo Tormentoso* (The Cape of Storms), was far more fitting than the change to *Cabo de Boa Esperança* (The Cape of Good Hope) made by King John II. Then one day the sky became overcast with scurrying clouds and the wind began to howl and whistle in the rigging; darkness fell suddenly, black as night, and the full force of the storm struck the vessel. It lasted for days, and in its fury it washed several luckless sailors from the rolling deck into the raging sea. The mass of humanity crowded under the hatches suffered keenly from cold, hunger, and seasickness, and it was a sorry-looking ship's company that finally emerged when the storm had blown itself out, leaving the *São Bento* much the worse for her battering and still wallowing in the troughs of great seas.

onions were also a preventative, but shipowners were too parsimonious to lay in a supply for their crews. Yet these same owners knew that from 7 per cent up to the incredible but authentic figure of 65 per cent of the men carried on board were lost on each voyage because of scurvy. This failure to provide against the disease left little recourse for the physicians but bleeding, which resulted in a further weakening of the victims, making them less resistant to the disease. (It has been estimated that thousands of Portuguese lives would have been saved in the 103 years from 1497 to 1600 if a plentiful supply of dried onions had been carried on each ship.) Moreover, the carrying in each caravel of far more men than was sanitary or safe rendered the care of the sick extremely difficult, if not impossible. It was particularly so because in bad weather most of the men not on duty were forced to crowd into the cramped, limited space below decks, a practice which offered ideal conditions for the spread of every kind of infection, especially since many green recruits were not yet immunized to the infectious and contagious diseases of childhood. Still another hazard was the failure to issue clean uniforms to the crew or soldiers at the owners' or the government's expense; thus the men came aboard with their own clothes, often old, filthy, and infested with vermin. Bathing was not mandatory, and no inspections of the men were held. The water put aboard in casks in Lisbon or en route was often from polluted sources. With all these threats to health and to life itself, it is surprising that the toll of life—most of it sheer waste—was not greater on each voyage.

Luis noted well the storm and the sea's various moods. A verse of his *Lusiads* tells the story of the tempest in a few magnificent lines:

> To recite at length the terrors of the sea
> Were to tell a tale that no man would believe
> —The sudden thunder, the wild lightning bolts
> That seemed to set aflame the firmament;
> Black cloudbursts, long nights of gloom,
> Then more crash of thunder 'till it was
> As though the very earth from pole to pole were riven
> —Indeed, 'twere error to essay to tell it all,
> Even though with voice of iron did I speak.[4]

In like manner, and in detail, he described the sight of a waterspout, first forming, then bursting, and other occurrences at sea. Later in his epic he summed up what he had experienced in a single stanza:

> If the philosophers of olden days
> Who sought to learn the secrets of the earth
> Should have witnessed what mine eyes have seen,
> And raised their sails to such contrary winds,
> What profound books would theirs have been,
> What portents of planets and of stars!
> Yet no word of untruth in it withal,
> But purest verity.[5]

After the vessel rounded the cape, fair weather again prevailed and presently they reached Natal, where "they commonly used to take counsel of all the officers of the ship, whether it is best for them to sayle within the land of San Laurenso[6] or without it, for that within [the channel] they sayle to Mossambique [Mozam-

---

[4] *Lusiads*, V, 16.

[5] *Ibid.*, V, 23.

[6] São Lourenço was the early Portuguese name for Madagascar.

bique] and from thence to Goa, and sayling without it they cannot come at Goa, by reason they fal down bye meanes of the streame, and so must sayle unto Cochin." Since the *São Bento* was bound for Goa, she entered the channel and dropped anchor off Mozambique,[7] to the great joy of both crew and soldiers.

Thence the vessel sailed northward up the coast, her men largely recovered from their scurvy and refreshed by the few days on land. They remained some time at Quiloa, where the Portuguese had built a fort—already badly neglected—manned by a very small garrison and provided with scanty stores and munitions. Some of the soldiers who were stationed there had their wives with them, but there was also a colony of half-castes—offspring of Portuguese soldiers and Indian women. It was an unhealthy place where "divers of our men fell sick and died, by reason of the unaccustomed ayre of the place, which of it self is an unwholesome land, and an evil aire by means of the great and unmeasurable heat."

[7] "They have time enough there to refresh themselves, and to take in fresh water and the other victuals, and so to lie at anker ten or twelve days altogether—for that commonly they are sick of swollen legges, sore bellies, and other diseases."

II

- *Babylon* -

By the rivers of Babylon, there we sat down, yea, we wept, when
we remembered Zion.

—Psalms 137:1

CHAPTER X

Goa

Goa is the most principal citie which the Portugals have in India, wherein the Viceroy remaineth with his court. . . . It is a fine citie, and for an Indian towne very faire. . . . Here bee many marchants of all nations. And the Fleete which commeth every yeare from Portugal—commeth first hither

—RALPH FITCH, (Hakluyt, Maclehose V, 471)

FROM QUILOA the *São Bento* pointed her prow toward Goa, meeting calm seas and favorable winds all the way. Finally, one day at the beginning of September, 1553, the Indian coast was sighted, and before evening the anchor was dropped off the mouth of the river at Goa. Camoëns could now say, as did John de Castro some years before, that he had "reached the bar of Goa more by the goodness of Our Lord than by our deserts, art and science. Praise be to God."

The long, wearisome passage was over, and Camoëns was come to the land that was to be his home for some years—many more than the three which he had contemplated when the voyage began. Before him at last lay Goa, "the mother of all India, for thus it lieth in the midpart thereof."[1] That the vessel had arrived at its

[1] These were the quaint words of Viceroy Affonso de Albuquerque, conqueror

destination safely after "six evil months of my life at sea" was indeed fortunate, for it was not unusual for from one-third to one-half of the ships that left Lisbon for India to be lost at sea, shipwrecked on some foreign shore or burned to the water's edge.

There was every reason for the interest and excitement that pervaded the city when a fleet or even a single ship "from the Kingdom" was sighted in the offing, for the vessels were the bearers of the latest news from the capital. Stores were closed and all government business suspended, workmen left the shipyards and building jobs to meet the new arrivals at the quay, taverns and gambling houses prepared to receive the newcomers, and the women of the town rejoiced that sailors and soldiers, perhaps with money in their pockets, were to land. Malabarese, Negroes, and mulattoes, freemen as well as slaves, congregated at the water front to seek work in the unloading of the vessels, and agents and brokers were on hand, eager to negotiate early sales of spices, silks, and jewels for the return voyage. Citizens and their wives joined the throng in the hope of seeing long-awaited friends or relatives. Apart from the mob were rich citizens mounted on gaily caparisoned horses or lolling on the pillows of their canopied palanquins, while behind them were their wives or Indian or half-caste mistresses. And everywhere were people who had congregated in Goa to work for the government, for God, or for gain—Arabs, Chinese, Parsis, Gujratis, Tamils, Malays, and merchants from Holland and Italy—all in their colorful costumes: a motley, turbulent crowd.

Newcomers were always greeted with catcalls by the idlers, for recruits were the particular targets of the jeers and taunts of earlier arrivals, who called them *descamisados*—literally "men without shirts"—and told them in the foulest of language what fate was awaiting them in India. There was little semblance of law or order anywhere, for, except when the King was wise enough

---

of the city and its first Portuguese ruler. "A mãe de toda a India, por assi estar no meio d'ella."

(or fortunate enough) to select a strong and honest viceroy, Goa and the other Portuguese establishments in the East were lawless and uncontrolled centers.

The city was hot and humid under the blazing Indian sun, and since no provision was made for the reception and quartering of the soldiers arriving from Lisbon, they had to find lodgings for themselves as best they could. Many of the penniless wretches could not obtain food, and numbers of them, badly nourished as they had been aboard ship, died miserably during the first few days in India.

Here in Goa, the Portuguese, representatives of Western civilization, had changed their ways of dress and life; a handful of Europeans set in the midst of medieval India as conquerors, they seemed to have taken unto themselves every extravagance of the people among whom they dwelt—and to have added more of their own devising.

The Terreiro do Paço, where the Viceroy's palace was located, was in the very heart of the city, and there, in spite of the suffocating heat, the crowds were as dense as in the busiest streets of Lisbon itself. The gleaming cuirasses and helmets of soldiers contrasted with the white and black robes of Dominicans and the grey cowls of Franciscans. Both sword and cross symbolized Portugal in the East, and soldier and priest, in their proud bearing, seemed desirous of impressing all that by sheer force of will, rather than numbers, they were masters here, and, large as was the throng —a mingling of every race of Europe, Asia, and Africa—the few Portuguese dominated. Nonetheless, their greed, cruelty, and corruption, from the highest officials to the common soldiers, and the inexorable hand of time had marked their period of power as pitifully short in history. But as with men in every age and in every nation, they were, with a few exceptions, blind and oblivious to the approaching debacle that was soon to sweep them from their mastery of the Eastern seas.

Through the native mobs on the streets rode *fidalgos* on Persian horses, their bridles embroidered in gold and silver thread and adorned with pearls, their stirrups encased in silver, and the reins hung with tiny tinkling bells of precious metal, while before and behind trotted black slaves on foot. No carriages were used in the busy quarters of the city, and residents who did not ride horses or walk were borne in litters by two or four slaves. Only the Portuguese appeared abroad with arms, which were forbidden to the natives. Many of the men wore heavy rosaries about their necks "and continually told their beads in apparent devotion."[2] Most of the Europeans were accompanied by slaves carrying boxes of areca nuts and lime, for they had taken up the South Asian custom of chewing betel.[3] One of the familiar sights of Goa at this time was a Portuguese barber. But such a barber as was never seen in Europe! When he called at a client's house, it was in full state: before him marched his slaves, one carrying his basin, another his razors, scissors, combs, brushes, and the other implements of his profession, another his boxes of soap, lotions, and cosmetics, while he himself strutted pompously down the street under a great silken parasol carried by a fourth slave. Dressed in silks and wearing a plumed hat with a jeweled cockade, girt with a fine sword, his fingers heavy with rings set with large precious stones, he appeared more magnificent than a grandee of Lisbon.

From time to time palanquins passed through the crowd, these also carried by slaves. Within them were women, some of them Portuguese, but the greater number half-castes. Their faces were veiled, and their hands, often dangling languidly over the side of the palanquin, were so covered with rings that only the hennaed tips of the fingers were visible. They were followed by women

[2] Visitors to Egypt will have noted that many Egyptians (Moslems for the most part) carry rosaries and use them in the same manner, even while engaged in conversation.

[3] One French visitor of the period said of them: "In a word, they are very vain and proud, and as the [Spanish] proverb has it: 'Pocos y locos'—'there are but few of them—and they crazy.' "

94

slaves, many of them in fine silks. In fact, by far the greater number of people on the streets were slaves, for even the poorer residents owned from ten to thirty, since the Europeans considered it beneath their dignity to engage in trade or perform the slightest piece of manual labor. Good-looking women slaves loitered alone or in pairs along the more frequented streets and in the squares, soliciting passers-by with barefaced effrontery, which was taken as a matter of course by all and caused no offense to those addressed.[4]

Although Goa was called a dourada (the golden), it was, even in the busiest part, filthy beyond description—but probably not much more so than the great cities of Europe—for every kind of refuse was indiscriminately thrown out of houses and shops, and many of the streets, as well as the river banks, were used as latrines.

The Rua Direita,[5] like the Via Nova in Lisbon, was lined with the finest shops, where bankers, goldsmiths, and lapidaries carried on flourishing businesses. Many of the artisans were natives, but some of the master craftsmen in jewelry were French, German, Italian, and Flemish, for rich Goa had attracted adventurers from every corner of Europe, Asia, and Africa. Even bearded Englishmen from the distant shores of the Thames were to be seen on the streets. Peddlers of fruits, vegetables and cooling drinks made the center of the city a Babel with their shouting and soliciting in

[4] The number of half-castes, many of them accepted on equal footing by the Portuguese, was very large and ever increasing. In fact, Albuquerque, while governor in the early part of the century, realizing that the drain on Portuguese manpower in exploring and maintaining Portugal's conquest was rapidly becoming too great, had encouraged and fostered intermarriage with the Indians so that the offspring of such unions might populate and protect the Portuguese settlements. When he died in 1515, there were five hundred such mixed families—and they were most prolific—and in addition to these there were uncounted children of irregular unions between native women and soldiers, sailors, and civilians. (The greater part of the half-caste population was baptized into the faith of the conquerors.)

[5] It was called Direita (straight) because it differed from most of the streets laid out by the Portuguese in quadrants or other curves.

every language of Asia. The side streets were always filled with the sound of clanging hammers, the click of flying shuttles, the hum of bows flailing cotton, and the chatter of men and women sewing garments, and over all hung the dusty odor of sandal and teak, mingled with musk and attar of roses from the perfumers' shops and the acrid tang of leather from the saddlers' and harness-makers' stalls.

The Portuguese residential quarter revealed another side of Goanese life, especially when shops and offices were closed during the siesta or after business hours. Then groups of men gathered in doorways, seeking what cool shade was available, lolling in loose pajamas and talking over the topics of the day, while slaves fanned the flies away from their masters. The women sat apart on balconies on the upper floors, whose windows were trellised or screened to hide the occupants while giving them a good view of the street beneath. There they spent much of their time, watching the life below them, chattering, eating sweetmeats, and drinking cold juices and coconut milk. For these women, life in India was for the most part a dull, monotonous existence. Many of them were uneducated and unable even to read, and the enervating heat, rich foods, and day-long indolence led to intrigues, constant quarrels, and scandal, which kept the social life of the city in a perpetual ferment, supplying unending occasion for gossip.

This was the Goa of Camoëns' residence-years; he quickly absorbed its atmosphere, and we find much of the local color in his verses. Unlike his masters, Vergil and Dante, he was not writing of imaginary places or of those which he had never seen. The geography of his epic was not that of ancient or medieval myth or legend, but of Portugal, the coasts of Africa and Asia, and of the seas he had traversed; the descriptions were of people whom he had seen and whose life he knew well from personal contact.

The poet was certainly too intelligent not to have recognized his power in verse and his fertility of imagination, but from the way he came through his experiences in the East unscathed, he surely had early realized that if he was to succeed he had to win a decisive victory over himself, to discipline his body as well as his mind, and to remember always that drunkenness and carousing would inexorably lead to the destruction of his talent. At the same time he was a man of his age, and had not the slightest desire or inclination to be a hermit. The blood in his veins, the taste of life that had been his in Coimbra and at court, his experiences with women thereafter—all these continued to call imperiously for the affection of a woman, as well as for the eternal quest of the ideal. This appears in poems which were most likely written at this time, though, as so often, Catherine de Ataide was the theme:

> What are they doing, those beautiful eyes,
> So dimmed with tears that day?
> Who knows if they take thought of me,
> Or if any memories cling?
> Are they laughing with others
> While I am so sad?
> Are they longing with me
> For that day of all days
> When again I shall see that bright smile?
> Are they counting each minute and hour?
> Are they living long years without number
> Each moment that we are apart?
> By chance do they ever seek tidings of me
> From the winds and the birds of the air?
> Ah! Happy thoughts and dear fancies are these,
> To lighten my grief-stricken days![6]

There were times, however, when Luis' resolution and courage evidently weakened, as witness several of his poems written during this same period.[7]

[6] Soneto "Aqueles claros olhos que chorando."
[7] See Appendix I, Poem 61.

CHAPTER XI

Soldiering in India

Never did the pen blunt the lance.
—Couto, *Diálogo*

THE YEAR 1553 was nearing its close, and now Luis' weeks of idling in Goa came to an end, for a proclamation was posted ordering soldiers to report to their headquarters for active duty. Among the small states on the Indian coast lay the kingdom of Pimenta, consisting of a few villages whose inhabitants had but two sources of income: fishing and piracy. The King and his people were always turbulent and rebellious. Now they had seized some islands, the property of the King of Porca, an ally of the Portuguese, and the Viceroy determined to punish them.

All day long drums were beaten up and down the streets and notices were posted on the public buildings, granting amnesty to soldiers who had committed crimes, even murder, if they would sign up for the expedition. Many reported with alacrity, for they had been literally starving, not having received any compensation since the last expedition, and those who had come to Goa with Luis on the *São Bento* had had no pay since their arrival. Some, however, were reluctant to enrol, for, having obtained a little capital by devious means, they had been making a comfortable profit in dealing in pepper and other spices in small quantities. As each soldier was entered on the Viceroy's list, he was paid his stipend for three months in advance, most of which either went to redeem personal effects pawned during the weeks of enforced idleness or was squandered in riotous living.

All the efforts of the Viceroy to collect a sufficient Portuguese force were in vain, and on the last days before the expedition was to sail, soldiers began to drag Negro slaves—often bloody from beatings received when they resisted—to the *casa de matricula,* or recruiting station. Though they had been seized as they were going about their masters' business, the latter were not notified nor did they receive any compensation for the human property thus stolen from them.

Finally the troops were issued the necessary equipment: arquebuses, pikes, partisans, small shields, bows and arrows. Each also received a leather gorget, a broad collar, as protection against swords and arrows. Shoes and stockings were not supplied, and those who did not possess them went barefoot.

At last all was ready and the flotilla set sail, led by the Viceroy aboard the *Reliquias.* The first port reached was fortified Cananor, which had been long in the possession of the Portuguese. There lay the tomb of D. Henrique de Menezes (1496–1526),[1] fifth governor of India, in the Chapel of Santiago. He had died at the early age of thirty; having had a brilliant career in Morocco and the Moluccas, he had served but two years as governor of India. A crudely carved epitaph was set in the pavement beside the altar:

> The noblest knight,
> The most Roman of governors,
> The most humane and the most excellent,
> In all things the first of the first

[1] See Appendix I, Poem 62.

Both in war and in peace
Was he who lies here,
Dom Enrique de Menezes
—And he lived so few months.

After a short stay for food and water the ships moved on to Chale for a council of war and thence proceeded to the assault on Chembé.

At break of dawn the ship's captain gave the signal to disembark, and the chaplain, standing before the men on the foredeck, recited the confiteor, accompanied by the soldiers and crew. Immediately upon receiving a general and plenary absolution they all rushed ashore, scattering in bands, each man following his captain. Control of the men by their officers was hardly more than nominal, and as soon as they landed they set up a shout of "Santiago!" Thereafter each followed his own will or whims. This headlong advance by heavily armed and armored troops was irresistible; the islanders were thrown into the utmost confusion and fled, the soldiers pursuing them to the town, where the old men, women, and children were gathered. Thereupon an unbelievably cruel massacre, senseless and inexcusable, began. Every living being found was killed; even little children, the maimed, the crippled, and the sick did not escape. The carnage was frightful, the ferocity of the soldiers more wanton than that of wild beasts. Pregnant women were ripped open, their unborn babes torn from them and dashed to the ground, and with knives the soldiers stabbed and cut to pieces the breasts of nursing mothers. All pleas for mercy were in vain. The appetite for blood was not glutted with the killing of every human being in sight; even cows, donkeys, dogs, and cats were slaughtered. Nothing found was left alive, and for days corpses lay rotting in the sun. Then all the standing crops were burned and the coconut trees chopped down, thus depriving the people of their sustenance.

After the massacre, the soldiers (it is to be remembered that many were savage slaves impressed into service) started looting, the men entering huts and shops, seizing everything portable that struck their fancy, and smashing or destroying what they did not want or could not carry off. At this juncture, while many were drunk or had laid aside their arms, the better to gather up their plunder, a number were killed by natives who, having escaped the initial onslaught, crept up and stabbed them unawares, then fled before the heavily laden soldiers could pursue them. The pillage over, the town fired, and the troops mustered onto the ships, the Portuguese sailed away, leaving behind them reeking, smoking desolation—and a smoldering hatred that never died.

Camoëns, brave man as he was on the field of battle, revolted at the blood lust of his fellows-in-arms when the indiscriminate killing of the helpless noncombatants began. His sensitive soul writhed at the cruelty and unbridled savagery, and he never forgot the dreadful picture. Later, in six bitter lines of his *Lusiads,* he concentrated the horror and nausea it caused him:

> On brute cruelty and bestiality
> Do you bestow the names of "valor" and of "bravery,"
> And hold possessed of virtue great
> Him who despises human life,
> —Life ever to be prized,
> For He who gave it shudders at its loss.[2]

True it was—and Luis recognized it—that cruelty was common in warfare, but he could not subscribe to the inexcusable destruction of human life, even though his superiors proclaimed that it was necessary to instil terror of the Portuguese name, since they were few and the Indians innumerable. The spark of resentment and shame for the actions of the unworthy descendants of his country's heroes flared up in him, to be poured out in acid vituperation in verse when finally he could no longer contain himself.

[2] *Lusiads,* IV, 99.

Leaving a few score men to complete the campaign, the Viceroy returned with his fleet to Goa, arriving in February, 1554. The expedition was a success from the military point of view and had been accomplished in a matter of weeks, though the actual fighting lasted only two days. The story was later touched on by Camoëns in one of his elegies, impersonally and dispassionately, but without details; he was a soldier by compulsion, not by choice, and was disinclined to do more than sketch the incident. Although he devoted few lines to this, his first conflict with the Indians, the campaign and its revelation of the disgraceful conduct and lack of military discipline of the Portuguese impressed him profoundly.

The days following the return of the soldiers were wild and boisterous. As ever, when the city was crowded with troops laden with loot, gambling was rife. The streets were scenes of continual brawling, and the hospital was kept busy dressing wounds received in stabbing and shooting affrays.

Gambling was a real business in Goa. The houses were licensed and paid rent to the government. Profit was made not only on the games, but on eating, drinking, and sleeping quarters, for these were all at the disposal of the patrons. They were cheerful, bright, well-kept places made attractive not only to the soldiers and sailors, most of whom had no fixed places of abode, but also to the residents of the town. The large number of priests in the city made an effort to control their flocks, but, as in all wars (and in the sixteenth century the Portuguese were waging a continuous war up and down the African and Asiatic seas and coasts), the soldiers knew that their lives were precarious, that a native spear or sword, poison, or disease might carry them off at any time. So they resolved to enjoy all that was offered them in drink, gaming, and women while they could, giving no thought to the morrow, for it might never dawn for them. At such times the citizens were especially careful to bar their doors at night, for soldiers, drunk or desperate for money, often broke into homes, and when they did, the householders had to defend themselves as best they could, for there was no police protection, and neither they nor their womenfolk or property were safe from the lawless marauders.

There were for Camoëns but a few weeks of respite and repose, for 1554 was still in its second month when the troops were mustered for a move against the Turkish ships on the Red Sea route from Egypt to the East. Determined as they were to monopolize the sea-borne trade between spice-rich Asia and the European markets, the Portuguese constantly sent out fleets to capture or destroy all vessels in the Eastern seas not flying the flag of Portugal. Such ships were deemed enemies, for they dared to challenge the Portuguese mastery of Asiatic maritime commerce.

Of all this Luis had heard much in Lisbon, and now, in Goa, the policies of his fellow countrymen and their ruthless application were becoming painfully clear to him. Already he could, with his background, see the lack of vision and the shortsightedness of Portuguese policy, the weakness of Portuguese statecraft, and the dry rot that had set in throughout the bureaucracy both at home and in India. He was caught up in the machine, however, and though he might write to friends in Portugal of his disillusionment and forebodings, he could not speak his mind in India as long as he was bound by the contract of military service made part of the royal pardon.[3]

[3] A few days before Camoëns reported for duty on the Red Sea expedition, the *São Bento*, on which he had come to India, sailed for Lisbon. The intervening months had been spent in careening and repairing her and finally in loading her with Indian merchandise for the home voyage. The vessel rode far lower in the water than she had when she sailed down the Tagus from the capital. Not only was her hold loaded to the hatches with merchandise, but bales, barrels, and chests were heaped high on the decks, and swarming everywhere were soldiers and officials returning to Portugal, as well as a cargo of slaves destined for the auction block. Such overloading of Portuguese vessels was the cause of many shipwrecks and losses at sea.

Now the soldier-poet was to move from the coast of India onto a larger stage and engage in a Portuguese campaign against the Moslems at the entrance to the Red Sea, fittingly named by the Arabs *Bab-el-Mandeb* (The Gate of Tears).

CHAPTER XII

The Red Sea Campaign

> They enter the Persian Gulf where still abide
> Memories of Babel, though now confused.
> —CAMOËNS, *Lusiads*, IV, 64

THE END OF FEBRUARY, 1554, arrived, and with it sailed a Portuguese flotilla of more than thirty-five vessels carrying twelve hundred soldiers.

Camoëns had received, as had the other veterans of the Pimenta campaign, a certificate from his captain setting forth his time of service and his conduct, for such a certificate was issued after each expedition in which a soldier had engaged. If a man could accumulate a minimum of twelve of these in his years of compulsory service, they brought him his release, permitting him to return to Portugal or to enter the Indian government civil service.

The course was set for the Arabian coast, the soldiers happy and carefree, already looking forward to killing unbelievers, gathering loot, and returning to Goa and its fleshpots, for they considered every foreign vessel a prize whose cargo was a legitimate spoil of war. The crew and passengers, most often helpless, unarmed, and innocent of any crime against the Portuguese, were regarded as outlaws, to be killed if they resisted or perhaps sold into slavery.

Although the fleet watched the straits and scoured both the African and Arabian coasts near by, their search for Turkish ships was in vain. One of the African roadsteads in which Camoëns' vessel dropped anchor was off Cape Guardafui (the Arabic *Jard-Rafun*), near Ras-ef-Fil (the Elephant Head), at a point called Cape Felix, and there, in sight of the bare, burned, sterile hills, Luis found himself lonelier than ever. Time hung heavily on his hands, until, affected as he so often was by the landscape about him—the arid, bleak mountains and the calm sea, with never a ship in the wide expanse except those of his own fleet—he wrote one of his finest *canções,* or songs.[1] In it, as in the elegy describing the expedition against the King of Pimenta, his innermost thoughts reverted to Portugal and the hours with Catherine de Ataide, for one Portuguese proverb was ever fulfilled in Luis de Camoëns: "O que enche o coração, transborda pela bocca."[2] Thus, in the midst of a campaign in which all others' hopes and plans were of blood and loot, did Luis compose some of his most poignant verse.

Failing in their mission to the Red Sea—the Turks were wary and did not risk the seizure of their vessels—the Portuguese sailed away along the Arabian coast into the Persian Gulf, finally casting anchor before the island of Ormuz.

[1] See Appendix I, Poem 63.
[2] "What fills the heart overflows through the mouth."

CHAPTER XIII

Ormuz

The world is a ring and Ormuz is the precious stone set therein.
—Barros, *Decadas*

In this city [Ormuz] are many merchants of substance, and many very great ships. It has a right good harbor where many sorts of goods are handled which come hither from many lands, and from here they barter them with many parts of India.
—*The Book of Duarte Barbosa*, I, 92

THE ISLAND OF ORMUZ was sterile and devoid of cultivation, but it was picturesque from a vessel approaching its anchorage, for its fortress, with eight towers, resembled a castle half-surrounded by the sea. With no water supply of its own, four great cisterns filled by boats from the mainland supplied its needs. In addition, the climate was particularly unhealthful, especially when the hot wind, called by the Portuguese *abrasador,* blew. It usually rose in the afternoons, filling the air with a fine suffocating dust.

The barren island produced nothing but sulphur and salt, but it was an important entrepôt for the products of India, Persia, and Ethiopia. Dominated by the Portuguese, it was crowded with folk from all the East, and Indians and Persians rubbed shoulders with

Levantines and Turks, Abyssinians, Armenians, and Arabs. In its markets and warehouses were great stores of spices, carpets from Turkey and Persia, from Bagdad and Damascus, and fine-woven silks from China, together with sacks of precious stones and pearls. From its quays were shipped to the ports of India great numbers of Arabian horses. Ships were constantly arriving from the Moluccas and Ceylon, from Malacca and the Indian coast, and others sailed away in every direction to the harbors of Asia, East Africa, and the Spice Islands. From the mainland, but a dozen miles away, goods were transported across deserts and mountains to far countries, and caravans came down out of Syria and Arabia, Afghanistan, and the northern lands.

Life in Ormuz was much like that in Goa, save that in the Persian city there was even more of the age-old voluptuous life of the East, as yet hardly touched by contact with Europe. Men still dressed in their flowing robes, used perfumes, and wore many jewels, and the rich had their harems, filled with women brought from every land, harems guarded by eunuchs, bought for the most part from Arab traders who imported them from East Africa. Here spread the roots of the same moral corruption that had penetrated into the life of the Portuguese in India. They, whose forebears but fifty years before had made these great seas and ports their own, had now sunk to adopting the vices and degrading practices of sixteenth-century Asia, destroying their own birthright and that of their gallant nation, not caring, probably not even realizing, that in their blind stupidity they were rendering all profitable future for their people in Asiatic lands impossible.

As July wore into August, news came to the Portuguese commander that Alecheluby, a rich and powerful Arab, once treasurer of Cairo, was preparing to send sixteen Turkish galleys from the Persian Gulf to Suez, on the Red Sea. In fact, the message asserted that the ships had already left Basrah. Five galleons were dispatched to intercept them. The wily Alecheluby learned of the ruse

and escaped, following a course near the coast of Arabia, whereupon the whole armada set out in pursuit, finally sighting the
sixteen ships a few miles off Muscat (Muskat) on August 25, 1554.

Spreading all sail, the Portuguese swiftly overtook the slower
galleys. Meanwhile, cannon were loaded, slow matches lighted, and
swords unsheathed, the soldiers venting their joy at the approaching slaughter and looting with snatches of songs and yells. Alecheluby's ships, though also armed with cannon, were heavily laden
and, designed to carry cargo, were clumsy and difficult to maneu-
ver. As the Portuguese drew near, their cannon raked the Moslem
vessels fore and aft, bringing down the rigging, masts, and sails and
throwing the decks into confusion. Then the galleons closed in on
six of the ships; the soldiers lashed the vessels rail to rail with grap-
pling irons and ropes and swarmed over the bulwarks to engage
the terrified enemy with sword and dagger.

Soon all was over. The decks, strewn with dead and dying men,
were slippery with blood; the hand-to-hand struggle had become
a carnage and slaughter, not a battle. Although many of the crews
threw down their weapons in surrender, they were cold-bloodedly
killed, to a man, their bodies and those of the dying being tossed
overboard to the sharks.

The vessels—Alecheluby had escaped to Cambaya in India with
several of his ships—were towed to Muscat. There they were
stripped of everything of value, including fifty pieces of bronze
artillery, after which they were cleaned and repaired, solemnly
blessed by the priests who had accompanied the fleet, and divided
among the *fidalgos* and captains of the expedition. After a short
stay in Muscat, where the Portuguese dead were buried and the
wounded treated, the fleet, rejoicing in its success, turned its prows
southeastward toward its home port of Goa.

This piratical foray—for it was nothing else—had sickened
Camoëns even more than the savage assault in the south of India.
At least in Chembé there had been an enemy drawn up in battle

array, whereas the capture of Alecheluby's ships was like the slaughter of cattle for the market. He hated his part in it and hoped for the day when he could lay aside the sword forever and take up his pen. Though not lacking in courage, he longed to be far away from such scenes, for he had seen and learned enough by now to know the Portuguese rule and the men who were its agents for what they were. Anger and indignation were growing stronger and stronger with him—to burst forth in a few short months and to bring him naught by greater suffering and sorrow.

CHAPTER XIV

Follies in India

> Ever in this world saw I
> Good men suffer grave torments,
> But even more—
> Enough to terrify—
> Men who live out evil lives
> Reveling in pleasure and in content.
> —CAMOËNS, Redondilha "Ao desconcerto do mundo"

AT THE BEGINNING of November in the year 1554, the Portuguese fleet, loaded with the plunder of Alecheluby's galleys and with music playing and flags flying—as though a glorious and hard-fought naval victory had been won—sailed into the harbor of Goa, to be met and congratulated by the Viceroy, whose son[1] proudly felt that he had covered himself with honor and distinction by the capture of the Turkish ships.

Meanwhile, during the eight months' absence of the fleet, changes had taken place in the government of Goa. The three-year term of Viceroy D. Afonso de Noronha was over, and he had, as was customary, moved from the palace and was preparing

[1] See Appendix I, Poem 64.

for the voyage back to Portugal. His departure revealed his incredible corruption and greed, for an entire vessel had been set apart to convey to Lisbon the goods he had plundered from enemy ships, looted in captured Indian towns, or taken by extortion—and worse—from rajas and princes under the domination of Portugal, as well as wealth stolen from the government treasury. These thefts and ill-gotten gains were accepted as normal by the Portuguese of Goa, for such was the custom of most of the viceroys and governors: to spend the first year of their service exploring the financial possibilities of their position, the second and third in gathering all they could in every possible manner, legal or illegal, and in preparing to leave upon the arrival of their successor.

In the three years of his incumbency, D. Afonso and his son had accumulated enough wealth to make them rich beyond any expectations which they may have had when they arrived in the Indies. In January, 1555, they sailed for Portugal. Many months later, news came that their ship had become separated from the remainder of the home-going fleet and was not heard from again. It was never learned whether it sank in a storm, was wrecked on the African coast, or was attacked and destroyed by the Moslems. Whatever happened, D. Afonso, his son, and their treasure vanished forever.

The new viceroy, D. Pedro de Mascarenhas, an old man already far gone in tuberculosis, had arrived in Goa to take over the government on September 16. No sooner had he settled in the vice-regal palace than he began to distribute lucrative positions to his favorites, irrespective of their abilities or the lack thereof. The announcement of these appointments caused much comment, even in cynical Goa.

The city was officially in mourning when the fleet arrived from Ormuz, for upon his arrival the new viceroy had published an announcement of the death of Prince John, the only surviving son of John III and the hope of the nation. He was only seventeen,

Labels within image: PRINCE HENRY OF PORTUGALL. — HONI·SOIT·QVI·MAL·Y·PENSE — CEUTA

From Richard Fanshaw (trans.), *The Lusiad*, London, 1655

Prince Henry the Navigator

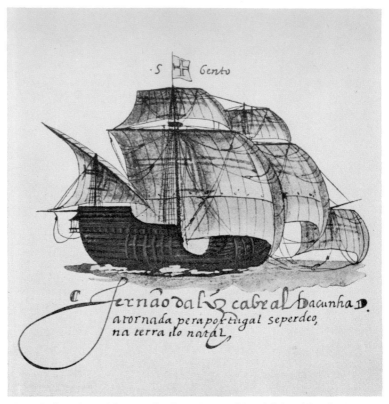

From José Maria Rodrigues and Afonso Lopes Vieira (eds.), *Lírica de Camões*, Coimbra, 1932

The *São Bento,* on which Camoëns sailed to India

and although he was very sickly, he had been married thirteen months to D. Juana, daughter of Charles V, when tuberculosis carried him off. Eighteen days after his death, his son was born and at baptism was given the name Sebastian.

Camoëns received other tidings which for him overshadowed the national calamity: young D. Antonio de Noronha, whose tutor he had been, was dead. Luis was deeply grieved, for he had loved the lad as though he had been his own brother, but with it all there was in his sorrow a pardonable pride in the brave way in which Antonio had met his death.

Shortly after Camoëns had left the service of the Noronhas, King John had conferred upon Antonio the singular honor of selecting him as the companion and partner of Prince John in a great tourney in Enxobregas. There, though he was but fifteen years old, Antonio had fallen madly in love with one D. Margarida da Silva. His father, D. Francisco, who had higher ambitions for his son, opposed the young lovers and used his powerful influence to have Antonio sent to Ceuta as an officer, believing that he would win his spurs there and at the same time forget his passion; as the Portuguese proverb has it: "Longe dos olhos, longe de coração."[2] By good fortune—or so, mistakenly, thought D. Francisco—this was easily accomplished, for Antonio's uncle was *capitão-mór* of the Moroccan city, and there, in frequent skirmishes with the Moors, Antonio learned how to acquit himself in battle.

One day, however, the Arab *alcaide* of Tetuán challenged D. Pedro de Menezes, the *capitão-mór* of Ceuta, to a combat between equal numbers (about three hundred) of Arabs and Portuguese, fixing the day and place near Mount Condessa, a league from the city. Though D. Pedro had been warned to beware of treachery, he refused to listen and rode rashly out to the rendezvous with his three hundred men, Antonio at his side. Suddenly, as they neared the place, more than three thousand wildly shouting Arabs, some

2 "Far from the eyes, far from the heart."

on horseback, some on foot, swept out from behind the hills, brandishing swords, spears, maces, and muskets. The Portuguese were surrounded; they could neither flee nor retreat, even had D. Pedro so desired. Quickly turning to his aide, Antão Pacheco, D. Pedro asked: "What's to be done?" Pacheco, who had strongly urged D. Pedro not to accept the challenge, replied bitterly, with a shrug, "Your lordship wanted it so. Now there's nothing left but to die with honor."

The Portuguese charged with drawn swords, but it was in vain. Spears hurtled through the air on the little group, arrows and bullets rained on them, and the ambush became a massacre. It was soon over. Three hundred and seven Portuguese, all but a few of those who had ridden out that day through the gate of Ceuta, lay dead. These men, who had sold their lives dearly, were men whom Portugal could ill afford to lose, and only a handful escaped in the dust of conflict to bear the sad news to the garrison.

Among the slain, lying close to his commander and Pacheco, his young body covered with wounds, was Antonio, heir to the house of D. Francisco de Noronha, killed on the eighteenth of April, 1553, at the age of seventeen. Little profit it was to the King that one of those who escaped saved the royal banner; little did it comfort D. Francisco to learn later that D. Margarida, so adored by his son, became the bride of a count from Portalegre.

This was the tragic tale that came to Camoëns the day the flotilla arrived from Persia with flags flying gaily and drums and trumpets and pipes making merry music. With the untimely death of Antonio, one of the few ties that still bound Luis to his old life, to the happy days of feasts and love, music and poetry in Lisbon, was severed. Never again was there to be a meeting and conversation with one of those nearest and dearest to him, one whom he had so often looked forward to seeing when his three years' tour of duty should be over. As ever, when his emotions swept over him, they were sublimated into verse. When grief had ceased and only the long, dull ache of an irreparable loss remained with him, he wrote of his erstwhile young companion:

> Alas, beloved Dom Antonio,
> In the flower of your years were you struck down
> By unkind fate;
> There on the field of battle
> You did with your good right arm
> Bedim the fame of the fighting men of old.
> I have this one comfort in my grief so great,
> That if such a thing as honor be in death
> You could earn no greater earthly meed
> Than is yours now.
> If the Muse would only touch my verse
> And to my heartfelt prayer let halting pen respond,
> In long and mournful song by you inspired
> E'en though you died at the hand of cruelest Mars,
> Yet shall you live 'mongst men in fragrant memory long.[3]

Luis enclosed this sonnet in a letter[4] to a friend in Lisbon. From the tone of the letter he appears to have been at least partly adjusted to his new life, but still yearning for the homeland. There is a significant line which foreshadows the indignation—a mild term —at the conduct of his fellow Portuguese that was soon to find vent in bitter verse.

I longed so much for a letter from you that I believe that just because of my desiring it so it did not come, for this is the most certain practice of Fortune, that she allows that most to be desired which she is the most ready to refuse. But that other ships may not commit for me so great an offense as to make you think that I do not remember you, I have determined to oblige you with this letter, in which you will learn more or less what I wish you to

---

[3] Soneto "Em flor vos arrancou, de então crescida."

[4] Although the addressee is unknown, the letter has survived time and destruction by fire and earthquake.

write me from over there. In return for which I am paying you in advance with news from here (which will not be bad for the bottom of a chest) about some adventurers who think that every jungle shrub is marjoram and who do not know that there are fairies both here and there.

When I departed from my native land as one who was bound for the other world, I ordered whatever hopes I had nourished up to that time hanged, with a public proclamation—"Hanged as makers of false coin." And I disentangled myself from those thoughts which I had harbored, for they could in no way profit me. And so, finding myself in a position where I could not distinguish between hawk and buzzard [in a twilight zone—i.e., confusion], the words which I last spoke on boarding ship were those of Scipio Africanus—"Ingrata patria, non possidebis ossa mea."[5] For when I reflect, through no fault that would condemn me to even three days of Purgatory I had to endure three thousand slanderous tongues, the worst of plots and evil intents, born of pure envy at seeing "their loved ivy torn from their walls, and clinging to another's "[6]—and because of this, friendships weaker than wax developed into hatreds which did more damage to my good name than does fire to the skin of a roasting suckling-pig. Then the fact should be added that they ascribed to my skin the quality of Achilles, who was invulnerable save on the soles of his feet—mine they never saw, though I caused many to show theirs[7]—or to add stories of like character, by which cowards stab with evil names, striking with their tongues that which they cannot [strike] with their weapons. Finally, Senhor, I don't know how to reward myself for knowing so well how to escape all these traps that were laid for me in the homeland, and for finding my-

---

[5] "Ungrateful fatherland, thou shalt not possess my bones."

[6] This quotation, written in Spanish by Camoëns, is from a poem by Garçilaso de la Vega (Eclogue I, 1, 135, 136) and probably refers to jealousies or enmities known to Camoëns' correspondent.

[7] That is, although he himself had never been laid low in combat, duel, or quarrel, he had stretched many another on his back—a reference to his rowdy days in Lisbon after his return from Morocco.

self here, living more respected than the bulls of Merceana, and more at peace than if I were in the cell of a Preaching Friar.

As for where I am, I can tell you that it is the mother of evil villains and the stepmother of honest men. For those who set out to find wealth here always float on top like bladders on water, but those whose inclination is "to arms, Moorish style"[8] are as dead bodies which the tide casts up on the beach, and I know that ere they ripen they waste away. . . . Now that I've told you this, I may say that here I have seen João Toscano who—as is found in any gang of ruffians—is, as it were, ready to eat raw flesh and to drink hot blood. . . . But a certain Manuel Serrão who, *sicut et nos,*[9] lacks an eye, is here. . . .

If you want to know about the Portuguese women, then know that all are fallen from grace. . . .

The letter closes with these lines:

For the nonce, nothing more, except the sonnet accompanying this, which I have written on the death of D. Antonio de Noronha and which I send that you may know how heavily it weighs upon me. I have also written the above eclogue on the same subject which treats in part on the death of the Prince, which [poem], it seems to me, is better than many others that I have done. I also send it that you may show it to Miguel Dias[10] who, because of his great friendship with D. Antonio, will be pleased to see it. But the occupation of writing many letters to the Kingdom [Portugal] gives me no leisure. I am writing to Luis de Lemos[11] there, in reply to one of his [letters]. If they don't arrive it should be understood that the fault lies in the voyage, in which all perishes. *Vale.*[12]

Camoëns evidently found it very difficult to make ends meet,

[8] A quotation from an old Spanish romance.
[9] "Just like me."
[10] This person has not been identified.
[11] This person has not been identified.
[12] "Farewell."

even with his pay and with what he received after the military expeditions in which he was engaged. His remark about his occupation in "writing many letters" to Portugal cannot mean that his personal correspondence left him no leisure, but that here, as probably in his last years in Lisbon, he was eking out his scanty income by writing letters for other soldiers and for sailors and inhabitants of Goa, the greater number of whom were illiterate or nearly so.

When he could not obtain coin, he was not too proud to accept clothing in lieu of payment for any service he might have performed. Shortly after his return from Ormuz a fellow Portuguese promised him a shirt instead of money. Luis, after patiently waiting a long time for the much needed garment, finally sent a reminder in the form of a short *redondilha*. Although he had scribbled it in joking fashion, Luis was desperate, and the request was made in all seriousness:

> He who in this world would be
> Distinguished from the rest of men
> Must ever, to exalt himself,
> Make the giving meet the promise.
> And now, since you, good sir,
> Have ta'en for all the world to see
> "GENEROSITY" for your blazon,
> 'Tis needful, to maintain your name,
> That you send the shirt you owe.[13]

Further bad news was brought by another vessel arriving from "the Kingdom," as Portugal was called by the residents of Goa. Luis had spoken rightly in his letter when he referred to the return voyages as those "in which all perishes." The *São Bento,* the largest, strongest, and in all ways the best of the five galleons that sailed so bravely—but so criminally overloaded—out of Goa

[13] Redondilha "Quem no mundo quiser ser."

that January day had been lost. An account of the shipwreck was told (and later written) by one of the survivors, Manoel de Mesquita Perestrello, who spoke of the ill fortune that seemed to have pursued the vessels.

They first touched at Cochin, whence they sailed on Friday, February 1, 1554. One, the *Cerveira,* was forced to put back to India after some days of sailing. The *Barrileira,* which remained behind the others at Mozambique, was later lost. The *Santiago* vanished one evening after sunset. For several days the crews of the other two ships anxiously scanned the horizon for her, but in vain. She was never heard from again. The *São Bento,* running before a gale, was wrecked on the coast of Natal. The captain and the retiring commander at Ormuz, together with some of the crew, were drowned; the others managed to get ashore on improvised rafts. Having lost everything but the clothes they were wearing, the survivors set out in a body to tramp along the unknown coast. After many days of privation and suffering, they finally made their way back to the Portuguese settlement at Mozambique. Only one of the five vessels eventually reached Portugal.

This shipwreck was but one of many that came to Camoëns' notice during his residence in India. Another, the subject of many a tale, was the loss of the galleon *São João,* perhaps the most tragic of the long list. It made a profound impression on the poet, for he told of it, even though briefly, in his *Lusiads* in stanzas of deepest pathos.[14]

So the time passed. No new military expedition summoned Luis to arms, and he had leisure to work on his epic, which was probably by this time nearing completion in a rough draft. Other poems

[14] *Lusiads,* V, 46–48. The tale describes the wreck of the galleon *São João* in 1552 and the sufferings of the survivors. The first Portuguese edition of the story is dated 1591 and was translated by Charles D. Ley in the Everyman Series in 1947 in *Portuguese Voyages, 1498–1663.* The subject is also fully treated by James Duffy in his *Shipwreck & Empire.*

also came from his pen—verses in all the fashionable forms of the day—and as these were circulated among his friends and acquaintances, his talent was gradually recognized by the officials and *fidalgos* of Goa. Month followed month, during which he learned more and more of the life of the foreigners in India, as well as of native manners and customs, until more than two of the three years of his compulsory military service had passed.

During this time Camoëns was far from happy. Though only in his thirty-first year, he had wandered far and had had many varying experiences, most of them tragic or near tragic. His nature, moreover, made it impossible for him to sever himself from some of the most poignant memories of his earlier life, and these, suffused as they were by the ever present *saudade* in his temperament, found their expression in tender, melancholy song.[15]

And Catherine? We know nothing further of her life, though she, too, probably walked lonely through the world. She may have longed to write and to receive letters from Luis, but no messages exchanged by them have as yet been found.

June of 1555 was at hand, and Goa was agog with excitement. D. Pedro de Mascarenhas, the second viceroy under whom Camoëns had served in Asia, died after only ten months of his term had expired. He was succeeded as governor[16] by D. Francisco Barreto, who was in India at the time and whose name headed the sealed list of those designated by the King to fill the office in such an emergency. The whole city joined in the traditional welcome to its new lord, and Luis, who had been absent in the Red Sea and Persian Gulf expeditions when Mascarenhas was installed, took part in the celebration.

First Barreto and his entourage were received by delegations

---

[15] See Appendix I, Poems 66 through 70.

[16] Some of the Portuguese rulers were called viceroys, others governors. The difference was a matter of protocol, not power.

representing the *fidalgos,* clergy, nobility, and citizenry. Then all proceeded to the cathedral, where a solemn *Te Deum* was sung, the church bells all over the city ringing during the service and continuing their clangor throughout the day. At sunset, fireworks, imported from far-distant China, were set off, and the streets and taverns were noisy with carousing crowds all through the night.

The celebration, which lasted for several days, was rudely interrupted on St. John's Eve. Shortly after nightfall, during a display of fireworks, some unknown person lighted a rocket near the Church of Our Lady of the Rosary. Instead of coming to earth on the marshy ground near the river as planned, it curved downward toward the fleet landing stage and struck the galleon *St. Matthew,* which had been drawn up on the shore and roofed over with straw as a protection against the weather. As Luis later described it to the historian Couto, "the ship caught fire with such a blaze that it was terrifying—and it lay bulwark to bulwark with other ships drawn up alongside it. The wind was high and the flames leaped from one [vessel] to another with such a tremendous roar and crackling that it seemed as though the whole city might be destroyed."

The Governor, as soon as he learned of the conflagration, hastened down to the water front with all the citizens and soldiers whom he could get together, and everyone set to work to salvage what vessels and property they could. Those of the ships which were anchored out in the stream were safe, but the craft lined up on the shore were blazing furiously and little could be done to save them. "The governor," said Camoëns, describing the scene most graphically, "rushed here and there like one possessed, covered with mud and water, even daring to go onto the burning galleons, risking his life in the flames and among falling timbers, to do all he could to save the fleet. The soldiers, too, showed themselves as fearless as though in battle, and many of them were badly burned. As they reported to the governor, begrimed with smoke, their hair, eyebrows and clothes singed and blackened, he embraced them; to one he gave the gold chain from about his neck, to another the seal-ring from his finger, and to yet others gold pieces, as he ran hither and yon, urging on and encouraging his men to save what they could, promising rewards to those for whom he had no more gifts on his person."

At daybreak the blaze had not yet died down, and when at last nothing remained but the water-soaked keels of the ships and a few blackened beams floating in the harbor, twelve valuable ships belonging to the King and forming the greater part of the squadron in Indian waters had been consumed.

Barreto's daring courage and absolute disregard for his life in the performance of duty so won the poet's respect and esteem (for he had been in the thick of the firefighting and had seen all that had occurred) that when the interrupted merrymaking was resumed, he resolved to write a drama as his contribution.

The play was *Filodemo,* the earliest drama written by him and now adapted for the celebration, with the title[17] intended as a tribute to the Viceroy. It had a cleverly contrived plot, as complicated as that of most operas, recounting the adventures of Filodemo, orphan son of a Portuguese *fidalgo* and a Danish princess. Wrecked on the coast of Portugal, the young man becomes enamored of Dionysa, ignorant of the fact that she is his blood cousin. Dionysa's brother, Venadoro, is in love with Filodemo's sister, Florimera. The revelation of the real relationships by an old shepherd brings about a happy ending.[18]

The performance, a novelty in Goanese life, was staged by Camoëns himself, and he delivered the prologue as well, to a very different audience from that which had witnessed the unfortunate presentation of *King Seleucus* in Lisbon. Instead of the King and Queen and courtiers, here were the Governor and his

---

[17] *Filodemo*, taken from the Greek, means "loved by the people."

[18] As in the *Amphytrion*, some of the spoken lines are in Portuguese, others in Spanish. Part of the play is in prose, part in *redondilha* form.

entourage, officeholders, hangers-on in the government, *fidalgos,* tatterdemalion soldiers, half-castes, turbaned Indians, and native women.

The play was a success, the talk for days in the houses and taverns of the city, and Barreto summoned Camoëns, whose story by this time was known throughout Goa, to thank him. The meeting was the beginning of a real friendship between the two men, who found many interests in common. Moreover, both were well-educated men with vision and ideals, and such were far too seldom found in the city.

Just as his foot seemed set once again on the ladder of success —for Barreto's friendship gave promise of advancement for the poet, and the three years of military service to which he had pledged himself on receiving the King's pardon were drawing swiftly to their close—Luis, entirely innocent, was drawn into an affair which threatened to put an end to the life of comparative peace and content which he was beginning to find in India.

The great fire had brought the festivities of Barreto's accession to an abrupt close, but they were resumed at the baptism of a Singhalese prince for whom the Governor stood as godfather. Among the games was a *jogo de cannas,* a tourney in which the contestants used long reeds or bamboo sticks instead of lances. It was a sham fight in which the champions might be unseated but where no great bodily injury could be inflicted.

Some of the participants had imbibed too freely of the toasts to the Governor before entering the lists, and many of the European spectators were in no better case, acting disgracefully in their cups. Camoëns, who was present, felt humiliated and was highly incensed at the shameful spectacle of the Portuguese conquerors, who were abandoning all decency in the presence of the great crowd of Indians and other Asians gathered in the square, and most tactlessly and freely voiced his disapproval and disgust at what was going on.

A few days later a paper fell into his hands. A fragment without beginning or end, it was a satire on the tourney and was written partly in verse. At the top of the page appeared a statement that in the festivities following the installation of the Governor, "certain men came out to play in the tourney who could not hold their wine, and others who were well known for various vices." Then followed innuendoes without names, but the targets of the satire were easily recognizable by all who had been present.

To Luis' consternation, some of his friends, amused by the pungent racy, and often biting lines and verses, came to congratulate him—and he then learned that all Goa, knowing of his facile pen, believed that he was the author. The laughter at those thus pilloried was uproarious, but the anger of the victims was fearful. Many of them held high office, and though Luis vehemently protested his innocence, they would have none of it, and made life miserable for him. He, on his part, was goaded to fury, and in reply to his detractors he indiscreetly lashed out with a set of *redondilhas* which far transcended the "Jogo de Cannas" in cold irony and bitter recrimination. His temper had never been too well disciplined—as witness his brawls and quarrels after his return from Ceuta and the fracas with Borges, which had brought him where he was—and now he had castigated his tormentors in verse just at a time when self-restraint might have served him far better.

He called the poem "Disparates da India":[19] nine stanzas of verses, with Spanish words and phrases interspersed in the text, the whole a burning diatribe and a merciless flaying of the social and political shame of the Portuguese in India. Though he mentioned none by name, he attacked all of those who had brought low the proud name of his country and held her up to the ridicule and malediction of all good men—the overbearing rich, the educated but pretentious and ne'er-do-well youth, those who boasted of their bravery yet were cowards, the immoral moralists, the hypocrites hiding behind long faces, the greedy judges who released the

19 "Follies in India."

rich but were merciless to the poor and helpless. Each verse ends
with some old and apt proverb—"Who is born crooked, is slow in
straightening out"; "One does not find honor and self-interest in
the same bed"; "He seeks to cover the sky with a fan" (i. e., "He
tries to throw dust in the eyes of folk"); "A wolf in sheep's clothing"; "When figs are ripe, there are no friends"; "From a pig's
tail one can make no arrow"; "There go the laws, where gold is
found"—and he speaks bitterly of justice as "that of spider webs,"
catching the little fellows and allowing the big ones to escape.

Thus did Camoëns, in no uncertain terms, declare a one-man
war against the vice and corruption rampant in Portuguese India.
Now more friends fell away from him, many of them fearing the
wrath that might strike them if they were known as associates of
a man who had challenged all Goa to a duel between the right and
the wrong. He was foredoomed to defeat, for the pattern of conduct was too deeply and firmly set to be overthrown in his time,
and his contemporaries, content with their ill-gotten gains and
their unbridled lusts and greed, looked not to the morrow. That
could take care of itself, meanwhile, this red-headed one-eyed
soldier must be silenced, lest his voice be heard in far-off Lisbon.

To make matters worse for him, someone, perhaps the anony-
mous author of the "Jogo de Cannas," wrote an additional nine
verses, not at all in Camoëns' style, and circulated them as part of
the original, thereby adding more fuel to the flames. The thinly
veiled allusions of the "Follies" gathered the citizens of Goa into
two camps: those who knew that Camoëns was in the right and
took his part, and those who in their guilt felt the finger pointing
at them and who in their hearts heard the stern voice of the prophet
declaring "Thou art the man."[20] The latter were powerful in Goa;
they had the ear of the Governor, and he dared not oppose them
when they spoke.

Camoëns followed this satire with a bitter sonnet:

20 The prophet Nathan. See 2 Samuel 12:17.

Here in this Babylon,
Sink of the world's iniquity,
Here where reigns the mother of all lusts
And pure love lies unsought,
Where evil ever waxes worse
And all that's good is spurned,
Here, where tyranny in honor's seat doth loll
And blind blundering monarchs seek
With vain words to cheat their God,
Here in this foul labyrinth
Where valor, virtue and wisdom beg
At the gates of vice and greed,
Here in the chaos of the Pit
Where I must earn my daily crust,
O Zion,
Can I forget thee?[21]

Here in Goa, as in Lisbon, which now seemed Zion itself to him—
that Zion from which he had been exiled into Babylon—Luis again
saw his world fall to pieces, for he had unwisely shown the sonnet
to friends. It passed from hand to hand, and when it came to the
notice of those who believed he had lampooned them, it added to
the intensity of their wrath.

Luis was attacked more viciously than before: his accusations
were too pointed to be ignored. The poem consisted of only fourteen lines, but concentrated in them was the summation of his resentment and indignation at what he had ever before his eyes in
Goa. In this sonnet Portugal occupies an exalted place, for the
cruelties, vices, and corruption that were so evident in Lisbon and
the corroding luxury, extravagances, and political intrigues of the
kingdom had become dimmed and blurred in the rosy haze of time
and distance, so that all was suffused with happy memories of Luis'
boyhood and his idealized love for Catherine. The place where

---

[21] Soneto "Cá nesta Babilónia, donde mana."

he had been born, where he loved and suffered, was now a living personality, whence sprang all virtues and fine qualities, the beauties and amenities of civilization which her unworthy sons in India were dragging in the dust and trampling underfoot in their greed, false pride, and arrogance. His reading and writing (for now he was continually engaged in revising and polishing parts of *The Lusiads*) had gradually led him to look upon Portugal as the flower of European nations, possessing a spirit little short of sublime. Conditions in Goa, on the other hand, had become for him the antithesis of all he dreamed of the past and of the promise of the future for the land of his birth. Small wonder, then, that Portugal had become Zion to him and that, steeped in the Bible as he was, Babylon and Goa should seem synonymous.

His enemies were convinced that the sonnet, called forth by his growing revulsion at the conduct of his countrymen in India and by his prophetic vision of the doom of the Portuguese Indian empire, was a weapon aimed at them. Once more he felt alone, stripped of what little he had been able to build for himself in this alien land. The chill wind of failure again swept over him, leaving him only the tattered garment of his pride and dignity.

The resentment against Camoëns did not cease, for he had brought the roisterers, the scoundrels, and the thieving officials face to face with their own guilt. They finally decided that they must be rid of this man, this poet with a pen too sharp for his own good—or theirs. He must be removed from Goa at any price. He was too much on the alert, too light on his feet, too clever with the sword to be attacked physically, so they moved—and that swiftly—in another direction.

Barreto, courageous and an excellent administrator, had one deep-seated vice: greed. His own hands were not too clean; he had been in too many dubious affairs to allow him to feel comfortable. The next step was simple. Luis had completed his term of compulsory military service and had no employment in sight. There was a position open, one within the Governor's gift—and one which would take the offending, belligerent, overzealous poet to a far-off post. It would rid the city of him, at least until he, Barreto, should have finished his term and returned safely to Portugal with his spoils. It meant a voyage to distant, almost unknown China and a long, lonely, isolated residence there, but once he boarded ship and sailed from Goa, all would again be calm and serene in the city.

So Luis was offered the position of *Provedor Mór dos Defuntes e Ausentes*[22] in the newly founded settlement of Macao, on the southern bank of the Pearl River at its mouth, about eighty miles from the great metropolis of Canton. He accepted the post and was soon aboard ship, eastward bound.

[22] Trustee for the Dead and Absent [Portuguese].

CHAPTER XV

Macao

The next morning we left the island of Sanchao and arrived as the sun was setting on another isle called Lampaco, six leagues to the north. There the Portuguese carried on their trade with the Chinese, and this lasted until the year 1557, when the mandarins of Canton, at the request of the local merchants, gave us this port of Macao, where the business is now transacted. In which, where before was a desert island, our people built a noble settlement of houses worth three and four thousand cruzados, with a cathedral, a vicar and beneficiaries. And it possesses a captain, an auditor and officers of justice; they are so secure and safe there that they may feel themselves at home [in Portugal].
> —Fernando Mendez Pinto, *Peregrinução*, CCXXI

This place is the staple and emporium of all the merchandise from China and other parts of the world.
> —François Pyrard de Laval, *Voyage*

MACAO! The place almost legendary. Little was known of it in Goa except that it lay on the coast of South China, many weeks by ship from India, and that tea and fireworks, silks and fine porcelains, jades and carved ivories were brought thence. But what of the isolation, thousands of miles from Lisbon, in a tiny outpost where dwelt but a handful of Portuguese? Of this Luis could know little, save that so few of his fellow countrymen traded with China that his post would be a sinecure.

His responsibilities as *Provedor Mór dos Defuntes e Ausentes* were to be similar to those of the director of the *Escola da Santa Misericordia* in Goa. Too often theretofore when Portuguese had died during the perilous voyages in the China seas the captains of the ships (or others) had seized the dead man's goods as their own, for they had been a law unto themselves. The holder of the newly created post of trustee was therefore designated as the respository of the testaments of such of his fellow countrymen as sought his good offices. In case of their death, he was to execute their wills, take over and dispose of their properties, and transmit the proceeds to the School of Misericordia in Lisbon, where, after due proof was given, their heirs could take possession. That his tasks would be light could not have been unpleasing to Camoëns, who was still at work on his *Lusiads*. In spite of all his misfortunes, his persistence in writing gives evidence that he had confidence that in the end his work would be published and would make him widely known, though as yet not a line of his verse had been published— except for the manuscripts circulated in Lisbon and in India.

Luis could not have come to China ignorant of the Portuguese position there or its background. The story of the mission sent by Albuquerque to Canton in 1517, the subsequent quarrels with the Chinese and the suspension of all intercourse with the Portuguese for many years, and the verbal agreement made in 1554 between the Chinese and Leonel de Sousa (a native of the Algarve) which allowed his countrymen to resume trade—all this was common knowledge in Goa. The Portuguese had also found their way to Japan for trade and had need of a sheltered port on the China coast for the repair of their ships. To meet their requirements they used the Bay of the Goddess Ama on the peninsula of Amagao, where they could careen their vessels and obtain fuel, water, and some foodstuffs. The settlers in 1557 named the little town (which was the first European colony in the Far East (*Cidade de Nome de Deos na China* (The City of the Name of God in China), but both settlers and sailors found the name too long and cumbersome and always referred to the settlement by its Chinese name, which was soon shortened and corrupted into "Macao."

The Portuguese traded with the Chinese on a peculiar basis, since the King of Portugal restricted commercial privileges to a person designated "Captain-Major of the Voyage of China and Japan." This grant was made annually through the Viceroy of India, and the grantee had the right to sell his privilege and in addition exercised absolute control of all Portuguese ships and trade between Malacca and Japan; moreover, he was Portugal's representative—as far as the Easterners would accept such—to both Chinese and Japanese officials. In this way the traders who had the monopoly in the China Sea often amassed more wealth in a short time than did the merchants and dealers in spices between India and Europe. In spite of the arrogance of the Chinese, tradition has it that permission was granted to the Portuguese to settle on Chinese territory in recognition of the assistance given in cleaning out a nest of pirates who had made Macao their rendezvous.

The ship that was to take Luis to China was a slow, bluff-bowed merchant vessel fitted with light guns as a defense against pirates, but, built in India of teak, she was far stronger than the vessels constructed (for the most part of pine) on the ways of Lisbon and Oporto. She sailed from Goa with a full cargo—wines, woolen fabrics, silver for the purchase of silk, clocks from Flanders (highly prized by the Chinese), cotton cloth, jewelry, precious stones, scarlet dyes, glass, and crystal. One of her passengers was D. João Pereira, on his way to his post as governor of Malacca, which Albuquerque had won from the Malays in 1511 after a long siege. On this voyage Luis was no longer traveling as a common soldier in the crowded space between decks, but in more comfortable quarters as a government official.

The first port of call was Cochin, on the Indian coast, where some of the European merchandise was landed and more spices loaded. Then, after the vessel rounded the coast of India, followed the long, monotonous crossing of the Bay of Bengal to Malacca. Few vessels were encountered, and these only small dhows or Malay proas.

One day at twilight the lookout at the prow sighted a landfall Sail was taken in, and the next morning saw the rising sun gild the walls and turrets of the Portuguese fort at the crossroads of the East. The fair panorama, as seen by the poet that morning, made a profound impression, and in *The Lusiads* he said of it:

> Malacca, made noble by her trade,
> Whither every province of great ocean
> Sends its richest merchandise.[1]

The city was colorful and prosperous, for the Portuguese, though they were but two thousand in a population of nearly two hundred thousand, had made the most of the place where converged all the trade of Japan, China, Siam, the Spice Islands, Arabia, Persia, and Africa. Caesar Federici described it in his *Voyage:*

> Malacca is a Citie of marveilous great trade of all kinds of merchandise, which come from divers partes, because that all the shippes that saile in these seas, both great and small, are bound to touch at Malacca to paie their customs there, although they unlade nothing at all.

In the harbor lay ships from Suez, Jiddah, Aden, Java, Sumatra, India, and the isles of the tropic seas. The town was situated on both sides of the Malacca River, spanned by a bridge, and the streets were crowded with a throng even more motley than that

[1] *Lusiads,* X, 123.

of Goa, for in addition to the Indians there were Chinese, Japanese, Siamese, Pegus, Burmans, and the peoples of the Malay Archipelago. In the shops were heaped high the goods for which the Portuguese had come so far and made such sacrifices—and had fought hideous, bloody wars—to attain. Here were to be bought more cheaply than in Goa the products of the Orient: cloves, nutmeg, sandal, benzoin, gold, quicksilver, pearls, diamonds, and opium, the last introduced by the Arabs into Eastern trade. The shopkeepers were of every race, from Parsis of Bombay and Armenians of Asia Minor to the Javanese and Bugis of the Islands.

Malacca was distant from the center of Portuguese control, and the soldiers on the streets were even greedier and more insolent than those in India. Blood-chilling tales of their tortures, bribes, extortions, and rapacity were current in all the Portuguese ports in Asia, for, far from all fear of punishment, they stopped short of nothing in their cupidity and sadistic cruelty.

A stay of a few days, then the anchor was weighed, dripping and weed covered, to the tune of an old sea chantey, and once more were the sails with the crimson cross of the Order of Christ spread wide to the winds as the vessel slowly swung out of her berth into the Straits of Malacca on the last stretch of the wearisome voyage to Macao. She plowed her way among the islands at the tip of the Malay Peninsula, finally rounding Cape Romania and setting her course northeast across the South China Sea.

The days were long and lazy and sultry, the wind often dying down to an almost imperceptible breeze. On the surface of the sea lay great patches of weed, and near the shores of the islands the shallows were every color of the rainbow, from softest delicate pink through palest green to deep sapphire blue. The nights were unspeakably beautiful, with the multitude of stars in the velvet heavens reflected in the slowly heaving waves, hardly ruffled by the winds, and often the vessel passed through phosphorescent expanses, so that the sea seemed a great silver carpet unrolled to the very horizon. At other times storms played over the ocean, far-off waterspouts whirling across the world of waters, or sharp quick tempests raised mountainous billows, flailing the sails with rain that sounded like the roar of many drums. Ever and anon a clumsy, evil-smelling junk with tattered sails, plying down the coast to Poulo Condore or Singapore, would wallow by, but other than this, no human life was astir on this little-known sea. Great hydras floated alongside, transparent, jelly-like polyps, spreading out like umbrellas, and porpoises played about the bows of the ship. Often whales, roused by the strange monster approaching them, spouted great sprays of mist high into the air, then sounded to escape the threatened danger, and sometimes, on very hot days, huge sea turtles floated by.

Camoëns, fascinated by the waves of the seas halfway around the world from Lisbon, apostrophized them and wrote, keeping the poem (written in Spanish) in his ever growing collection.

> Waves that find your way around the world,
> Unceasing stirred and heaving in the winds,
> Take, and on your mighty bosom bear
> My thoughts to her, the cause of all my grief.
> Tell her my heartache doth abide,
> That all light hath vanished from my days.
> Tell her that my torment ceaseth never,
> And I no longer live in any hope.
> Tell her a wanderer did you find me
>
>   . . .
>
> And when you meet her give her news of me.[2]

[2] Soneto "Ondas que por el mundo caminando."

CHAPTER XVI

Dinamene

The Island and Towne of Machau or Makau is inhabited by the
Portingales, together with the naturall borne (countriemen) of
China. They trafficke with the men of Canton, from whence the
Chinayes bring all [their] marchandises, and resort thether to
buy wares.

—LINSCHOTEN, *Voyage*

AT LAST Hainan was sighted and the coast of South China drew
near. Another day and the vessel passed the island of Shang Chuan
(St. John), where Francis Xavier had preached during his last
years. There he had died, and there his body was first interred
before it was taken to India for entombment in Goa.

Finally, after long weeks, the first landmark of Macao, the ancient Temple of the Goddess Ama (from which the settlement
derived its name), was sighted. The ship dropped anchor in the
roadstead, and another voyage in the odyssey of Luis Vaz de
Camoëns was at an end.

The ship's crew settled down in the little town for a long stay, for
they were not permitted to go to Canton, the great city eighty

miles up the river, whence the cargoes for the Portuguese vessels were brought. The little colony itself received its revenue from duties levied on goods brought in by Portuguese ships, but only one arrived each year, so there was little income.

The Chinese were eager to obtain spices, and since the Portuguese had driven the Moslem traders from the seas, Chinese spice dealers were forced to purchase their stocks from the former. The beach air was redolent of sandalwood, of which great stacks were brought from the ship, for the Chinese used enormous quantities in the making of incense, carved boxes, and fans, and there were sharkskins in plenty for the fashioning of fine purses and serviceable sword scabbards.

As the hold of the vessel was emptied, goods were gradually moved from the warehouse and loaded into the cleared space. While waiting for the silk which was to come from Canton—for Japan valued Chinese silks far above her own—dock workers and the ship's crew loaded other Chinese exports for Japan, from sugar, wax, and the finest rice to great bags of whiting (refined chalk), brought to China from the island of Borneo and ground very fine. (The Japanese bought large quantities of it, for their women whitened their whole bodies with it, "even down to the legs.")[1]

A sojourner among strange people whose language, manners, and customs were to him like those of dwellers on another planet, Camoëns would dream of fair Coimbra, where he had spent his boyhood and youth, and often before his mind's eye came pictures of the lanes and countryside, the green slopes with their vineyards, the forests of red-brown cork oaks, the waving grain and the gray-green olives in the broad valley of the Mondego. He could hear the wind in the pines and the chestnuts, the singing of the birds and the murmur of the brooks, could smell the sweet fragrance of gorse and newly cut hay and honey-laden clover. The seasons passed before him: the freshets and the sprouting grass in the gusty days

[1] Even today many Japanese women, especially the geisha and maiko (young dancing girls), follow this custom.

of spring; the blue sky of summer with fleecy, lazy-drifting clouds, whiter than the sheep that grazed in the meadows, and fruits heaped high in the village market places; autumn with its harvest and the treading of the grapes to merry singing and dancing, autumn with its yellow and red leaves fluttering to the ground, its scent of wood fires and the gathering of nuts, reminding him that winter was on its way; then winter itself, bearing in its arms a blanket of soft white, covering hut and barn and village place with gentle touch, that the good earth might rest until again the warm sun should arouse it from its sleep to vibrant new life.

The dream took concrete form under his pen. It was one of his longer poems (twenty-eight stanzas), full of questioning and turbulence of spirit, well meriting its title: "On the Confusion of the World." But in it are two stanzas that shine forth—a simple prayer for peace and calm and a life far removed from the turmoil and strife which had been his for so many years. There is nothing artificial in these lines; Luis had learned that wealth and position were powerless to bestow happiness and that a quiet life was, after all, nearer to his heart's desire:

> Oh, that Heaven serene would grant me
> Some simple, humble, quiet home,
> In which, no longer exiled in a distant land,
> I might forever with the Muses dwell!
> There would I seek out none of high estate,
> But alone would I live with you, content,
> —With you, to whom content with ease could come.
> There would we lie together by a bubbling spring
> Which invites the nightingale to sing
> The sad tale of her parting from her mate
> In throbbing notes,
> Or, when winter clothes the far green hills with snow
> We would seek our hut, and there find joy
> In books, wherein the spirit has her true abode.[2]

[2] Oitava "Quem pode ser no mundo tão quieto."

Several weeks passed. At last the bales of silk arrived from Canton, the vessel was loaded and provisions put aboard, sail was set, and, with flags flying, the only tie between the few Portuguese in Macao and the outside world vanished among the islands to the north on her journey to far-off Japan, not to return for perhaps a year, and then only if she were fortunate enough to escape typhoons and the pirates who lurked among the islets and the greater island, called by the Portuguese *Formosa* (The Beautiful).

In his isolation, Camoëns' hunger for a woman's affection evidently grew upon him, so it was not surprising when he met a gentle, sympathetic, and attractive young Chinese woman, one who seemed to understand him, that he should have turned to her. That this young woman was of an alien race was not the slightest bar, for Luis came of a people which from its earliest days had accepted the mingling of blood as a natural occurrence—where Iberian and Goth, African and Moor, and the ancient Basques of the mountains had mated—and in Portuguese India, where such unions had even been officially encouraged, there was already an inextricable mixture of race.

In her was the warm, honest companionship that Luis had sought, and with her he seems to have found content and peace—peace not only with the world, which he had somehow felt always hostile, but peace within himself as well. He called her Dinamene, the nearest that he could attain to the pronunciation of her Chinese name, and, too, it was the name that he had met in Garçilaso de la Vega and in the Latin versions of Homer and Hesiod that had fallen into his hands: Dinamene, the lovely nymph, daughter of Doris and the sea-god Nereus.

Their friendship soon grew to be more than mere friendship; simply and naturally they lived their life together during Camoëns' sojourn at Macao. In this new-found peace of spirit his genius unfolded and expanded even more, soaring, seeking, and seizing upon both exalted thought and expressive word to carry forward the epic in which he lived more than in the real world about him. Moreover, he had leisure, for his position, except when the "silk and silver ship" was in port, called for but perfunctory duties.

The months that followed were happy ones for Camoëns, far removed from the insensate cruelties of Portuguese rule in India and from the corrupt, vicious social and political life in Goa. Undisturbed by any summons to arms, cut off from the degenerate luxury of his fellow countrymen, he was nearer the peaceful life of which he sang with longing in his verses than he had ever expected to be.

One person, however, he could not—did not seek to—forget. True to the ethics of the age, he found nothing incongruous or contradictory in his life with Dinamene and his love for Catherine de Ataide. During the years (for now more than four had passed since his departure from the banks of the Tagus), she had become less of a woman to be wooed and wed and more of a pure, ideal love. But the warm, human love of a man for a woman, honest, faithful, gentle, and kind, this Dinamene had from him.

On one of his excursions around Macao, Luis came upon a heap of granite rocks, three that in some mighty cataclysm of nature had so fallen together that they made a rude arch, which, with the hillside behind, formed a cave, or grotto, not deep enough for much shelter from heat or rain, but a natural alcove where one could sit and look out over the land to the sea. Trees[3] grew around the secluded spot, and the harshness of the rocks was softened by clusters of profusely growing ferns. Here, far from the sound of human voice, Camoëns often came to dream and to write.

Whenever the "silk and silver ship" was sighted on her return from Japan, the little community was agog with excitement. Some of the men stationed in Macao were due to return to Goa and Portugal, while others were to be invalided home, letters were to be writ-

[3] See Appendix I, Poem 71.

ten, and cargo was to be removed from the warehouses for shipment. News of the arrival was dispatched to Canton, where merchants were waiting to come down the river to bargain for the silver obtained in Japan in exchange for Chinese silks, and soon junks and sampans appeared before the settlement with goods for Malacca, India, and Portugal: furniture of hardwood (some inlaid with mother-of-pearl), lacquers, silks, porcelains, baskets, and ivory (both in tusks and carved into figures of gods, men, and animals). Bags of musk and civet, much in demand in Europe for perfumes, large quantities of beeswax for church candles, and stores of honey and fine paper—all these and much more vanished into the gaping hold of the ship, to make profit for the shrewd merchants of Canton and the Portuguese entrepreneurs who would convey these wares to Lisbon and sell them everywhere on the Continent. Then the galleon, heavily laden for the Indian and European markets, set sail for southern seas, and the little town, now to be exiled without news of the outer world until the coming of the next annual vessel, returned to its peaceful existence. Life often became monotonous, for ignorance of the language made social intercourse practically impossible. Since Chinese soldiers stopped the Portuguese at the frontier of the settlement, the latter could not explore the possibilities of the surrounding countryside, and because there were few women besides those married to the native fishermen, they were thoroughly unhappy, continually complaining, and longing for the fleshpots of Malacca and Goa.

Month followed month, until again the lookout on the point cried "Sail ho!" and soon those gathered on the shore saw the ship from Goa standing in toward land. Arriving opposite the group of huts, she dropped anchor and put off boats for the shore.

Amid the political and social gossip brought by the ship was a bit of news that disquieted Camoëns and seemed to forebode evil. He heard that Leonel de Sousa, who had negotiated successfully with the Chinese for permission to settle in Macao, had addressed the King, complaining that he had been treated scurvily in return for his services and mentioning especially that he had rightly expected, among other offices (he was *capitão-mór* of the "silk and silver ship"), that of *Provedor Mór dos Defuntos e Ausentes,* the very post that Camoëns was holding by appointment of Governor Barreto. Sousa himself was on board the ship in the harbor and landed soon after the news was received.

Camoëns was relieved when at last sail was spread and the ship departed for Japan, but from what he had learned of Sousa in India, he knew that he had not heard the last of the affair. He had seen enough of political dishonesty and maneuvering in the government at Goa to know, or at least to surmise, what would happen.

He seems to have been perfectly content to sit alone in his semi-voluntary exile. He was unknown, unnoticed; his poems had not been published and fame had not touched him, yet he went on and on, absorbed in the song of the great deeds of his nation, without ever questioning the eventual publication of his work. He was satisfied to sing the mighty exploits of Portugal's founders and explorers, to chant the praiseful saga of the people that had banished him. Living in spirit in the days of chivalry, when his native land had been fashioned from a rude province of Moorish Spain, he was able to lose sight of the hatred and enmity of the petty souls who had brought him where he was. While thus engaged, the stormy past, the precarious present, and the uncertain future evidently had little place in his mind or spirit, for he was writing a tale that he was certain would be immortalized in his verse.

Another year passed. Once more the Portuguese galleon, on her homeward voyage to Goa, arrived off the settlement to refit, unload, and take on cargo. The sight of her coming to anchor again stirred in Luis the vague feeling that all was not well. He had become aware that Sousa was most unfriendly, but could not divine the reason, except that he had been given his position over Sousa's head, so to speak. As far as he knew, his official documents were in order.

When he presented himself to Sousa, who was supreme commander not only of the Portuguese ships that might venture along the east coast of Asia but also of all land establishments, personal disaster again struck him. He was told that his reports were far from being in order. In fact, there appeared, in the judgment of Sousa, such glaring discrepancies between Luis' figures and those to which several witnesses had testified (witnesses who were not, however, produced) that there was grave suspicion of breach of trust, embezzlement, and malfeasance in office. Camoëns was informed that since there was no court established by the Portuguese government in China, he would have to return to India with Sousa to stand trial. He was not put under arrest; that was unnecessary, for there could be no escape, either en route or in Malacca, where the vessel would put in before continuing to India. Evidently, no question was raised about Dinamene's traveling with Luis, since such relationships were too common in the Indies to be the subject of discussion.

Camoëns had had three years of comparative peace and happiness, the first he had known since his far-distant days at court in Lisbon. Now those years were at an end.

CHAPTER XVII

Shipwreck

This Mekong will on its placid breast
The drowning manuscript receive,
Rescued from the misery of the wreck,
And from the shoals, tempest-tossed, escaped.

Behold where Champa's coast doth lie,
Its forests with scented woods adorned;
See Cochin China but little famed,
And Hainan's bay, yet unrevealed.
                    —CAMOËNS, *Lusiads*, X, 128, 129

LUIS WAS ON HIS WAY BACK to Goa, that Goa whose life and ways he detested. Once there and cleared of the charges of which he knew himself to be innocent, he would have to decide on his future: whether to remain longer in India or return to Portugal, from which he had been away nearly seven years.

Fair weather at first favored the heavily laden ship, which carried a great fortune of Chinese and Japanese merchandise in her hold, as well as a large crew and many passengers. It was, however, the beginning of the season of the dread typhoons—a new

143

word to the Europeans, adopted from the Chinese *ta fêng,* which means "great wind." The Portuguese who plied the seas off the China coast had not navigated them often enough to have learned their patterns and vagaries. So, when off southern Indo-China, near where the Mekong debouches in its wide mouths, the captain took little heed of the sultry, silent hours and threatening skies that are so often harbingers of the sudden, violent storms that whirl out of the area of the Philippines and sweep up with destructive force to the north and over the Japanese islands. The sun sank beneath a fiery horizon and soon after nightfall the wind, momentarily swifter and stronger, began to whistle in the rigging. Orders were given to shorten sail, but it was too late; the full force of the storm swept down on the ship almost before the sailors could leap into the shrouds. She was lifted on a huge wave, only to be half-engulfed in the trough of another. The great bellying sails flew off in shreds and ribbons; a mast was carried overside, rigging and all, and it was impossible to keep the vessel's head into the wind. In the dark, the howling tempest shrieked and clawed at the ship with irresistible force. Boats that were lowered overturned before they ever reached the water and their occupants were swept away into the darkness. There was but one chance of salvation: to take to the remaining boats before the hull was battered to pieces by the pounding seas.

Luis hastily seized his precious manuscripts, then struggled along the deck, which was canted and shivering with the repeated blows of the mountainous waves. Suddenly a towering sea crashed over the vessel and swept him off his feet. When he recovered full consciousness, he found himself clinging to a broken timber— but, as by a miracle, the box of manuscripts was still firmly grasped in his hand!

As he started to swim, keeping the plank before him, his feet struck a sandy bottom, and he finally struggled ashore. Sea and land were empty; he was alone and, as he believed, was the sole

From Albino Forjaz de Sampaio (ed.), *Historia da Literatura Portuguesa,*
Vol. II, Lisboa, n.d.

The title page of the first edition of *The Lusiads*

RHYTHMAS
DE LVIS DE CAMOES.
Diuididas em cinco partes.

Dirigidas ao muito Illuſtre ſenhor D. Gonçalo Coutinho.

MIHI TAXVS

Impreſſas com licença do ſupremo Conſelno da geʀal ·
Inquiſição, & Ordinario.
EM LISBOA,
Por Manoel de Lyra, Anno de M. D. Lxxxxv.
A cuſta de Eſteuão Lopez mercador de libros.

From Albino Forjaz de Sampaio (ed.), *Historia da Literatura Portuguesa,*
Vol. II, Lisboa, n.d.

The title page of the first edition of Camoëns' lyrics

survivor of the entire company that had sailed from Macao a few days before. Fortunately, he was found by some Cambodian fishermen, who conveyed him to their village on the Mekong, near whose broad mouths the vessel had gone to pieces. Here he was received and given shelter.[1]

Now ensued an indeterminate residence among the Cambodians for which we have no information whatsoever except Camoëns' own references to it in a few lines of his epic and in the poems wherein Dinamene is mentioned. That he grieved for her is very evident, for he sought relief for his sorrow at her loss in his gift of song:

> When fancy lulls my lids to sleep
> Against these my oft oppressing griefs,
> In my dreams does that dear spirit come
> Who was in life a vision of delight.
> There on a barren plain,
> Stretching far beyond my straining eyes,
> I pursue, but, driven by some occult force,
> On fleetest foot she glides away.
> I cry, "O blessed spirit, flee me not."
> She naught replies,
> But on me fixes saddened eyes
> As though to say,
> "Alas! This cannot ever be,"
> And turns away again.
> I call, "Dinam—"
> My lips have formed but half her name
> When I awake,
> Robbed even of this brief deceptive joy.[2]

[1] That Camoëns passed through more than one heavy storm besides this is evidenced by *The Lusiads*, VI, 70–79, from which details of the episode described above have been drawn and adapted.

[2] Soneto "Quando de minhas mágoas a comprida."

Again he wrote of his grief, but penned the lines as though the incident were one that had happened to a fictional person whom he called Aonio:

> The sky, the earth, the wind are hushed;
> The waves flood soft upon the shore;
> The fish disport beneath the sea;
> The night is calm.
> Aonio, the fisher lad,
> Lies sobbing on the sand,
> Where the breeze sweeps in the spray.
> In vain he calls the name he loves
> —That name, alas, of her who thence
> Will be no more than name.
> "Ah, ocean's waves," he cries aloud,
> "Before I die bring back my nymph
> Whom you dragged to death so young."
> No answer comes.
> The words are seized by the passing wind
> And are lost on the empty air;
> The waves break on the rocks afar
> In sullen roar,
> And silently the tree-tops
> In the forest gently sway.[3]

Still a third sonnet on the loss of the young girl has come to us with plangent force. In it Luis speaks as though her spirit were hovering near and could hear his plaint:

> Ah, Dinamene,
> Thou hast forsaken him
> Whose love for thee has never ceased,
> And no more will he behold thee on this earth!
> How early didst thou deem life of little worth!
> I found thee

[3] Soneto "O Céu, a terra, o vento sossegado."

—Alas, to lose thee all too soon!
How strong, how cruel the waves!
Thou canst not ever know
My longing and my grief!
Did cold death still thy voice
Or didst thou of thyself
Draw the sable veil before thy lovely face?
O sea, O sky, O fate obscure!
To live without thee, Dinamene, avails me not.[4]

After this he wrote of her no more. At least no other poem referring to Dinamene has ever been found.

The months (perhaps two years) during which Camoëns lived among the simple dwellers on the Mekong River are a blank in the story of his life, for as has been noted, the only information available is found in a few meager references in his poetry. Yet even from this dull existence he was able to extract material for his epic, though his lines reveal a woeful misunderstanding of the religious beliefs of the people of the Mekong.[5]

Just when Luis was almost resigned to what was to him an aimless, futile existence, he was able, in some way unknown to us, to obtain passage to India.

It was customary for the silk-and-silver ships to make Malacca a port of call, and it is a pleasing thought that Luis perhaps met the famous historian of the Portuguese conquest of India, Gaspar Correa,[6] who was living in Malacca at the time. Whatever may

[4] Soneto "Ah! minha Dinamene! Assim deixaste."

[5] See Appendix I, Poem 73.

[6] Gaspar Correa, a *fidalgo*, went to India in the spring of 1512 at the age of sixteen. Soon thereafter he obtained a position as secretary to the great Affonso de Albuquerque, chief architect of the Portuguese Eastern empire, and accompanied him on most of the military expeditions which established Portugal's power in Asia. After Albuquerque's death, Correa held many other important government positions and knew Vasco da Gama during the latter's short viceroyalty. Correa's work,

have happened, after a voyage of about forty days from Malacca, Camoëns reached Goa.

entitled *Lendas da India*, was not published until 1856–66. No translation has ever been made, except the chapters covering the voyages and viceroyalty of Vasco da Gama. For the latter and for the third voyage, Correa is the most important chronicler. For additional information, see Hart, *Sea Road to the Indies*, pp. 254ff.

CHAPTER XVIII

Last Years in India

See how long I have a wanderer been,
Singing of your Lusitanians and your Tagus' stream,
While Fortune has me a pilgrim led
New labors and new sufferings to behold.
—CAMOËNS, *Lusiads*, VII, 79

LUIS HAD SCARCELY LANDED in Goa when he learned that Leonel de Sousa and twenty-three others of the company on the wrecked vessel had been saved, having been picked up by a passing merchantman. And now, to his consternation, Luis heard that Sousa was in Goa.

The news from Lisbon was anything but cheering. King John III had died in 1557, just about the time Camoëns had sailed for China. He had left no will, but on the doubtful authority of some unsigned notes, the Queen, D. Catharine, had been declared regent during the minority of D. Sebastian, the King's grandson and only surviving male heir of his house. This decision had alarmed and greatly disturbed the people of Portugal, for Queen Catharine, a Spaniard and a sister of the Emperor Charles V, was extremely unpopular because of her nationality, her Spanish speech, her bigotry, and her support of the Inquisition. Quarrels had broken out between her and her brother-in-law, Cardinal Henry, over the question of the appointment of a guardian-tutor to Sebastian, and the Queen had announced her intention of surrendering the regency and retiring to a convent in Lisbon.

At the same time, Luis heard the dire news that Catherine de Ataide was dead. It seemed as though life were determined never to allow him peace of soul or happiness, but of all the ordeals he was called upon to endure, this was the most difficult to face. Again he sought the solace of his pen, and in that ineffable moment of sorrow and despair was born an immortal sonnet, the cry of agony of a soul in travail. They are the most famous verses in the Portuguese language, and are known to every Portuguese with the slightest pretense to education:

> Gentle spirit mine,
> Thou who didst depart this earth
> Before thy time,
> May'st thou be given rest eternal
> With the bless'd,
> Though I still bide in anguish
> On this earth.
> If, where thou dwellest
> In the realm on high,
> Memory be granted of this, our mortal life,
> Forget not, I beg,
> This heart that yearns within its breast for thee,
> Nor the pure passion that flames so ardent
> In these eyes.
> If thou findest aught of worth
> In this great love of mine that knows no cure,
> Pray God, who cut thy mortal years so short,
> At once to bear me hence to where thou art,
> And, swift as thy sweet form was snatched from me,

May I once more behold thy features dear,
And feast upon them with these hungry eyes.[1]

A few days later Camoëns found himself again in prison, summoned to answer Sousa's charges. His detention was, however, of
short duration, for no valid evidence was produced against him
and he was speedily released.

Taking up life where he had laid it aside on his departure for
Macao, he found little changed, for the same vices and corruption
permeated the European community in every stratum. Moreover,
the soldiers, often unpaid, were at their old games: breaking into
private houses, stealing, intimidating the menfolk, and abusing
and assaulting helpless women. Brothels had been opened, and at
their doors sat native and half-caste women, shamelessly soliciting
passers-by.

During his absence in China—in fact, just before his return to
India—the Inquisition had extended its operations to Goa and had
introduced a new and sinister element into the colony. Its seat was
old Sabaio Palace, on the cathedral square, which had been the
residence of the Indian ruler of Goa before the conquest and later
the home of the viceroys. There the dread tribunal held its ses-
sions and there it had its *aljube* (prison cells), the black stone of
its façade a fitting color for the ghastly scenes enacted within its
walls. The natives shrank at the mention of its name, speaking
of it as the *orlem gor* (great house). More than once the poet must
have witnessed the solemn autos-da-fé, with the procession of the
prisoners, their strangling and their burning, for the executions
took place in the presence of the Viceroy and the officials of the
colony.

Street quarrels were an everyday event and were often settled
by slaves sent to avenge their masters by assaulting, maiming, or

[1] Soneto "Alma minha gentil que te partiste."

even killing the avowed enemies, though sometimes for no other reason than that a Portuguese felt that his greeting had not been acknowledged by a low enough bow or sweep of the hat as he passed. The punishment and unspeakable tortures of slaves by their masters and mistresses were ignored by the authorities, and stories of the brutal treatment of these helpless creatures were rife in Goa.[2]

The return of Viceroy D. Constantine de Bragança from an expedition to Ceylon was the cause of a strange scene, demonstrating the utter Portuguese ignorance of the Indian mentality. The most important trophy brought back from the siege of Jafanapatam was a reputed tooth of the Buddha, the disposition of which was the subject of much deliberation by the Portuguese clergy and officials. At last it was decided to destroy the precious relic in a solemn public ceremony. The Viceroy ordered it delivered to the Archbishop, who placed it in a mortar and ground it to powder with his own hands, the fragments being immediately thrown onto blazing coals. The calcined ashes and coals were then carried carefully through the crowd, which thronged the streets, windows, balconies, and walls, to the north river, where they were thrown into the water, to be carried off to the sea.[3]

In 1561, Bragança's term of office expired. He was succeeded by D. Francisco Coutinho, Count of Redondo. A man of culture and refinement, Coutinho had met Luis in Lisbon; learning of the poet's presence in Goa, he immediately renewed the friendship.

[2] For example, one Portuguese casually remarked to his wife on the fine white teeth of her Japanese maid. On his return home that evening he found that all the unfortunate slave's teeth had been knocked out at his wife's order. Another woman, angered at the clumsiness of a female slave, ordered a horseshoe nailed to her back. Many more such incidents could be cited.

[3] Instead of realizing that such a wanton act only alienated them further in their dealings with the peoples of Asia, the bigoted Portuguese prided themselves on the performance of a most meritorious deed.

However, though he recognized Camoëns' great merits as a writer of verse and his excellence as a man, he was blind to Luis' pressing material needs.

Luis had scarcely begun to find life a little easier and happier because of the Viceroy's cordiality when he again found himself in trouble. While in Malacca he had borrowed a sum of money from a rich captain, one Miguel Roiz, a brave man, hero of many daring exploits, but nicknamed, because of his habits and rapacity, *Fios Secos* (Skinflint).[4] He now began to press Camoëns for payment of the debt and threatened imprisonment. Luis, not having the money, pleaded for time, but in vain. Finally, in desperation, he turned to the Viceroy for help, presenting his plea in a satirical but tactfully worded *redondilha:*

> What devil can so damnèd be
> Who fears not the blow
> Of Fios Secos' sword—
> That Fios Secos who Miguel is called,
> So brave in war's exploits?
> Since such a blow would cause
> The fiend of hell to quail,
> Why should I not flee him, too?
> Indeed would I with reason fly
> Did not your Lordship stand
> A mighty shield 'twixt him and me.
> He has me at his galley's oar enchained.
> Save, oh save me, I beseech,
> Ere the vessel does depart.[5]

Upon receiving the doggerel verses Coutinho summoned some of Camoëns' friends to take up a collection to pay off his creditor, thus relieving the poet of his fears.

[4] *Fios Secos* means literally "dry threads." It may also mean "blunt edge of a sword."

[5] Redondilha "Que diabo há tão danado?"

153

No sooner had the impecunious Camoëns accumulated a few more cruzados at letter-writing and copying documents than he planned a banquet to honor four friends he had met since his return from China. Among them was a fellow poet, Heitor da Silveira. Eleven years younger than Luis, he had been married twice, had left his second wife, and had come out to India as a soldier, landing shortly after Luis' arrival from Malacca. A doughty fighter, he had been on expeditions to Ormuz and the coast of Malabar. Now, his military service over, he found himself, like Camoëns, living from hand to mouth. The casual acquaintance led to a mutual liking and the discovery of many interests in common, as well as of sympathetic temperaments; a strong friendship soon sprang up between the men and Silveira moved into Luis' lodgings. Because Silveira was as shy and reticent in his private life as he had been brave and daring in war, Luis was never able to learn why he had left his wife, whom he appeared to love with a deep devotion. The other guests at the banquet were of noble families, some of them having come to India with D. Constantine de Bragança.

Camoëns had conceived a clever plan to make the dinner interesting for his friends, and carried it out most successfully. Having read of a banquet given by a Roman emperor, who ordered painted imitations of food set before the guests, the poet, in lieu of such facsimiles, placed a poem under each cover (saving copies for his ever growing collection of lyrics), the name of each friend appearing at the head of the lines addressed to him. Written as they were as diversions for the occasion and with no thought of their future publication, the verses hardly merit the name of poetry, but in them the poet revealed himself as open hearted, generous, and able to rise above his personal griefs to bring pleasure to his friends, no matter what their stations in life. The poem at the place of D. Francisco de Almeida gives an idea of the content and quality of the lines Luis penned for the occasion:

Heliogabalus, jesting with his guests,
As a prank did serve them painted food.
But fear not to be thus deceived, good friend,
For all that happened long ago.
This meal will be real, not simulate,
Though it comes set forth in rhyme.[6]

When the fourth guest, John Lopes Leitão, had read the verse addressed to him, he turned the sheet over and found in the lines there written the rhymed menu of the real dinner. The food was then set out on the table, amid laughter and merrymaking which lasted far into the night.

One woman, an Indian girl, was present when the meal was served, though she appeared only to bring on the various courses. Camoëns, though deeply affected by Catherine's death, had tasted of the happiness brought him by Dinamene and longed for the home and companionship which he knew only a woman could give him. In this mood he had purchased the young girl in the slave market and had made her his mistress.[7] Thus it was that Barbara entered his household—and his poetry. He became deeply enamored of her, and he who had sung so often of golden hair, roses and snow, and eyes of green or blue now found himself penning the praises of a dark Asiatic with black hair and eyes.[8]

The slave girl was soon dubbed Luisa Barbara, and those who knew the story of Luis' loves in Portugal and his poems in praise of them began to ridicule him on his latest infatuation. In defiant defense of his choice he wrote and circulated an ode,[9] referring to the "black but comely" maiden beloved of Solomon in the Song of Songs, to Briseis, the slave over whom Achilles quarreled with

[6] Redondilha "Se não quereis padecer."

[7] The matter of colored mistresses is treated at great length by Gilberto Freyre in his *Casa Grande e Senzala*, translated into English by Samuel Putnam as *The Master and the Slaves*.

[8] See Appendix I, Poem 74.

[9] Redondilha "Endechas a Barbara escrava: Aquela cativa."

Agamemnon before Troy, and to the union of Aristotle and Herpyllis after the death of his wife, finally exculpating himself by turning to Cupid, who "can do all things to all." What Barbara's final fate was, we do not know.

For some time after the banquet given his friends Camoëns seems to have prospered, having received an appointment to a clerkship from the Viceroy. There is no indication that at this time he considered returning to Portugal, for he had long been acclimated to India and, moderate in his habits and of a strong physical build, had successfully resisted the diseases and ills that beset so many of his contemporaries. Catherine was dead, there were no prospects that he could envision for himself in Lisbon, and he had no close relatives there except his mother (though there is no evidence that they corresponded); he was in the Viceroy's favor and accepted socially, and, moreover, he was becoming one of a small circle of men with interests and tastes similar to his own. During this period he seems to have lived from day to day, performing his routine official duties, working at his poetry, and meeting with his friends. We have but little information concerning these years, except such anecdotes as the following.

One day Heitor da Silveira came to Luis seeking assistance, confessing that he was completely out of funds. After much discussion the two friends decided that help should be sought from the Viceroy. So Silveira wrote his petition, and Luis, because of his friendship with D. Francisco Coutinho, felt no hesitancy in attaching an appeal in verse.[10] What the outcome was, is not known, but the poem has been preserved.

During these years Goa was constantly expanding and new activities were developing, and Camoëns was probably present at many important public functions, such as the laying of the foundation

[10] See Appendix I, Poem 75.

of the new cathedral[11] in 1562 and the extension of the city walls. But in spite of the comparative comfort in which he lived, he seems never to have found complete peace or happiness for he became more and more restless as time went on. One after another his dreams had been shattered by the cruel realities of life and even his short but happy residence in Macao had had a violent and tragic ending, so it is not surprising that a despairing, pessimistic note appears in many of the poems written during his last years in India. They seem to voice a belief that life could hold no more for him in the future than it had in the past.[12]

[11] The building was not completed until 1632.
[12] See Appendix I, Poems 76 through 81.

CHAPTER XIX

Garcia da Orta

> He knew the cause of everich maladye
> Were it of cold or hete or moyste or drye
> And where they engendred, and of what humour.
> He was a verry parfait practisonour.
> —CHAUCER, "The Doctour of Physick"

THE LATER YEARS in India brought to Camoëns two warm friends, men with whom he delighted to share himself, men nearer his mental caliber than any others whom he had met since leaving Portugal. One was Diogo do Couto, the historian, the other Garcia da Orta, the scientist.

Couto, born in Lisbon in 1543, had been a page in the royal palace when ten years old, and later received an excellent education from the Jesuits. Thereafter he enlisted as a soldier for Indian service, arriving in 1559 and immediately going into action in several expeditions against Malabar. It was between two of these forays that he and the poet met in Goa, and, though Couto was away fighting a great part of the time, the friendship became a firm one cherished by both. Couto was drawn to Camoëns by the latter's poetic genius and sterling character, while Camoëns admired the other for his

158

learning, his courage, and his alertness of mind. He was also much interested in Couto's notes for a projected history of the Portuguese exploits abroad.

On Luis' return to Goa from Macao he found that a bookstore —the first in the city—had been opened on a corner of one of the main streets of the town, and it was probably there that he met the famous Dr. Garcia da Orta, also a great lover of books. A familiar figure to all on the streets of Goa, he was a friend of the Governor, had been physician to a succession of viceroys, and was renowned for his almost fabulous knowledge of the drugs and herbs of the East. He lived alone in a luxurious house, for he was very rich, and besides surrounding himself with every comfort, he possessed many slaves, most of them women. His housekeeper, Antonia, also a slave, was a highly intelligent woman and seemed to manage Orta's whole life; she possessed the keys to all the rooms and storehouses and knew the trees of the garden and the contents of the physician's various collections. He also had an excellent cook, and we can well imagine that the meals she served were no small attraction to Camoëns, who could not have lived too well on his own small income. Moreover, the physician had a large and well-selected library, and these allurements, together with a host who was a veritable mine of valuable and curious Eastern lore and history and a warm-hearted and generous counselor, surely helped Luis content himself with his lot in having such a friend.

But the giving was not all on one side. We can be sure that the companionship of an alert, intelligent young man was most welcome to Garcia da Orta, who was isolated intellectually in crass, vulgar, and largely illiterate Goa. In addition, he discovered in Luis one who knew and could tell him much of Portugal and events that had transpired there since his (the Doctor's) departure from Lisbon; moreover, Orta enjoyed the younger man's conversation and his profound learning in literature. Camoëns knew but few in Goa who could appreciate his verse, full as it was of classical allusions and delicate use of rhyme and rhythm. The reading of poems led to more intimate discussions, and the Doctor, a shrewd student of the human mind, most likely soon drew from Luis his tale of mistakes, heartaches, and frustrations. In his turn the Doctor related the story of his own rich and interesting life and his dreams, ambitions, and experiences.

Orta recounted his boyhood in Elvas, near the Spanish border, where he was born in 1490. Although his father was but a small landowner, he was able to give his two sons a good education, and Garcia was sent to Spain, where he studied medicine, first at the University of Salamanca and then at Alcalá de Henares, the birthplace of Cervantes. After his graduation he became the village doctor of Castello de Vide, near Elvas, where he practiced with such skill that a few years later he was appointed lecturer in Lisbon.

In 1534, Orta came out to India as body physician to Martin Afonso de Sousa, who later became governor. He had been present at the cession to the Portuguese of the important city of Diu, and was familiar with most of the ports on the west coast of India. His renown continued to spread, and between campaigns he was often summoned to treat the potentates of friendly states. The Goanese government granted him land on the island of Bombay, which he sublet, thus adding to his already large income. This, then, was the wise, influential man whose friendship was won by Camoëns.[1]

As the Doctor's confidence in the poet grew apace, he discussed with Luis a literary work that he had long been planning: a volume which was to contain the results of his years of study and practical experience with the drugs of India. He had already made a summary compilation in Latin, but now, after conversations with Dr. Dimas Bosque, he had determined to expand it and have it pub-

---

[1] At Orta's home Luis also became well acquainted with another learned physician, Dimas Bosque, a Spaniard, who had come to India in 1558 in the suite of Viceroy D. Constantine de Bragança.

lished in Portuguese. As a simple method of combating the rigid, unscientific teaching of the time (still based on the acceptance of ancient writers rather than on personal observation), Orta cast his work in the form of dialogues between himself and several other real persons, among them Bosque, as well as with a fictitious figure called by him Ruano (the man on the street). Of course his own discourse always refuted that of the straw men he set up as his opponents.

The volume expanded rapidly, until it embraced fifty-nine *coloquios*, as they were called. They were far from being dry catalogs and learned dissertations, for the humorous though often stubborn Doctor poured into them his cyclopedic knowledge of Indian politics, history, legend, and gossip. He would leap from a description of Indian chessmen to scandalous tales of the effects of *datura* on men and women, and from Yoga to the etiquette of betel-chewing; then he would write of his home and garden and the faithful Antonia. With it all he found a malicious joy in disproving the theories and dicta of other writers.

All this was fascinating to Camoëns, to whom, as to Bosque, the *coloquios* were read by Orta. The only interruption to these pleasant days was some news that came from Malacca at the beginning of 1563: Gaspar Correa, the historian, had been murdered. It was believed that some person had learned that Correa had written of his malfeasance in office and had hired men to stab Correa to death at night. Although the murderers were known, nothing was ever done to punish or even arrest them, and careful inquiry concerning the fate of his bulky manuscript was in vain; it had mysteriously disappeared without a trace.[2]

At last the text of Orta's book was finished and there remained only the preparation of the introduction and dedication. The au-

[2] The only edition of Correa's great *Lendas da India* appeared in eight quarto volumes, comprising 3,500 pages, in Lisbon in 1858–66 after lying in manuscript form for three hundred years.

thor realized his shortcomings—that the volume was badly written, full of repetition and clumsy phrases, and in places most difficult to follow—and now that the manuscript was complete, he was, in spite of his fame, hesitant about publishing it, and turned to his friends, the physician Bosque and the poet Camoëns, for literary help and support. He dedicated the book in a long poem to Martin Afonso de Sousa, whom he had accompanied to India nearly thirty years earlier. This was followed by verses (in the writing of which Camoëns may have had a hand) laudatory of the same Dom Martin. Then Bosque, speaking of himself as a "Doctor of Valencia" wrote a short address in Portuguese to the "discreet reader," enjoining him to "receive the fruit of this garden of simples and plants of India which Dr. Garcia da Orta offers him."[3] An epigram in praise of Orta by Thome Dias Cayado, an excellent Latin scholar of Goa, was followed by an ode by Camoëns addressed to the Viceroy, D. Francisco Coutinho, who had granted a three years' copyright on the volume.

After thirty-six stilted lines of classical allusions, Camoëns' ode develops its real theme, the invocation of D. Francisco's blessing on the undertaking:

> Grant favor to that ancient art
> Which e'en Achilles held in high esteem.[4]
> Behold, how in your own bright years
> The fruits are ripe
> In the garden of far-famed Orta,
> Where burgeon forth new plants and herbs
> Ere now to the learned world unknown.
> Behold how in his fields of Ind
> An Orta caused such herbs to grow
> As Medea and Circe never knew,
> Though they both excelled in witches' magic lore!

[3] Bosque here puns on the word *orta*—a garden where vegetables and fruits are planted—and the learned author's name.

[4] Achilles was instructed in the art of medicine by the centaur Chiron.

See how, with wisdom born of many years
And knowledge in all fields profound,
This agèd man, who, with science taught
By the muses of great Ganges' tide,
In the subtle, sylvan art of Aesculapius' son[5]
Doth excel old Chiron's self,
Who did Achilles teach.

This man now seeks the favor of your grace,
That the noble volume from his hand
May forthwith see the light of day,
And, printed, shed radiance on his art,
And give to us
Those secrets to the ancients unrevealed.

Thus, I beseech you, do not this gift refuse
To him who for you a great renown would win,
As one, who already famed in war with Turk and Moor,
Now lends support to him whose struggle is 'gainst death.
Then with the noble Greek of old
Will your name be linked.[6]

Orta found it much to his liking, and the whole sheaf of manuscript was then taken to the shop of João de Endem for printing. The latter was pleased to receive the work, for he was desirous of establishing himself in business in Goa and so far only two books—and those on religious subjects—had been printed in India. Eagerly Luis awaited the publication of the volume; it would present the results of the lifework of his benefactor, Garcia da Orta, and would give to the world the first of the poems of which Luis had so many score laid away. There seemed to be endless delays. First Endem had to leave Goa on business, and then he was ill and away from his shop. He was confined to his bed so long that he finally entrusted the typesetting and proofreading (if, indeed, any of the

[5] Aesculapius' son—Podaleirius, the surgeon of the Greeks at the siege of Troy.
[6] Ode "Aquelo unico exemplo."

latter were done) to his assistant, who, poor fellow, was neither expert nor careful in his work.

At last, on the tenth day of April, 1563, the *Coloquios dos Simples e Drogas da India* appeared, and there, for the first time, Camoëns saw one of his poems in print. The type was so carelessly set that the lines were full of inaccuracies and the rhythm and sense were broken here and there because of the ignorance of the printer, but even that slight disappointment quickly vanished as Luis assured himself that at last he would become known and recognized, as was his due, in this association with the famous Garcia da Orta.

The book was an instant success, and is a famous landmark in the history of pharmaceutical research, though Luis' contribution probably received small notice.[7]

In spite of the real affection Camoëns had conceived for Coutinho and the obligation for the latter's protection and employment, his soul rebelled at the continued cruelties of the Portuguese acting under the Viceroy's orders, for the maltreatment of the natives never ceased. Not content with defeating the petty rulers of the coast, the Europeans, with little or no excuse, destroyed native plantations to the extent that the inhabitants of many districts were reduced to such starvation that some even resorted to cannibalism. These injustices not only continued, but seemed to grow more flagrant with the passing of the years.

One example will suffice. In January, 1564, Coutinho heard of attacks by Malabarese vessels on Portuguese ships. Refusing to accept the vehement protest of the Malabarese ruler that the marauders were not from his country, the Viceroy ordered eighty native craft to be seized, even though all of them carried Portuguese passes. Their crews and passengers, innocent of any wrongdoing,

---

[7] Only eight copies of the first edition of the book have been found. In no collection of Camoëns' poems does the ode appear in the exact form found in the 1563 book. Four versions are known.

were put to death in cold blood by the European commander, Domingos de Mesquita. The greater number were beheaded; the remainder were sewn in their own sails and thrown overboard alive, after which the ships were sunk. Thus perished two thousand helpless Indians at the hands of the Viceroy.

Even as this devilish work was in progress Coutinho fell ill, and, in the words of Couto, "so brief was his illness that he did not realize it until he was pronounced dead." The historian implied by this entry that the Viceroy's sudden demise was the laying upon him of the finger of God for the terrible crime he had committed. The very next sentence was surely written by Couto in bitter sarcasm: "The which [i.e., the death] terrified all greatly, and caused general sorrow, for he was very much beloved by all." A long paragraph of formal, empty laudation followed, but nothing could erase the black pages of Coutinho's days.

The villainous acts of his countrymen in India had but increased Camoëns' love for his native land. As seen through the memories of his youth, Portugal still seemed to him a veritable paragon of civic, religious, and martial virtues. Fired as he was by his reading of the knightly exploits of the founders of Portugal's greatness and by the tales of Correa, Orta, and Couto, to Luis the glory of his home seemed to glow the brighter in comparison with the misdeeds of the Portuguese in the East. This great love Luis had woven as a golden thread throughout his epic, which was now almost complete. If only men would read it, he believed, they would be inspired by their national heritage, and instead of setting up lucre and lust as their gods, they would repent and seek to emulate the great heroes of their country.

In the absence of D. Antão de Noronha, who was viceroy designate, D. João de Mendonça governed India for six months—and ruled well and justly. That he was far different in both character and acts from the majority of India's Portuguese rulers is affirmed by Couto in two brief sentences. "He arrived in Portugal poor, for in Malacca he took little or nothing, and much less from the governorship, which lasted but a short time. And, according to his character, I believe that if his rule had continued longer, he would have taken less."[8]

With the arrival of Mendonca's successor, D. Antão de Noronha, the Portuguese resumed their wars against several of the Indian states of the western coast; they were as ruthless under Noronha as they had been under preceding viceroys. Cananor was besieged by the Nairs of Malabar, but they were driven off by the Europeans, who then proceeded to wreak a terrible vengeance. In feuds between native states, coconut plantations had been held inviolate and never destroyed, since they were the chief means of subsistence, but no such consideration restrained Noronha, and forty thousand of these invaluable trees were cut down in one campaign. Several of Luis' boon companions, among them Heitor da Silveira and John Lopes Leitão, engaged in this siege and in other small coastal wars, but the poet remained in Goa. He retained his official position under Noronha, but since the Viceroy was not interested in literature or learning, no warm friendship sprang up between the two men and Camoëns lived much apart, always working on his epic and lyrics, ever seeking to polish and better them.

[8] Mendonça perished with King Sebastian in the battle of Alcácer Kebir on August 4, 1578.

CHAPTER XX

Homeward Bound

I long for thee,
O land where I was born.

—GIL VICENTE

As THE MONTHS WORE ON and the years glided by, Camoëns became
ever more restless and dissatisfied with the life he was leading.
There was no opportunity of advancement in his government position; the work was monotonous and so unrewarding financially
that he, even living frugally as he did, could lay nothing aside. Most
of the friends he had made during his long residence had passed
away and lay in foreign soil or in watery graves in the seas between Europe and the Indies, and of those who had survived, by
far the greater number had returned to their homes in Portugal.
He was weary of the vicious, artificial world about him, a world
which (though he was successful in retaining his physical and
mental health and vigor—no easy accomplishment in the unhealthy
climate of India) never ceased to cause him unhappiness and shame.

The homeland held little promise of a future, for he was now
unknown there and well past forty, but he was eager to have his

epic, which he had entitled *Os Lusíadas,*[1] published, that it might not perish unread by the folk for whom he had written it: his own fellow countrymen. Life had given him little in the way of financial gain or other rewards, but in spite of all, he had confidence in the worth of his poetry. He realized, too, that it might be difficult to arouse an interest in his verse and that in the event of publication he himself would have to be present to supervise the book through the press. So, in the spring of 1567, he finally decided to seek passage back to his native land. Long forgotten was the foolish vow of his youthful years (that his country should never possess his bones); indeed, at the very thought of setting foot in Lisbon once more, some of the old dreams of fame, glory, and perhaps even wealth must again have been rekindled within him. And though Catherine, whose memory was ever with him, was no longer alive, at least he would have redeemed himself in his own eyes if the pages to which he had given all his vast knowledge, his poetic genius, his sufferings, and his deprivations could be printed.

It was one thing to make up his mind to leave India, but quite another to obtain space on a ship bound for Lisbon. During the early period of the conquest and exploitation of the Eastern markets by Portugal, captains of vessels returning to Europe often gave free transportation and food to soldiers who had completed their military service in India, and during the first years of Camoëns' sojourn in the East, some former soldiers were still accorded this privilege. Moreover, if the captain were unusually softhearted, biscuit and water were supplied as far as the African coast. But now the greed of both masters and crews had so increased that they even rented their own cabins, hammocks, and berths to passengers at exorbitant prices. If the latter had slaves with them, these were charged as freight and an additional "entry card" was demanded, the fee for which was supposedly paid to the King.

[1] "The Deeds of the Sons of Lusus." Lusus was the legendary ancestor of the Portuguese people.

The price of the voyage made it impossible for Camoëns to buy his way back.[2]

Something else caused Luis to hesitate: he had suffered one disastrous shipwreck off the Mekong, on the Indo-Chinese coast, where he had lost not only Dinamene but all of his worldly possessions as well, and he knew that shipwrecks on the homeward voyage were far more common than on the outward journey. Sometimes the vessels lay off the Indian coast for many months, their hulls accumulating barnacles and weeds and the masts, yards, and other wooden parts deteriorating or rotting in the damp climate. In addition, the avarice of the merchants, officials, and ships' crews was such that all too frequently the returning ships were overladen and the cargoes badly stowed, often even encumbering the deck to such an extent that maneuvering, especially in the storms encountered in the vicinity of the Cape of Good Hope, was rendered difficult if not impossible. Besides these deterrents, many of the pilots were thoroughly incompetent.

In spite of all these obstacles and his own misgivings, Camoëns persisted, for he was convinced that in some manner not yet clear to him he would be given an opportunity to leave this land which had been his home for more than fourteen years and that he would succeed in having his treasured epic and lyrics published. His faith was finally justified, for in September he was approached by an official, one Pero Barreto Rolim, better known as Pedro Barreto, a man of little education, who had been appointed to the captaincy of Sofala and was about to depart for his post. Hearing that the impecunious poet was seeking to return home, he made a bargain with Luis. It is supposed that Barreto had need of someone to act as his secretary and keep the ship's books and that he agreed to Camoëns' taking on these duties in exchange for passage and food as far as Mozambique. Luis, realizing that this would at least take him part of the way and trusting that he would soon find another

2 According to Linschoten, the passage cost two hundred cruzados.

ship to carry him further, accepted the offer with alacrity and made preparations to depart.

Couto, Heitor da Silveira, and others were shortly to follow him to Europe, so his adieus to them were probably brief. With Garcia da Orta, however, it was different, for he was seventy-seven years old and had resolved to remain in India for the rest of his life. The learned doctor had been a father to Luis, who had sought his advice and guidance for years, and was most likely one of the few to whom Luis had read the verses of his *Lusiads*. Neither man could have dreamed that one would become famous through the centuries as the first modern writer on tropical medicines and their uses (he is often called "the father of scientific pharmacology") or that the other, the gaunt, threadbare, one-eyed, poverty-stricken Luis, would one day be hailed and immortalized as the greatest of Portuguese poets. So it was that these two great sons of Lusus, one on the brink of the grave, the other to live and suffer for many years more, parted forever.

The voyage from Goa to the African coast was uneventful. Relations between Barreto and Camoëns were friendly enough at first, but their temperaments were bound to clash. Barreto, an unlettered man, was probably envious of Luis' schooling and talent, and that, taken with Luis' mercurial and violent temper, exaggerated as it was by his many years in the tropics and the repeated blows of ill fortune, caused, we may easily believe, much friction during the fifty days of the passage to Africa, so that the two men were at swords' points by the time the low-lying coastline of Mozambique was sighted. Barreto, who, after all, had done the poet a great favor in taking him without cost a goodly part of the way to Portugal, had had enough of him and put him ashore with scant ceremony, leaving him to his own devices to make the remainder of his way to Lisbon.

CHAPTER XXI

Mozambique

O Sea,
How much of thy salt
Are Portugal's tears!

To win the way across thy waves
What mothers mourned,
How many sons have prayed in vain,
How many brides have died unwed
That thou might'st be ours,
O Sea!

Was it worth the toil?
All is worth the toil
If the spirit be not commonplace,
For he who would round Cape Bojador
Must be steeled to perils all unknown.

God gave to the sea the terrors of the Pit
—But behold! 'Tis the mirror of His Heaven, too.
                    —FERNANDO PESSOA (1890–1935)

MOZAMBIQUE WAS AT BEST a dreary place with an unhealthy climate, and Goa was a veritable Paradise in comparison. A small island half a league from the mainland, it was discovered by Vasco da

Gama, who found there an excellent harbor, on March 7, 1498.[1] Part of the beach was sandy, but much of the shore consisted of mud flats overgrown with skeletal mangroves, most evil smelling at low tide (and here the tide rose and fell some twelve feet). The place was occupied by a few dozen Portuguese soldiers, most of them living with native women. Camoëns was probably received at first as a welcome addition to the tiny, isolated European community, but since he had no money and was reduced to doing menial jobs or seeking charity, he was left much to himself. In fact, the coastal natives were probably kinder to him than his fellow countrymen, and among them he found many bits of local color which he later wove into his *Lusiads*. A less valiant man, one who had not the courage and determination to maintain his morale, could not have lived through those dreary months without "going native," nor could one with a weaker physique have withstood the combination of a deadly climate, the constant dampness, poisonous insects, malaria, and, probably, insufficient nutriment. Yet not only did Luis successfully meet these challenges to mental, physical, and moral health, but he found time to add and at least partially arrange a compilation of the poems in his possession, some of them composed in Morocco and Portugal, others in Asia. Ever a lover of ancient literature, he called the collection his *Parnaso*—after the mountain at Delphi where dwelt the Muses.

At long intervals vessels from Portugal came to anchor in the bay, and from them he learned of events in the kingdom. Ships put in from India, too, en route to their home port of Lisbon, but their crews would have none of him, for he had not the wherewithal to purchase a passage or food for the long voyage to Portugal.

---

[1] In 1505, a Castilian, one Poro de Noya, was sent to occupy the island. He erected a fort on the mainland near it, and two years later another fort was built on the island itself to protect its good, landlocked harbor. Though there were orchards and fertile fields, no drinking water was to be found there, all water used being ferried over from the mainland and stored in earthen vessels and cisterns.

One day, after two long years, when the hope of ever seeing home again had almost died within him, Camoëns sighted a galleon rounding the point and entering the bay. As the vessel drew near, he recognized her as the *Santa Clara,* homeward bound from India. Aboard her was Viceroy D. Antão de Noronha.

Luis' happiness knew no bounds. Here at last was deliverance, for he knew that Couto and Heitor da Silveira had planned to sail from India on the *Santa Clara.* His friends' hearts were touched at the sad tale of his misadventures and his present plight and quickly collected enough money from the ship's company to pay his passage to Portugal with them.

The vessel remained at anchor in the harbor of Mozambique for seven long months after the poet joined her, waiting in vain for the arrival of the other ships of the fleet, from which she had been separated in the crossing from Goa. Finally it was assumed that the missing galleons had continued their voyage to Portugal. Preparations were made for departure, and at last anchor was weighed. It must have been with unrestrained relief that Luis saw the low-lying island sink below the horizon, for now he was really homeward bound.[2]

To Luis the remainder of the voyage must have brought a leisure that he had seldom known, for he bore no responsibilities and had the time to work on his poetry, as well as to converse with his friends. For Diogo do Couto the presence of Camoëns was a windfall that repaid manyfold his efforts in securing the poet a passage. Couto was busily engaged in compiling and collating notes for

[2] The vessel had scarcely spread sail when Noronha fell ill, and before she had reached the islands of Angoxas (or Angoshas, a group of tiny coastal islands south of Mozambique), he was dead. His testament was read immediately after his death in order to ascertain his last wishes. To the surprise of all and the horror of many, he had directed that he be buried at sea but that his right arm be amputated at the elbow and taken to Ceuta and there placed in the tomb of his nephew. The ship's surgeon performed the operation, and Noronha's body was consigned to the waters where so many of his fellow countrymen had found their last resting place.

his history of the Portuguese in India,[3] and now good fortune had brought him copious eyewitness material covering the years before his arrival there.[4] Camoëns profited vastly, too, from the presence on board of Heitor da Silva, in whom he had an educated, sympathetic, and kindly critical audience. He had discussed, we may be sure, parts of his work with Silveira in their lodgings, but now he could read the poem aloud, for it was complete, except for some verses which he was planning to include as a dedication to King Sebastian—if he could secure royal patronage for his book.

One may visualize the scene as Luis began to tell his listeners, who sat on deck in the shade of the sails, how he had conceived of the poem. Then he outlined its main features. He had taken Vergil's scheme for the development of his own theme: the noble deeds of the Portuguese people from the beginning of their history to the poet's own time. Just as Vergil had placed part of his story in the mouth of Aeneas, who recounted the fall of Troy to Dido, so, too, was much of the Portuguese saga recited by Vasco da Gama to the King of Malindi, on the East African coast, while events that took place after Vasco's departure from India were presented as a vision and prophecy revealed to him.

Into his epic Luis wove his great knowledge of the classics and of Portuguese history and legend, as well as material drawn from his personal experiences on land and sea. To these he added a colorful myth of his own creation, that of the giant Adamastor,

[3] This history, a continuation of Barros' *Decadas* in many volumes, had a varied and often unfortunate career. Some of the volumes were published before Couto's death (December 10, 1616), some were tampered with, one was destroyed by fire, another captured and thrown overboard by an English privateer, and two were stolen. Couto rewrote them, and the work was finally printed in a definitive edition in 1778–88.

[4] Two books by Couto, *Dialogue of the Practical Soldier*, which treats of the mistakes and disillusionments in India, and *Dialogue of the Practical Portuguese Soldier*, were so frank in their revelation of the corruption, abuses, and vices of the Portuguese in India that the manuscripts were stolen from him. He rewrote them from memory, but they were suppressed and were not published until 1790.

son of Mother Earth, who, as punishment for his rebellion against the gods, had been transformed into the Cape of Good Hope.

The circle around the poet was surely entranced from the moment he began the tale:

> Of the arms and heroes unmatched in fame
> Who from Lusitania's western shore
> E'en beyond Taprobana's isle did sail
> O'er seas ne'er traversed by man before
>
> And of these whose great and valorous deeds
> Have them from the grave's oblivion saved
> Shall I sing, that all the world may know
> —If art and genius but lend their aid.[5]

Silveira and Couto must have realized that their companion was one of the immortals. Couto was even more impressed than the others, for he was well acquainted with the best verse his countrymen had written, and he himself had composed poetry with considerable success.[6] He now recognized in Camoëns, whom he thought he had known well in India, a transcendent literary genius, greater than any Portugal had given to the world. He had found Luis' lyrics to be far superior to those of the other poets who had gone before him, and now he was convinced that Camoëns was worthy of walking in the great company of Homer and Vergil. Couto felt humble in Luis' presence and spoke of him thereafter as the Prince of Poets—beholding him already seated on Parnassus' heights. Because of the historian's recognition of the work and his encyclopedic knowledge of the exploits of the Portuguese, Camoëns suggested that Couto write an historical commentary on

---

[5] *Lusiads*, I, 1, 2.

[6] Couto left a volume of poetry, which has been lost. He referred to Camoëns twice in his books. In his *Dialogue of the Practical Soldier* he quotes a line from *The Lusiads* (V, 97): "He who knows nothing of art cannot measure its value." The second reference is in his *Decadas* (VII, Liv. X, Cap. xi, p. 532), wherein he cites the poet in discussing the marriage customs of the Nairs of Malabar.

The Lusiads. Couto felt honored by the request and forthwith set about making notes, convinced that the poem would be printed and would receive the world's acclaim and that he, Couto, would, by his commentary, bask in reflected glory.[7]

Favored by fair weather, the voyage continued until the island of St. Helena was sighted. After a stay of twenty days there (in the vain hope of meeting other vessels of the convoy), the captain ordered the anchor weighed and the *Santa Clara* proceeded northward alone.

[7] Couto wrote a commentary on the first four cantos, but it was never printed. His work was interrupted by Philip II's order to write a history of India.

III

- Zion -

The Lord hath accomplished his fury; he hath poured out his
fierce anger, and hath kindled a fire in Zion, and it hath devoured
the foundations thereof.

—Lamentations 4:5

CHAPTER XXII

Lisbon Again

Thus they fared, ploughing the sea serene,
With gentle winds and waves ne'er tempest-stirred,
Until they had first glimpse of land,
The land that gave them birth,
—The land of heart's desire—
And entering Tagus' peaceful stream,
At last dropped anchor by its well-loved shore.

—CAMOËNS, *Lusiads*, X, 144

This is my own, my happy, well-loved native land,
To which, if Heaven but grant that I return
Unharmed, with this my enterprise complete,
Then may the flame of life die out for me.

—CAMOËNS, *Lusiads*, III, 21

THE LONG-AWAITED DAY arrived at last. Camoëns saw the hills of Cintra looming blue in the haze and knew he was really nearing Portugal after an absence of seventeen years.

On Friday, April 7, 1570, the *Santa Clara* entered the estuary of the Tagus. Hardly had she dropped anchor when a small boat flying the royal pennon put out from the shore to bring her cap-

179

tain a terse, grim message. The plague was raging in the city, the harbor was closed, and no vessels were to proceed further without a certificate from the King's physician and an order from him personally.

Young King Sebastian had been on the throne little more than a twelvemonth when in June, 1569, a new visitation of the devastating pestilence began to spread over Portugal. In less than a year it had claimed more than fifty thousand victims. Often five or six hundred died in a day; there was no time to prepare coffins, and mass burials of the heaped-up bodies, clad in linen shrouds, were the rule rather than the exception. The streets were deserted; grass grew between the paving stones, and the few healthy citizens who went from place to place avoided each other in fear of the dread contagion. Finally, however, the scourge began to diminish, the number of deaths decreased, and the inhabitants who had fled the city slowly returned, though great danger of a recurrence of the disease, as well as famine, still threatened. The *Santa Clara* was therefore ordered to allow no one to disembark except some person to be selected by the captain. The man chosen was to proceed at once to Almeirim, where the King was residing, with documents bearing the latest news from India.

Couto was assigned the mission. Hardly had he departed up river when Heitor da Silveira, who had so long been Camoëns' companion in India and on shipboard, died. He had been ailing during the voyage, but his illness was not considered serious. His sudden death was a terrible shock, adding one more to the miseries that seemed to assail Luis unceasingly.[1]

Among Silveira's papers were found letters indicating that he, too, had had great sorrows, which he had borne heroically and in silence, for he had not only lost his first wife and a baby—his only child—but his second wife had also preceded him into the great unknown. That he loved her dearly was evident everywhere in the

[1] The genealogical records of the Silveira family imply suspicions of poisoning.

packet of letters and, in one of them, in the fragment of a poem which ended with a sad apostrophe to her:

Oh, my steadfast Northern star,
My clear light and my guide,
Beliza, who dost cheer my soul,
I called to thee in vain.[2]

Thus had death taken from the poet another of the few loyal friends left him.

Shortly thereafter Couto returned on board with the information that the *Santa Clara* might proceed to her moorings.

Even the death of Silveira could not entirely damp Camoëns' joy as the great galleon sailed slowly up the Tagus and one by one the familiar hills and streets and buildings, which he probably never expected to see again, came into view. But when he went to his cabin to gather his few effects, he found to his dismay that although his *Lusiads* and a large bundle of other poems were intact, his *Parnaso*, which contained the labor of years and which he treasured almost as much as he did his *Lusiads*, had vanished. He searched everywhere on shipboard and traced every possible clue, but in vain. The manuscript, wherein he had begun to arrange his lyrics in the order in which he desired them published, was lost forever. At one stroke he had been deprived of much of the fruits of his genius.[3]

Luis de Camoëns and his companions set foot once more on their native soil. Many of them came with worldly wealth—loot from the wars in Asia or gold from the Indies—or with investments sufficient to insure security and comfort for the remainder of their

---

[2] Fragment "Tudo nos roubam cá, té o desejo."

[3] It is probably because of the loss of this collection, called by one commentator "the collar of pearls," that even now, more than 350 years after his death, scholars have difficulty in collating Camoëns' poems and deciding which are authentic and when and for whom they were written.

lives. Luis was the least of all those who stepped ashore that April day from the boat of the *Santa Clara*. He must have bethought himself of the welcome which he dreamed might have been his, a dream once so vivid that he had set it down in his *Lusiads*:

> The joy their native land to reach again,
> Their loved household gods and kith and kin.
> To tell of strange wanderings o'er the sea,
> The various skies and people seen;
> Home to enjoy the fruits they earned
> By labors long and happenings unforeseen,
> Emotion wells up in each breast so strong
> That the heart proves a vessel all too small.[4]

Just as Ulysses returned to his home in Ithaca after many years of wandering by land and sea and was not recognized in the guise of an old beggar, so, too, did Camoëns, drawing his cloak about him, return to the city of his birth, unknown and an outcast. Unlike Ulysses, however, who was restored to his own youthful self, there was no gray-eyed Athena to give back to Luis his youth, sapped by war and hardship, no one to buoy up his manly spirit, weighed down by the invisible chains of the years of struggle against ill fortune. Exhausted, old long before his time, Luis had to take up the burden of his life alone. Even so, as he entered the narrow streets at the waterside he hugged close to his breast a wealth greater than that possessed by any man who had ever entered the kingdom: the manuscript of his *Lusiads*, the great, the immortal song of his people.

On the night of Camoëns' arrival, Lisbon was celebrating the cessation of the plague. The King had ordered that on the eve of April 20 prayers were to be offered up in all the churches which were still open, that every citizen should place a lighted candle or

[4] *Lusiads*, X, 17.

lantern in his window, and that lights should burn on every vessel, great or small, in the harbor. The city, scourged for many months by the deadly disease, looked as if it were decked out for a festival, the lights shining like a myriad of stars, and all ugliness was mercifully obscured by the velvety blackness of the night. Still more weird did the actions of the citizens appear, for in the abandon of their joy at the departure of the dread pestilence they had built huge bonfires at crossroads and in the public squares, and now they sang and danced madly about them all through the night. The following morning, the streets and public places were crowded, for a procession of thanksgiving was held in honor of the Virgin. All the clergy marched together with the brotherhoods and parishioners of the various churches, carrying relics and statues of the saints and allegorical figures, while long lines of people bearing crucifixes, great wax tapers, and painted banners paraded for hours, the ceremony lasting more than half the day.

Tradition tells us that after his arrival Luis set out in search of his mother and learned that she dwelt in the ancient Mouraria, on the slope of the hill where stood the royal Castle of St. George. None but the poor lived in the crooked lanes and squalid little courts where the Moslems of the capital had dwelt for centuries before their expulsion from the country. The reunion of mother and son may well be imagined. Luis' father had died many, many years before (some accounts state that it was in a shipwreck on the Indian coast), and since then his mother seems to have lived alone, although no story of her experiences during the intervening years has come down to us. Luis had probably carried the picture of her as she was in his boyhood: a handsome, happy young woman. He found her old, gray, bowed. And she? She surely must always have had in her heart the image of a golden-haired, blue-eyed, stalwart young lad as he stepped forth from their home on the hill of Coimbra so many years ago. It must have been difficult for her to believe that this man who stood before her in worn, patched garments, that golden hair shot with gray, darkened and burned by the tropic sun and the winds of the sea, with but one tired eye and a sunken socket where once had been the flashing, merry blue eyes of her boy, was really her son.

Luis' first inquiry concerned Catherine's resting place. When he learned where she lay, he hastened there, and with the memory of the lonely grave before him, he wrote:

> She lies beneath this stone entombed,
> Whose noble beauty so rejoiced the world,
> And whom death through cruelest jealousy
> Carried off before her time.
> Her excellence did naught avail,
> Nor the radiance of her gentle soul,
> That turned dark night to brightest day
> —And eclipsed the sun itself.
>
> By that same sun in envy
> Wert thou bribed, O Death,
> And by the moon,
> Whose silver rays before her paled?
> Hadst thou power, Death, to work such change?
> And even if thou hadst,
> How couldst thou in such short space of time
> Turn this world's light to coldest clay?[5]

It took many months for Luis to adjust himself to the scene about him, for the capital was not the city he had left so many years before. Then, though signs of decay were evident to the discerning eye, Lisbon was the most important city in Europe, seething with life and sustained by the wealth pouring in from the Indies.

In spite of the austerity of the court, the Lisbon of 1570 was still rich and extravagant and, like most of Europe, was plagued by religious intolerance and unbelievable profligacy. During Camoëns' absence, money had been devaluated and poverty had

[5] Soneto "Debaixo desta pedra sepultada."

increased. The clergy were preaching that the plague was a visitation in punishment of the people and that a great earthquake was imminent. There were more beggars on the streets than ever before; the almshouses and orphan asylums were crowded, and the slums where Camoëns lodged were a swarming hotbed of disease and vice. The kingdom seemed topsy-turvy, for the farm lands were being depopulated, the peasants filling the cities or clamoring for places on the ships bound for India.

Luis learned that the most loved poet of his youth, Sá de Miranda, had died in 1558. Hearing this, he must have recalled one of the poet's phrases whose meaning he could not fully grasp before he had gone to Goa but which was now all too clear. Writing of the stream of fortune hunters leaving the kingdom, Miranda spoke of them as "dead of starvation but living for greed."[6] And all the while the continual processions of the victims of the Inquisition passed through the streets, with the doleful tolling of the church bells adding to the depression and desperation of the people, whose morale had been severely undermined by the ravages of the plague. Camoëns, student of the past and present, reflecting on what he had observed in India and now in Portugal, sadly faced the bitter fact that he had come home in the empty, chaotic years between his country's marvelous, brilliant past and her inevitable, hopeless future.

The two men who probably rejoiced most at seeing Luis once again were Antonio Ribeiro Chiado, the unfrocked Franciscan monk, and Andre Falcão de Resende, writer of verse, both rollicking friends of the poet's Lisbon days after Ceuta. Resende was, as usual, working on his ballads, lampooning the Englishman Sir Francis Drake, and writing clever satires, while Chiado was carrying on a mutual abuse with Afonso Alvarez, the keen-minded mulatto servant of the Bishop of Evora.

Camoëns had not been long in Chiado's company when he met

[6] *Mortos de fome, mas vivos de cobiça.*

a painter of some local renown, one Fernando Gomes, who claimed to have been a pupil of Michelangelo. One day, in an idle hour, Gomes suggested that Luis allow him to paint his portrait, and the poet, nothing loath, agreed. The painter, who had only red pigment with him, set up his easel and with rapid strokes quickly sketched a small but spirited likeness. The picture of Luis' long, thin, scarred face, with the right eye missing (but treated kindly, without a patch, so that the features were not distorted), was true to life. His left eye had the dreamy, faraway look of a poet and philosopher, and the thinning hair and roughly trimmed beard, the fine, high intellectual forehead, the bedraggled ruff and threadbare pourpoint were all there. When the portrait was finished, Gomes wrote Camoëns' name in the upper right-hand corner in fine, large Roman letters, then signed his own name in black in the lower left-hand corner and presented it to the poet.[7]

Luis' patriotic temperament could not have beheld unmoved what was transpiring in court circles. Very little of the truth had seeped through the messages and documents and highly colored or biased reports of the kingdom that came to India with the arrival of each vessel, but now, piecing together information from all sources, one could only be deeply disturbed at current events.

Of the nine children of Manuel the Fortunate and the six of his son, King John III, only one had survived—and he a Cardinal—so at John's death in 1557 the throne passed to his grandson, D. Sebastian, born January 19, 1554. Sebastian's mother, a Spanish princess, had retired to her native land shortly after her son's birth, leaving the royal child, who had inherited various signs of physical

[7] This portrait was not known until July 23, 1925, when it was found in the effects of Dr. Carvalho Monteiro, one of the most famous collectors of Camoniana, and presented to the Lisbon Academy of Sciences. It is the only portrait known to have been painted in Camoëns' lifetime; all others are deformed copies or imaginative representations. The portrait, about six by nine inches in size, is torn in several places and has been very inexpertly mended.

degeneration from his father, in the care of his grandfather, John III. At the death of the latter, the grandmother, Queen Catharine, became regent, but in 1552, eight years before Luis' return, she had surrendered the regency to Cardinal Henry, an unattractive man in his late sixties.

According to the stories current in Lisbon, the young King was increasingly revealing in his actions the evil results of the inbreeding in his family. He had developed into a morbid youth, spending most of his time in hunting and praying, finally becoming so pathologically fanatical that all of his dreams and plans centered on a chimerical new crusade to drive the Moslem infidels out of North Africa. Meanwhile, his family persisted in trying to arrange marriages for him to one foreign princess after another, in spite of his physicians' (and at one time he had eight of them) vigorous protests that the youth was fitted neither physically nor mentally for matrimony. In 1569, when he attained his fifteenth year, he was declared of age; the regency came to an end and he ruled thenceforth in his own right. When the plague broke out, he left Lisbon and traveled through the provinces with his court, displaying during the months of his absence from the capital so many vagaries and aberrations from the normal in both word and action that the wiser heads around him despaired of Portugal under his rule. This, then, was the incompetent King Sebastian whom Luis desired as his patron.

Not only was the kingdom afflicted with an irrational ruler, but Portugal's entire political and social structure was threatened with disaster. The empire of King Manuel had been erected on an insufficient foundation, and in spite of her many brave sons still alive, Portugal's situation was a most serious one, both at home and abroad, for the administration had fallen into irresponsible, greedy, and corrupt hands and was rapidly decaying, both from the top and at the roots. The fine native virtues which had brought Portugal from a small, obscure country to one important in European affairs was vanishing beneath fictitious prosperity, in which men seemed to live for the day only, caring nought for the morrow. Thus, in addition to his concern for his own fallen fortunes, Camoëns grieved over his country's ills—grieved so deeply that he was impelled to write a despairing, pessimistic verse, inserting it into the last canto of *The Lusiads*. It was a cry of personal disillusionment, and though he probably read and reread the epic many times before it was finally published, he was never moved to strike the stanza from the page:

No more, O Muse, no more,
For now my lyre is out of tune
And my voice grows faint.
I weary not of singing,
But of folk whose ears are deaf to song,
And whose hearts are hard.

That one gift which fires the poet
More than all
My country will not grant;
Sunk in greed and avarice,
In ignorance and gloomy vice
Morose it lives, content.[8]

[8] *Lusiads*, X, 145.

CHAPTER XXIII

The Epic of the Lusiads

To serve thee with arm well trained in war,
Mind devoted to the Muse.
                              —CAMOËNS, *Lusiads*, X, 155

EVIDENTLY, as soon as possible after his return to Portugal Camoëns turned his energies to the difficult task of having his *Lusiads* recognized and published. With his ardent love of country and his concern for what he perceived of her social and moral deterioration, as revealed in many of his verses, it would seem that he desired it to be published and widely read as much for the purpose of arousing his fellow countrymen from their apathy to some vigorous action as for the gratification of his own personal ambition to see his work in print.

The approval of the book by the King was essential to give it the necessary publicity, and Luis turned successfully to the only one of his old friends who had access to the throne, D. Manuel de Portugal, who, we can believe, had pity on the man who had suffered so many hardships through nought but youthful folly, and, a poet himself, he probably recognized the genius of the younger man. Knowing that Sebastian, vain, headstrong, and deeply impressed with his own importance, could be won by flattery, he suggested that since the remains of John III, Sebastian's grandfather, were to be transferred to the Monastery of the Jeronymos at Belem, just outside Lisbon, where King Manuel was also interred, Luis write a sonnet on the late King which he, D. Manuel, would contrive to have read before Sebastian on the occasion.

The poet consented, though he surely bore a deep resentment against John, who, with Catharine, had ordered his exile, but he was far wiser in the ways of the world than on that far-off day of the performance of *King Seleucus*. Fortunately, the sonnet[1] received the King's approval. D. Manuel next suggested that before *The Lusiads* was presented to the King some stanzas directly applicable to Sebastian should be inserted in it. D. Manuel was wise enough to realize that the King, a willful, abnormal young man, would never be patient enough to listen to a reading of the entire poem or even a substantial part of it, yet he was confident that if Sebastian could be induced to listen to the opening stanzas, especially if they exalted him and appealed to his vanity, his approval and patronage would be given the work. Though Camoëns knew of the vacillating, fanatical, and unstable character of Sebastian and undoubtedly revolted at prostituting his talents by flattering such an unworthy occupant of the throne, he must have understood that there was no other likely way of gaining his desired end, so thirteen stanzas lauding the King and his high destiny were inserted in the first canto of the epic.[2]

In these verses Luis apostrophized the King as

> Thou, the high-born champion
> Of ancient Lusitanian liberties,
> Thou, the new terror of the Moorish lance,
> The wonder foretold of this our present age,
> Given the world by God, to rule it all.

[1] See Appendix I, Poem 89.
[2] *Lusiads*, I, 6–18.

And further:

> Mighty sovereign whose high domain
> The sun in his course doth first behold.

And then, before he launched into the body of the poem,[3] he offered his book to Sebastian thus:

> And while these heroes—but not thee—I sing
> —For King sublime, I dare not so high aspire—
> Take thou in hands the reins of this, thy state,
> And create deeds for still another song
> As yet unsung.
>
>   . . .
>
> Thy favor grant to this, my daring song,
> That these my verses, may be thine.

Camoëns' honesty of spirit must have cringed within him as he wrote these lines, but his experience in the court of King John III had taught him that such fawning adulation was demanded of a courtier by such a king as Sebastian.

The work was finished, the last touches given the bulky manuscript to which he had devoted more than half his life, on land and on sea, from the farthest confines of China to Portugal, and now it was to pass from his hands, to be approved or rejected at the whim of a witless king. He could do no more; he had to rely entirely upon the discretion of D. Manuel de Portugal.

The date was the twenty-fourth of September, 1571. Luis had probably been impatient, like all authors awaiting approval of their work, but on that day he received a document bearing the royal seal:

> I, the King, make known to those who may read this decree that it pleases me to grant authorization to Luis de Camoëns to

[3] Stanza 19.

cause to be printed in this city of Lisbon a work in outava [*sic*] rima entitled *Os Lusíadas*, which contains ten excellent cantos in which in poetic fashion are set forth in verse the principal exploits of the Portuguese in the regions of India since the sea road to them was discovered by order of the King, D. Manuel, my great-grand-father (may he be in saintly glory). And this is with the privilege that for the period of ten years, beginning on the day when the printing of the book is completed and thereafter, it may not be printed or sold in my kingdom or dominions nor be taken beyond them, nor from the said parts of India to be sold without the license of the said Luis de Camoëns, or by any person to whom the power may be deputed by him, under the penalty, in violation hereof, of fifty cruzados and the confiscation of the volumes so printed or sold, one-half [to go] to the said Luis de Camoëns, and the other half to him who brings the charge—and before the said volume is printed it is to be submitted to and examined by the Board of the Holy Office of the Inquisition that it may receive its permission to be printed, and if the said Luis de Camoëns should increase [the work] with any additional cantos, they are also to be printed, ob-taining therefore the license of the Holy Office as above stated. And this my decree is to be printed in the front of the said work and will have the same force and effect as though it were a letter made in my name, signed by me and passed by my chancellor. . . .

Drawn up by Gaspar de Seixas in Lisbon the twenty-fourth day of September, 1571. Written by Jorge da Costa.

The King had given his permission for the printing of the epic. Joyously, Luis expressed his gratitude to D. Manuel in an ode.[4]

There was another—and very important—step to be taken be-fore the manuscript could be confided to the printer. The royal de-cree had specifically stated that the *imprimatur* of the Board of the Holy Office of the Inquisition was necessary before anything fur-ther could be done. Luis was presented to Frei Bartolameu Fer-reira, chief censor of the Board, who had the last word in the

[4] See Appendix I, Poem 90.

matter. Frei Bartolameu and the poet must have discovered kindred souls in one another, for Camoëns' reception was most
friendly. Then followed the reading of the poem, with questions
and answers, for the censor's duty was to assure the Holy Office
that there was nothing sacrilegious or contrary to the Faith in any
book approved by it. Luis, fearful lest the number of pagan and
mythological references throughout *The Lusiads* arouse insur-
mountable objections on the part of the censor, had inserted an
additional stanza in the last canto.[5] Frei Bartolameu (who probably realized that it would be bad policy to withhold his consent
to the publication of a book whose printing the King clearly desired) ignored the extravagant tales of Adamastor and the erotic
episode of the "Isle of Loves," for doubtless the interpolated stanza
calmed any doubts he may have had. It was all over in a matter of
minutes. The scratching of quill on paper, sand shaken on the
page, and Luis possessed the last precious document necessary to
set the press in motion to turn out his book:

By order of the Holy and Universal Inquisition I have examined
these ten cantos of *The Lusiads* of Luis de Camoëns, concerning
the valorous exploits in arms which the Portuguese performed in
Asia and Europe, and I find in it nothing scandalous or contrary
either to the Faith or to good morals. Only it is necessary for me
to warn readers that the author, in order to impress them with the
difficulties of the Portuguese in finding the route and the entrance
into India, has made a fictional use of the gods of the Gentiles.—
Nevertheless, since this is a poem and pretense, and the author, as
a poet, intends no more than to ornament his poetic style, we do
not find it improper to introduce this fable of the gods into the
work, recognizing it as such, and without detriment to the truth
of our Holy Faith, that all the gods of the Gentiles are "demons."
And for this reason the book appears to me worthy of printing,

[5] This stanza (X, 82) declares that the gods are all fabulous and are introduced
as mere fantasy to render the poem more harmonious.

and the author shows in it much talent and much learning in the humane sciences. In testimony whereof I affix my signature hereto.

FREI BARTOLAMEU FERREIRA

All the preliminary obstacles had been overcome; Luis now had to find a printer who would be willing to undertake the work. He was forthcoming in the person of Antonio Gonçalves, who had already published a number of volumes and who foresaw that with the patronage of the King and the protection of the Holy Office he might expect many sales and a good profit. His shop, however, was full of work, and Camoëns was forced to wait his turn—a protracted delay, for the volume did not come from Gonçalves' press until the summer of the following year.[6]

At last the first copy of the book was in his hands:

> The Lusiads of Luis de Camoëns, with the royal grant or copyright, printed in Lisbon with the authority of the Holy Inquisition and of the Bishop of the diocese, in the house of Antonio Gonçalves, printer, 1572.

The title-page was well arranged and dignified, and so were the leaves (there were 186 of them), but the book was full of grave errors in printing and the type was not always as regularly set or as clear as one would have liked. However, many of the Portuguese books of the day were full of such mistakes, and Gonçalves' publishing house (which had been chosen because it offered the best terms) was notorious for its defective typography and the carelessness of its proofreaders.

What joy it must have been for Luis to walk on the Rua Nova, where he could see his volume stacked in neat, clean piles in the book stalls! What excitement when he could, from some corner, watch a passer-by stop, thumb through the pages, take out his

---

[6] The exact date is unknown, and there are two editions dated 1572, with numerous variations in type ornaments, in the text and elsewhere. One of these may be a pirated edition.

purse, and buy a book written by him, the poor, half-blind outcast, Luis de Camoëns! We may easily imagine the scene.

The small first edition of *The Lusiads* was soon sold. Favorable comments were heard on every side, and men began to quote from its verses. When reports of the success of the work reached the King, he made inquiries about Camoëns and upon learning of the poet's pitiable condition granted Luis a pension. But Sebastian, lavish as he was in some ways, was extremely parsimonious in others, and the most he would give the poverty-stricken poet was the annual sum of 15,000 reis ($150.00).

Accordingly, on July 28, 1572, a rescript from the royal chancellery was delivered to Luis:

> I, the King, make known to those who may see this document that, having respect for the services which Luis de Camoëns, knight of my household, has rendered me in the parts of India for many years, and for those which I hope he will perform for me in the future, and because of the knowledge which I have of his genius and cleverness, and the ability which he has shown in the book which he wrote concerning the affairs of India, it is my will and pleasure to grant him an annual pension of 15,000 reis for the period of three years, beginning the twelfth day of March of this present year 1572; that award is granted and will be paid him by my chief treasurer or by whomsoever's duty it may be for each of the said three years. . . .
>
> Drawn up in Lisbon July 28, 1572. And I, Duarte, caused it to be written.

The smallness of the pension was almost an insult, for it was barely enough to hold body and soul together, let alone sufficient to relieve the poet from want and worry, but in his condition anything must have been acceptable.

Meanwhile, the book was selling and Camoëns was becoming known through it. He may have had hopes that the rich and powerful Gama family, whose ancestor he had made the protagonist of his epic and whose name and fame he had sung throughout its stanzas, might come to his assistance, but in this, too, it appears that he was bitterly disappointed. They accepted the praise of the great admiral, in whose reflected glory they shone, but there is no record of their having moved to recompense the man whose verses had immortalized Vasco and his discovery of the sea road to the Indies.

Even though the monetary reward was negligible, the book had created a sensation among many discerning readers, who realized that *The Lusiads* was great literature, towering far above anything ever before produced by a Portuguese. The sweetest praise, probably, that Luis received was in conversation with Count Pedro da Alcaçova Carneiro. In discussing his book the poet asked Carneiro what he considered the greatest mistake he had found in it. "The error is a very great and grave one," answered the Count, smiling. "It is that your poem is not short enough to be learned by heart and not so long that one need never cease reading it."

Immediately upon its publication, the book was bitterly attacked by the poets of Lisbon, who showed their petty natures and envy in their carping, adverse criticisms, claiming that Camoëns had invented words theretofore unknown in Portuguese and that he had employed expressions foreign to the language. For months there raged a battle between these critics and those who, recognizing the grandeur of the work, defended it with might and main.

The advances on the small edition of *The Lusiads* were soon consumed, and Luis was compelled to do hack work—prologues, dedicatory poems, and other bits—for aspiring individuals unable to versify for themselves. Fortunately, however, through Frei Bartolameu he met the monks of São Domingos and became very friendly with them. They made every effort to assist him, sending him persons in need of literary services and inviting him to share meals with them—when he would otherwise often have gone hungry.

From the day Camoëns landed after the subsidence of the plague, one misfortune after another befell his country. With the disappearance of the pestilence, financial difficulties became even greater, the price of copper fell, and inflation set in. Sebastian was called upon for aid by Charles IX, the boy king of France, who, under the influence of his mother, Catherine de Medici, had declared war against the Turks and Lutherans. In answer to the summons, and not heeding his own country's pressing needs, Sebastian gathered a fleet of thirty vessels. He borrowed money from nobles and high dignitaries of the Church, confiscated funds, and seized ships, pardoning large numbers of convicts to man them. In August of 1572 all was ready, but before the fleet could sail, Nature stepped in and ended the adventure: a great storm swept in from the Atlantic and wrested from their anchorage all thirty vessels, strewing their hopeless wreckage on the shores of the Tagus estuary.

Wise men could discern the rapid disintegration of the state. Her people were not traders by nature, and she had no middle class versed in business and banking. Moreover, by the discovery of the sea road to India and their greed for empire the Portuguese had disorganized the centuries-old land and sea trade routes between Asia and Europe and had failed to import Oriental cargoes in sufficient quantity either to satisfy market demands or to make spices cheaper. Gradually, shrewd and experienced bankers and middlemen from Venice and other Italian commercial centers, from Germany and the Low Countries, had forced their way into the Indian trade, and by advancing funds to the Crown and money to Portuguese merchants they were channeling the profits of Eastern commerce from Lisbon to their own cities. Those who loved their country saw, with a deepening sadness and a growing feeling of helplessness, that all the exploits of their countrymen had been performed in vain. Portugal was rapidly mortgaging itself and its future, and there was no apparent way by which, under the rule of a Sebastian, it could redeem the pledge.

In 1572, Lisbon was visited by a most destructive flood. Camoëns must have escaped this, for though the Mouraria was an area far from desirable for decent living, it was on a steep hillside, well out of reach of the greedy waters of the Tagus.

In February of the next year Pope Gregory XIII—he who in 1582 revised the calendar—sent as a gift to King Sebastian one of the arrows which supposedly had slain the martyred St. Sebastian.[7] Conveyed personally by the Papal Secretary, it was presented to the King, who was sojourning at Almeirim. Enthused by the gift of the relic, which still bore the stains of the blood of his patron saint, Sebastian ordered its reception by the highest church dignitaries and decreed that it be carried in procession, that all his people might behold and venerate it. The streets were crowded, and it was with difficulty that the cortege made its way through the narrow thoroughfares. The arrow, wrapped in a transparent veil of crimson silk, lay in a coffer of silver lined with vermilion cloth, while over it was borne an ornate canopy, the poles of which were carried by the King, Cardinal Henry, the Ambassador of Castile, and the highest officials of the court.

The arrival of the arrow seems to have aroused Camoëns to perceive in it a plan by which he could obtain the extension of his pension. He therefore wrote nine stanzas of *oitavas*, flattering Sebastian as though he were the world's greatest monarch, the poem opening with these lines:

> Most mighty king, to whom the Heavens have given
> The name, august and most sublime,
> Of the knight who in his death for Christ
> Was by a thousand arrows slain.[8]

Knowing of the King's desire and ambition to lead a new crusade against the Moors, Camoëns continued by declaring:

[7] One of Portugal's churches already possessed one of the Saint's arms, which has now vanished.

198

We have sure forecast and hope most clear
That yours will be an arm supreme in strength
Against the boastful Mauritanian sword.

His plan succeeded. The poem was read to Sebastian, whose weak nature could resist no flattery, and the pension was forthwith renewed for another three years.

It was during this period that Camoëns met and became very friendly with Manuel Correa, curate of the Church of San Sebastian, not far from the poet's home in the Mouraria. Correa was a learned man, a barrister as well as a priest, and one well versed in literature. At the time, he was translating Tacitus[9] and carrying on a lively correspondence with the famous Flemish Latinist, Justus Lipsius.[10] During one of their discussions, Camoëns suggested that the priest edit and annotate his *Lusiads*; Correa consented with alacrity and forthwith worked on the project.[11]

During these same years, however, Luis met with great difficulty in earning a living. He suffered still more because of the irregularity with which he received his pension, often being turned away from the Treasury with some flimsy excuse. His irritation was constant, and one day he exploded with: "Such a niggardly amount, and so much trouble to get it that I'm tempted to petition His Majesty to commute the fifteen thousand reis into fifteen thousand lashes on those fellows' [the bureaucrats'] backs!" Many times in the few years left to him he was heard to complain about the payment of the sums due him, for although the pension was again renewed in 1578, he always had difficulty in collecting it.

With the passing of the months the poet's health began to fail, the

[8] Oitava "Mui alto Rei, a quem os Ceús, em sorte."

[9] This exists in manuscript only.

[10] Justus Lipsius—the Latinized form of Joest Lips (1547–1606).

[11] Correa's annotated edition was published in Lisbon in 1613, thirty-three years after the poet's death. Although the "Address to the Reader" gives a few paragraphs on Camoëns' life, the information is both scanty and unreliable.

inevitable result of his hard life in India and his ill-nourished poverty at home, and he became ever more querulous, even with those who sought to give him employment. One day Ruy Diaz da Camara, a *fidalgo* well known in Lisbon, called on Luis to make a verse translation of the Penitential Psalms. He accepted the commission but kept putting off the work for many months, until finally Camara angrily upbraided him for his failure to keep his promise, "being such a great poet and having composed such a famous poem." Camoëns drew himself up to his full height and answered proudly, yet pathetically: "When I wrote those cantos I was a young man, living in the lap of luxury, loved, sought after and honored, and loaded down with the multitude of favors and gifts of friends and of women—those things which added fuel to my poetic fire. Now I have neither my heart nor contentment in anything, for all these fail me."[12] Whereupon he turned away, and Camara departed without his verses.

Meanwhile Portugal was assailed by one calamity after another. In 1573 the dowager Queen, D. Catharine, who to the very last had done her best to dissuade her grandson from his wild idea of a new crusade against the Moors of North Africa, died. The next year, a famine swept the land, and in June, 1575, a tremendous earthquake wrought far-reaching destruction. Again Luis and his mother were spared, as they were, likewise, in a great fire which shortly afterward demolished whole districts of the city. As though these catastrophes were not enough, terrible rainstorms brought on floods in the winter of the same year—deluges that swept away large portions of the streets—and on every side people shook their heads and, in fear of the outcome, recalled an old proverb: *Nadando vem a fome a Portugal.*[13] The threatened famine followed swiftly on the heels of the flood; starving people swarmed into the capital, seeking succor, and the streets were crowded with beggars, many

[12] From Pedro de Mariz, cited by Storck.
[13] "Famine comes swimming into Portugal."

of them lepers. The influx of country people brought many diseases, some of them spreading into almost epidemic proportions.

In 1576, Camoëns was again called upon to write an introductory poem, this time for a serious work in prose. Although he had been neglected by the court circle and the nobility, for whom *The Lusiads* was written (for the mass, even of the reading public, could not know or enjoy his countless classical references), he had earned the respect and high esteem of the men of literary worth in Portugal, among them Pedro de Magalhaes de Gandavo, a resident of Braga. Gandavo had been a great admirer of the poet, and in his colloquy (written in 1574) on the superiority of his language over Spanish, a Portuguese declares proudly to a Castilian: "And if it appears to you that you outstrip us in heroic verse, just look at the works of our famous poet Luis de Camoëns, over whose renown time will never triumph."

Gandavo had just finished a short history of Brazil (called, for some years after its discovery, Santa Cruz) and, desiring an introduction by a prominent literary figure, sought Luis' assistance, requesting him to write two dedicatory poems for the work. The first, to D. Leonis Pereira, late governor of Malacca, consisted of an elegy, in tercets, opening with the lines:

> Since Magellan wove his brief historic tale
> Which told of Santa Cruz, then scarcely known . . . .[14]

This poem of 110 lines was followed by a sonnet dedicated to Pereira as victor in a fierce battle against the ruler of the kingdom of Achin in Sumatra.[15]

Gradually Luis drew more and more within himself, seeing but a small circle of close friends and the friars of São Domingos.[16]

[14] Elegia "Despois que Magalhães teve tecida."
[15] Soneto "Vós, ninfas da gangetica espossura."
[16] Couto had returned to India, depriving the poet of this prized friendship.

These companions, realizing Luis' condition, urged him to gather and arrange his lyrics for publication. He consented and began the task, writing a poem which he planned as an introduction to the volume. In this sonnet he seemed to forget the tortures, disappointments, and failures of love and entrusted his poems to the tender and understanding hands of those who themselves had been the victims of Cupid:

> Since Fortune has so willed
> That I have some portion of repose,
> The inclination of both mind and pen
> Has led me to tell of loving—and of being loved.
> Yet, fearing that I may betray his confidence,
> The god beclouds my art in use of words.
> O you whom Love bends to his will
> In ways diverse,
> When you read in one small book
> These pure truths—and I speak in simple way—
> Whosoever and wheresoever you may be,
> Remember that only as you love and know of love,
> Can you understand the meaning of my verse.[17]

The project of bringing his scattered poems together was never completed during his lifetime.

[17] Soneto "Emquanto quis Fortuna que tivesse."

CHAPTER XXIV

The Field of Alcácer Kebir

Whom the gods would destroy they first make mad.

—EURIPIDES

THE YEAR 1576 found Portugal in even greater chaos. Sebastian had not married; there was no heir nearer the throne than the aging Cardinal Henry, son of King Manuel, and both court and people feared that if the King died without children the kingdom would fall to Philip II of Spain. He was Sebastian's uncle, his closest blood relative, and was waiting eagerly for the time when he might seize upon hapless Portugal and add it to his dominions, which already covered much of Europe and the lands across the Atlantic. Although marriage to the Spanish Princess Clara was proposed to Sebastian, nothing came of it.

Soon events began to move swiftly. The preparations for the King's senseless crusade in North Africa were gathering speed, to the alarm of all thinking people in the kingdom. In 1557 a comet appeared in the skies; an astrologer gloomily declared that it foretold the death of the King in Africa and the destruction of his army, a prophecy which terrified the population. Then the Infanta Maria, who had received Luis in audience so many years before, died, and D. Manuel de Portugal, who had befriended Camoëns, departed from the country.

Outside the Hall of Swans in the royal palace at Cintra lies a tiny terrace planted in flowers. At one side of the wall that surrounds it is a sheltered loggia of old tiles in delicate shades of green, gold, and blue. There, one sunny day in the spring of 1578, young King Sebastian summoned his council of courtiers about him and made the final plans for his projected expedition to North Africa. Maula (or Muley) Ahmed ibn Abdallah, usurper of the throne of Morocco, had been driven out by his uncle, Abd-el-Melik, and, after being refused asylum by Philip II of Spain, had appealed to D. Sebastian for aid. Here, the King declared, was the heaven-sent opportunity for which he had been longing. His counselors earnestly urged him to abandon the idea (for Portugal had neither men nor arms sufficient for such an enterprise), but Sebastian was obdurate—and his word was law. "Call for volunteers," he ordered, "and if we cannot obtain enough men in that way, then let all healthy men, single or married, be drafted—and use force if necessary."

Once more was heard the ruffle of drums as recruiting officers walked the streets of Lisbon, but this time there were no rosy-cheeked youths in search of adventure, eager to enroll, as Luis had seen them years before when he first arrived in the capital. Soon it became necessary to draft men, even to seize them on the streets or at their work, thus inevitably opening wide the way to bribery and corruption, for though the poor were taken even when married and with families to support, those with sufficient money were able to buy themselves off. Women, to rescue their menfolk, sold their homes, their very garments, and in some cases even themselves. In the end, only the miserable and destitute were taken.

Rumor had it that Sebastian was contemplating taking a poet with him to Africa to observe the campaign and (so sure was the

King of victory) to celebrate it in heroic verse. Camoëns was the logical choice, for he had sung, as had no other in the land, the great story of his country's sons and their deeds in war and peace. But the feckless King, altogether unmindful of him, confirmed the rumor by selecting for the honor Diogo Bernardes, a far lesser poet. So the man who had devoted his life to his country, in his own words "ever in one hand the sword, the other the pen,"[1] was forgotten and denied even this recognition of his genius and worth. Surely there must have come home to Luis the ironical truth of his own line in *The Lusiads*:

O vain desire of this empty thing that we call fame.[2]

Lisbon's streets were humming with activity. The nobles were riding in from their castles and palaces throughout the land in their finest clothes and armor, accompanied by retinues, coaches, and baggage more fitting for a coronation pageant than for a serious military campaign against a formidable enemy.[3] The capital's fickle population was delighted by the influx of strangers —many of whom had generous purses—and the marching and countermarching of the troops, the colorful parades of cavalry, the tents of multicolored silk and canvas, and the strains of martial music aroused the people to a high pitch of excitement and blind enthusiasm. The wives of many of the nobles had followed their lords as if going to a tournament, and receptions and feasts were held throughout the city, while prostitutes and camp followers

---

[1] *Lusiads*, VII, 79.

[2] *Lusiads*, IV, 95.

[3] With all their efforts the officers of the King had been able to recruit only some nine thousand men. To these must be added three thousand men grudgingly sent by Philip of Spain, five hundred supplied by the Pope, and those of the Moorish allies of the King, the number of whom is unknown. Yet this small army planned to cross the seas to Africa to meet and conquer a seasoned host of untold numbers of fanatical Moslems, fighting on their own soil and filled with an intense hatred of the Portuguese.

gathered in great numbers to greet the soldiers and reap their brief but rich harvest. Lisbon was drunk with pleasure and the thrill of a victory which the people, in their ignorance of the real state of affairs, believed certain. The King rode through the streets to the cheers of the populace, blind to the poverty, the degradation, and the slavery about him. He saw only the glitter and display of his army; he knew only that he had won his point, and his warped mind was filled with visions of a speedy conquest, a return to Lisbon as triumphant as that of Caesar entering Rome, a crowned victor at the head of his invincible legions.

June twenty-fifth arrived, the day of departure for the armada. Crowds from all quarters of the city streamed down to the river bank, where eight hundred vessels awaited their complements of men. There was a fanfare and a roll of drums as the King and his entourage entered the canopied and tapestry-hung royal barge and a great display of gay banners, gleaming armor, silken garments, and tossing plumes as the nobles came down to the shore and were swiftly rowed to the ships in the stream.

Luis could have been interested in none of this. Life was over for him. Resentment of fate and all it had brought welled up within him and once more he found relief for his pent-up heartbreak in impassioned verse:

> Now may the day that saw my birth
> Be curs'd and die!
> May it be struck from Time's long roll
> And its like be seen no more.
> But, if perchance it comes again,
> May its sun be black in deep eclipse
> And its light be blotted out!
> May the earth give signs of its coming end;
> May hideous monstrous things be born
> And blood rain from the air!
> May the mother fail to know her child
> And the terror-stricken, blinded folk

206

Await the doom of the world!
Ah, ye who fear this, let your hearts be calm;
It is not so.
It was that on this day was born
A child of grief and woe.[4]

It was the last poem he wrote.

The city waited breathlessly for news of the campaign, for an announcement of the early and easy victory which had been promised. A month passed, then five weeks, but only vague rumors drifted into the country. Brought by fishing boats from the Algarve, these reported that the King had taken matters into his own hands, refusing to accept the counsel of his experienced officers, far better versed than he in fighting the Moors. Then more disquieting dispatches came: the enemy was massing in huge numbers; Sebastian was marching on Alcácer Kebir in the face of the urgent entreaties of his generals and his Moorish allies not to engage in battle there. Suddenly, like an exploding bomb, came the terrible news of the battle itself.

On August 4 the King, rejecting all reports and pleas from spies and scouts, ordered his men to draw up to attack. The Moorish horsemen swept down upon the little army in a great crescent whose horns quickly enveloped the Portuguese troops. Sebastian appeared both blind and dumb to the threat and hesitated to give the order to open fire until it was too late.

From the first there was much ineptitude and stupidity. The Portuguese lines were broken and the soldiers, isolated in groups, were slaughtered like cattle or surrounded and captured. The two Moorish claimants to the throne died in battle, one from heart failure, the other by drowning. D. Sebastian, too, was slain, tragically fulfilling the foolish motto he had selected for himself when he was crowned: *Un bel morir tutta la vita honora.*[5]

---

[4] Soneto "O dia em que nasci moura e pereça."
[5] "A fine death honors a whole life." The motto comes from Petrarch.

On that fatal day there fell eight thousand of the King's men. Fifteen thousand more were carried off to the slave markets of Morocco. Of the entire army, only some fifty men escaped to bear the tale of the tragedy to Lisbon, arriving there on August 10, six days after the disastrous defeat.

On the battlefield were found ten thousand Portuguese guitars!

The tidings were held back as long as possible, though garbled accounts were heard on every side. Cardinal Henry, the dead King's granduncle, had been summoned from Alcobaça, and when the news could no longer be suppressed, he was proclaimed Sebastian's successor. His first act was to begin to collect money for the ransom of the captives, and the wealth of Portugal went to fill the coffers of the Sultan of Morocco.

The future of the little kingdom was now most doubtful and precarious. The young Sebastian had died without heirs and was succeeded by a man who, though only sixty-six years old, was already senile but who dreamed of marrying a girl of thirteen and begetting sons. Even had he obtained a papal dispensation it would have been too late, for he fell ill soon after his succession and was periodically bedridden thereafter. Added to this burning question of the succession to the throne was the very serious problem raised by the loss of the flower of the nation's manhood at Alcácer Kebir, and always in the background could be seen the grim visage of Philip of Spain, whose claim to the Portuguese throne was paramount and who hovered like a vulture waiting to swoop down upon its dying prey.

Camoëns was growing ever more frail, and he no longer found zest or interest in living. It was as if the blow of the Moslem scimitar that had taken the life of his sovereign had wounded him, too, in a vital spot. On Christmas Eve, 1579, he dragged himself to the palace treasury, for the provisions of the grant of a pension required him to present himself in person to collect the sums due. This was the last money paid him by his country.

Lisbon was a strange, weird place that Christmas. Few able-bodied citizens in the prime of life were to be seen; only women, old men, and children were on the streets, and there was none of the cheerful bustle which of old had characterized the holidays, for the husbands, sons, or fathers of many had been lost in Africa. It was as if the city were on the eve of some dreadful catastrophe, rather than celebrating the birth of the Prince of Peace. Portugal was living the last hours of her freedom.

CHAPTER XXV

The Mysterious Judgments of God

Great hearts to lowly stations sink
. . .
To die—in paupers' beds.
—CAMOËNS, Lusiads, X, 23

O softly and gently sing to me,
Songs that are sad as the sea and the night,
Songs that perchance will bring release
For my soul to find peace and rest in sleep,
When death comes to seek me anon.
—GUERRA JUNQUEIRO

THE YEAR 1580 was a crucial one for Portugal. Cardinal Henry lay on his deathbed, vacillating and unable to decide on his successor, while the populace, enraged at his failure to proclaim a Portuguese as their monarch and terrified at the thought of enslavement under a Spanish master, sang in the streets and under the window of the dying man:

> Long live King Henry
> In the kingdom of Hell,
> For in his will he gave our Portugal
> To the King of Castile.

The King died miserably on January 31, and civil war immediately threatened to rend the country asunder. The last harvest had been destroyed by a long-continued drought, and famine clamored at the gates, for France, Flanders, and Germany could not supply enough grain to feed the people. And now a worse calamity came to the prostrate folk, for the plague that had been devastating England and the Continent was brought to Portugal by travelers from foreign lands and in some of the goods and foodstuffs which had trickled in towards the end of 1579.

At first there were few victims in Lisbon, but with the coming of spring the pestilence suddenly spread like wildfire and there was no street, lane, or alley which did not have its victims. Before many months had passed some forty thousand people died in the capital, and the hospitals set up by the government and the religious orders were unable to care for all the cases that called for help. Heaps of uncoffined corpses were carried through the streets; soon the churchyards were filled and graves were dug in open squares and even in the fields, while the bodies of slaves were tossed on the garbage heaps and dunghills outside the walls, there to be preyed upon by famished animals. The terrible scenes of 1570 were enacted once again, but this time there was no king to give aid. Those who could, deserted the city, and the roads east, south, and north were crowded with refugees. Many of the sufferers died at the roadside or carried the dread plague with them, spreading it still farther in town and village. Soon, since there were few left to bury the dead, convicts were released from the galleys to aid in the grim task, their sentences being commuted in exchange for their labor. The part played by the rat and the flea in spreading the plague was not yet known, and the people's ignorance of all sanitation provided ever spreading centers of contagion. Most of the stores were closed, and looting of abandoned houses and robbery of the sick, dying, and dead were so universal that it was well-nigh impossible to cope with it. Lisbon was more a necropolis than a metropolis, so that one might walk for hours through the stricken city and not meet half a dozen healthy people. For a time Luis moved about the streets in the Mouraria, until illness forced him to take to his bed. As the plague thrust its tentacles ever deeper into the city's life, one by one his friends ceased to go to the little tenement—all except some of the friars of São Domingos.

As he lay ill he wrote a letter (the last time his pen touched paper) to D. Francisco de Almeida, captain-general of Lamego, who was gathering patriots about him in a vain endeavor to resist Philip of Spain's seizure of the country. Only a fragment remains, but in it Camoëns reveals the anguish of his soul:

> Who has ever heard it said that Fate would choose such a small stage as a poor bed in which to act out such great misfortune? And I surrender, because to endeavor to resist such evils would appear a kind of effrontery.
>
> And so I come to the end of life, and all will see that I loved my native land so well that I was content to die not only in it, but with it.[1]

The will to live had passed from him. The wasted body which had so long carried his heroic soul could not resist the plague as it spread through the crowded lanes of the Mouraria, and on June 10, 1580, he died in the arms of Frei Josepe Indio of São Domingos, who administered the last rites and closed the poet's eyes.

Some time later the kindly Frei read a copy of *The Lusiads* and recalled the pitiable death of its author. So affected was he by the sublime lines of the epic that he wrote on one of its pages for all to see:

> What a grievous thing to behold so great a genius sunk so low! I saw him die without having even a sheet with which to cover him, after having triumphed in the Indies and sailed 5,500 leagues

[1] Visconde de Juromenha (ed.), *Obras de Luis de Camões*, Vol. I, p. 126.

at sea. What a great warning for those who wear themselves out by profitless study night and day, like spiders spinning webs to catch flies![2]

Thus Portugal's immortal poet died without even a shroud in which to bury him, but a member of the house of the Count de Vimioso, D. Francisco de Portugal, who had heard much of Camoëns from his uncle, D. Manuel, sent a winding sheet as a pious tribute to the man who was past all pain and all wants. Luis' last request had been that he be buried in the neighboring little Church of Santa Ana. No coffin was available, and so on Friday, June 10, 1580, without religious service or attendants, he was laid away, with other victims of the pestilence, in the subterranean charnel house of the Church of the Franciscan Sisters of Santa Ana, with no mark of any kind by which the body of the sweet singer, the prince of Portuguese poets, could be identified.

> No more, my song, no more,
> For I could without surcease
> Declaim a thousand years;
> And if perchance thou art e'er charged
> With being over-sad and long drawn out,
> Say unto him who blames,
> That Ocean's flood
> Cannot be in vase so small confined.
> I sing not in 'broidered poet's phrase
> That seeks the praise of men,
> But tell the honest verity
> Of what to me has come.
> Ah, would to God
> That it had been
> But the fantasies of dreams![3]

---

[2] Aubrey F. G. Bell, *Luis de Camões*, p. 65 and p. 143, Note 102.
[3] Canção "Vinde cá, meu tão certo secretário."

Epilogue

How easy 'tis for man's body to find a grave!
The waves of any sea, a mound in any foreign land
Will receive our bones,
As oft they have of many an illustrious man.
                                             —CAMOËNS, *Lusiads*, V, 83

I

THE PESTILENCE RAN ITS COURSE at last and Lisbon slowly returned
to its normal life. Only a few knew of Luis' death, and his place
of burial was forgotten. But his *Lusiads* and lyrics lived on, were
translated first into Spanish, then into other languages, and men
began to realize that a genius had moved among them, had written immortal poetry, and had died poor and neglected.

In 1595, Gonçalo Coutinho, who had known Camoëns, resolved
to locate the poet's remains and erect a memorial in the church
where they lay. The body of a plague victim could not be exhumed
(for fear of contagion), so D. Gonçalo had to content himself
with placing a slab on the wall near the place where Luis was supposed to have been interred. The inscription was simple:

HERE LIES LUIS DE CAMOËNS

PRINCE

OF THE POETS OF HIS TIME

HE DIED IN THE YEAR 1579[1]

THIS STONE WAS ORDERED PLACED FOR HIM

BY D. GONÇALO COUTINHO

LET NO OTHER PERSON BE BURIED IN THIS PLACE[2]

At an unascertained later date the Abbess of the Virgins of the Lord (the nuns of the Church of Santa Ana) decided to raise the floor of the choir and in so doing destroyed all vestiges of the grave,[3] though later other commemorative tablets with Latin verses were reportedly placed near Coutinho's inscription.

In the terrible Lisbon earthquake of 1755 a large part of the church roof collapsed, the slab that marked the traditional place of burial, together with the other inscriptions, was broken into fragments, and all were removed when a restoration of the edifice was commenced in 1771. By this time a new abbess and a different group of nuns occupied the premises, and none of them knew the location of the grave. Thus later, in 1818, when a move was made to find the poet's remains, there existed no information by which the precise spot could be identified.

In 1825 the epic poem *Camões*, written by the famous João Baptista Almeida-Garrett, aroused the first great interest in Camoëns the man, 245 years after his death. Eleven more years were to pass before another poet, Antonio Feliciano de Castilho, proposed to the municipality of Lisbon that a systematic search be

[1] An error. The correct year is 1580.

[2] In a newly discovered manuscript of part of the *Decadas* of Couto, the historian quotes an additional paragraph of the epitaph. It does not appear in the 1614 edition of the *Rimas*, which gives the epitaph as above. The Couto addition reads: "There in the Kingdom he met the same fortune as in India, and it is not to be wondered at that he who is born melancholy cannot be joyful."

[3] It is curious to note the remarkable coincidence of the manner in which the graves of both Camoëns and Marco Polo were obliterated. (See Henry H. Hart, *Venetian Adventurer*, pp. 245ff.)

215

made for the bones of Camoëns, that they might be interred in a place which was to be set aside for the tombs of Portugal's famous men. On September 7, 1836, a commission was named to try once more to locate the grave, but hardly had it begun its labors when civil war broke out and the investigation was suspended, not to be resumed until a new commission was appointed by Regent D. Fernando on December 30, 1854.

A diligent search was made and many documents were studied, but the results of the investigation were inconclusive; every clue led to an impasse, and even the traditions were too vague and contradictory to be of value. The Church of Santa Ana had gradually been modernized and was no longer similar to the structure of 1580, and, to make matters even more difficult, many other burials had been made there, both in Camoëns' time and later. The commission dug in the area which they considered the most likely—and of course unearthed many bones. Then, reasoning that Camoëns' remains must be among these, the commission ordered all the bones collected and deposited in a casket of brazilwood, which was then placed in the choir of the church where they had been exhumed. This was done with the proper ceremonies on May 15, 1855, and there the remains lay for twenty-five years.

In 1880 a move was initiated to celebrate the three-hundredth anniversary of Camoëns' death. At that time what were supposed to be the remains of Vasco da Gama[4] were brought from the church at his home in Vidigueira and they and the chest of bones in the Church of Santa Ana were conveyed to the Monastery of the Jeronymos at Belem, on the north bank of the Tagus, just outside Lisbon. There they were received with religious and military pageantry by King D. Luis and Queen D. Maria Pia on June 8. Silver wreaths were placed on the caskets by the sovereigns, and the day ended in festivities throughout the capital. Shortly thereafter, the caskets were placed in elaborately carved stone sarco-

[4] See Hart, *Sea Road to the Indies*, Chapter XXIII.

phagi, on whose respective lids were recumbent effigies of the great admiral and of the poet who had sung of his exploits. The tombs lay near that of D. Sebastian, whose supposed bones were brought back from Africa four years after the debacle of Alcácer Kebir.[5]

Thus at last, three hundred years after his death, the poet received the honor due him from his nation, but, in truth, to this day

Portugal knows not the humble place
Where repose the ashes of Camoëns.[6]

II

ON JUNE 28, 1862, King D. Luis laid the cornerstone of a monument to Camoëns in the Praça de Camões, at the head of the short, steep Rua Garrett, the busiest shopping street in Lisbon. Unveiled on October 9, 1867, it consists of a bronze figure of the poet, twice life-size, on a lofty pedestal, around which are grouped eight smaller bronze statues of famous writers of his era.[7]

III

WHEN THE UNFORTUNATE D. Sebastian asked for the hand of the daughter of Philip II of Spain and discussed his projected crusade in Morocco, Philip remarked cynically: "If he win, we shall have a good son-in-law; if he lose, a good kingdom." He lost, and immediately after the death of Cardinal Henry, Philip moved to enter into his inheritance. Fitful civil war broke out, for there were several Portuguese claimants to the throne, but the insurrections were put down by the Spanish Duke of Alba and a Portuguese cortes, summoned for the purpose, chose Philip as King of Portugal at Thomar on April 3, 1581, though he had crossed the frontier at the end of 1580.

[5] There is grave doubt about whether the bones are those of D. Sebastian.

[6] The lines are translated from João Baptista Almeida-Garrett's *Camões*.

[7] June 10, the date of the poet's death, is celebrated yearly throughout Portugal as a public holiday.

Tradition has it that upon Philip's entry into Lisbon one of his first inquiries was for Camoëns. When he learned of the poet's death, "he showed much grief, for he had desired to see him because of his renown, and in order to confer rewards on him."[8] In any event, Philip's government sought out the poet's mother, who had survived him, and saw to it that she received, in 1582, two years after his death, 6,765 reis, the unpaid portion of his pension for 1580. The memorandum of this payment, still preserved in the National Archives of Lisbon, recites:

> 6,765 reis in the treasury of the chancellery of the House of Civil Affairs to Ana [*sic*] de Sá, mother of Luis de Camoëns—whom may God have in His keeping—for so much as was due her son from the first of January of the year 1580 to the tenth of June, on which [day] he died, of the pension of 15,000 reis per annum. In Lisbon, November 13, 1582, by Don Duarte de Castelbranco.[9]

On February 5, 1585, by order of the King, Camoëns' mother was granted the continuation of the pension "for each year of her life."[10] The date of her death we know not, but this document, the last one referring to the poet, makes it certain that she survived her famous son by at least five years. With her passing the line of Camoëns became extinct, for he had no brothers or sisters.

That Luis' mother appears only at the beginning of his life story, then vanishes until his return to Portugal, and that there is no reference to her in any poem may at first appear mysterious to the reader. We must remember that Horace, who speaks so lovingly of his father in his works, never mentions his mother. Furthermore, only four of Camoëns' letters are extant, and we have no way of knowing whether or not correspondence was carried on between him and his mother. The very frequent loss of ships on the Indian

[8] Manuel de Faria y Sousa, "Cintra," in Thomas Joseph de Aquino, *A Vida de Camões*, 127V.

[9] Archivo Nacional, Liv. III de Ementas, fl 137.

[10] *Ibid.*, Liv. XI de Doações de Felipe I, fl 132.

voyages might account for the lack of letters, finally making it impossible for the two to keep in touch. A consideration of what happened to millions during the recent world war should make very clear this matter of separation with no news for years.

IV

We are acquainted with Camoëns' physical likeness in his later Lisbon years from the life portrait by Gomes. His appellation of *barbaruivo* would indicate that his hair and beard were of a reddish gold, and his eyes were reportedly large and blue.

Camoëns' character is revealed in great measure in both his lyrics, where he is most subjective, and in *The Lusiads*, in which is also to be found a strong personal element, a part of which may still be undisclosed to us. His patriotism and courage are so apparent in all his work that they call for no discussion. A certain braggadoccio, in which he reflected the temper of his age, is evident in his early poems and letters, but it was an ephemeral part of his temperament and vanished with maturity and more experience of life. As a soldier, he was as brave as his fellows, but followed the profession entirely through external compulsion, not from choice. He first shrank from and later openly rebelled against the wanton cruelty and callousness which characterized so much of Portuguese conduct in the East from the time of Vasco da Gama down to his own day, and his attacks on the vice and corruption of his countrymen in Asia in both public and private life were largely responsible for his isolation and his failure to profit by the opportunities offered him for loot and extortion in India and China. Come what would, he remained consistent.

By nature, until suffering and poverty caused him to draw more and more within himself, Luis was a genial, convivial soul, rejoicing in the company of kindred spirits and in the pleasures of the table and of wine. Money was to him but a means to an end, and what he earned was soon spent or given to those whom he adjudged more needy than himself, so that on his return to Portugal he was as poor as the day he left.

His temper, judging from his poems and the affection given him by his close associates—Orta, Silveira, Couto, and others—was a gentle, understanding one. That his whole being was suffused with that indescribable *saudade*, the underlying sadness of the Portuguese outlook on life, appears everywhere in the melancholy surrender and resignation to fate pervading his poetry.

A sensitive love of nature and the peace and quiet of the country-side is evident throughout Camoëns' poetry and is in no way a slavish imitation of Vergil, even though echoes of his Latin master recur again and again in his lyrics. His contentment with little, his desire only for a modest abode and books, are expressed frequently in his verse, while "tears for the world's ills" and indignation at every kind of social injustice are most articulate.

His love for women (and his poems reveal that his was a sensuous nature) demanded a never ending search for one who might be his complement. But even though he could give devotion to a Dinamene or passing affection to a Barbara (and probably to other unnamed and unknown women), what he ever sought was an ideal to whom he could give his all and in whom he could find perfect response. Both tradition and many lines of his verses indicate that his whole life and his real love centered around the beautiful Catherine de Ataide and that even after her death his sublimated adoration found expression in poems to her memory. As Dante had his Beatrice, so did Luis de Camoëns find his ideal, in this life and for eternity, in his Catherine.

His willingness to accept a Chinese or Hindu (or half-caste) with whom to share life is not incongruous with the ideas of the Portuguese throughout their colonial history, for, as we have seen, such mingling of the races was even encouraged officially, and a color line has never been drawn by the Portuguese either in their homeland or their colonies. But—save for the incident of the "Isle of Loves" in Canto IX of *The Lusiads* and some frank expressions common to his age—there appears nothing of the offensively erotic in Camoëns' verse. Delicacy and good taste, even in the most passionate passages of his poetry, are the rule. In the words of Richard Burton, the poet "holds the mysteries of love too sacred for the vulgar eye," and in all his writings he is as far from the prurient as he is from the complacent or smug.

Impulsive Camoëns was, in love and in life—impulsive, ebullient, and liberal—but when at last he was able to return to Portugal he was frail, worn out, and ill adjusted to the feverish tumult of Sebastian's realm and reign. Fortune had failed him from his early youth even to his dying day, and we find the concentrated expression of his surrender to life and its demands in what is perhaps the most pathetic stanza in *The Lusiads*:

> Now my years are in decline,
> And already from summer's days
> Is the road to autumn short.
> Fortune has turned my genius cold
> —Of which I can no longer boast or sing in praise.
> Me will misfortunes soon in the stream engulf
> Of dark oblivion and eternal sleep.
> But grant, oh grant, thou queen of the Muses great,
> That I may complete that work
> Which I would to my nation give.[11]

V

IN MANY WAYS Camoëns was the first Portuguese poet to appeal to the imagination of the general reader, for theretofore poems were largely written for the court or the small literary circles of the country, and those who wished to attain a wider fame composed in Latin or Spanish. He found the vocabulary of Portuguese confined and inflexible. He left it broader and richer, introducing in his

[11] *Lusiads*, X, 9.

poems Latinisms and phrases from the vernacular and demonstrating to his people that their language was worthy of a nation which, though small, had made a glorious place for itself in world history.

At times in *The Lusiads* and in his longer lyrics he becomes prolix, turgid, or pedestrian. These lapses, however, are remarkably few for such a large volume of verse, and though a gold mine cannot consist entirely of the precious metal, one finds but little dull stone or hard quartz in the rich treasure of Camoëns' verse. For the most part it flows clear as crystal, far more readable than much of the poetry in his or other European languages of the sixteenth century. In both thought and expression he reveals a style at once pellucid and natural; his imagination usually soars high, his figures of speech are unencumbered, and many of his lines are almost epigrammatic. Both epic and lyric are crowded with vivid pictures, ranging from original mythological conceits to homely similes and metaphors. His wide and deep experience of travel over half the world, his intimate knowledge of the classics, the varied events of his own full life—all these seem inexhaustible reservoirs from which he draws, with no apparent effort, in the painting of his canvases. Whether in the long epic, short sonnet, or *redondilha*, he reveals the master hand, be it with the bold stroke or the meticulous rendition of the smallest detail.

His *Lusiads* is a priceless possession, an epic still universally popular today in his native land, and a strong golden bond linking the mother country with her vigorous, vital child in the Americas —Brazil. In Portugal the poem has been an ever inspiring call to patriotism. As such it was a great force in keeping the national spirit alive and finally in arousing his people to throw off the yoke of Spain in 1640, thus ending the Spanish "captivity." What Homer was to the Greeks and Vergil's *Aeneid* to the Romans of Augustus' day, so even now is *The Lusiads* of Camoëns to the Portuguese: the incomparable literary monument to their early leaders and their glorious exploits.

The poet's vast store of scientific knowledge, as revealed in his verse both in direct statement and by allusion, is nothing short of cyclopedic, considering the age in which he lived, and book-length studies have been written on his accumulated information concerning botany, medicine, astronomy, navigation, and other subjects. He was thoroughly conversant, of course, with Latin, Spanish, Italian, and French literature, as well as with translations from other languages and the writers of his own country. All of this, added to his lyrical genius, intense patriotism, and chivalry, makes him, in the eyes of his people, even today, the ideal—if not the personification—of Portugal herself.

This, however, was not the only gift Camoëns gave his nation. It is no exaggeration to affirm that he, more than any other writer or factor in Portugal's long history, fixed her national language and that but few words have altered (except in spelling) since his time.

The forms of his lyrics are not only those of his native land, but many so adapted from the Italian that they became naturalized in Portugal through the magic of his genius.

VI

AT HIS DEATH Camoëns was known to the Portuguese public for his *Lusiads* only. Of his lyrics, only three had been published and these in the introductions to other men's prose works. The remainder of his verses were unknown except to a few of his circle—those to whom or for whom he had written them. By far the greater number were preserved among his own papers or scattered in the hands of his friends.

The lyric poems attributed to him were finally gathered together, probably first in 1594. The license to print and the approval of the Holy Office were granted in December of that year, and the book, dedicated to D. Gonçalo Coutinho (who had placed the epitaph in the Church of Santa Ana), was published in Lisbon in 1595 by

Estavão de Lyra. The "Prologue to the Reader," by Fernando Rodrigues Lobo Soropita, discusses Camoëns' genius and the variety of his verse. The editing was not too critical and the volume contains poems by other writers, several of the lyrics even having been printed in a collection published eight years before Camoëns' birth. Succeeding editors added more poems attributed to Luis. Indeed, of the sonnets alone the first edition contained 65, whereas the edition of 1875 contained 354.

Since then a more informed and critical editorship has eliminated many spurious sonnets and the latest edition, that of Alvaro J. da Costa Pimpão, published in 1953 by the University of Coimbra, accepts 147. However, down through the centuries no two editors have agreed as to which verses should be retained or rejected, so the canon of Camoëns' lyrics still remains uncertain.

Portions of them have been translated into English, the largest number, entitled "Lyricks," being in Volumes V and VI of *Camoens*, by Sir Richard Burton. Unfortunately, Burton used and translated all of those in the edition of Visconde de Juromenha (1807–1887), which contains many spurious poems. Moreover, his translations are in what he calls "archaicisms" and "eclectic style," thoroughly unacceptable to the modern reader.

The first edition of *The Lusiads* has been described. A second edition (perhaps pirated from the first) also appeared, dated the same year, 1572. A third edition was published in 1584 in Lisbon, and from that date down to the present a number of Portuguese editions, many of them annotated, have been printed. The poem has also been translated into at least thirteen languages, the first such edition probably being that of Benito Caldera in Alcalá de Henares (in Spain) in 1580. The author of *Don Quixote* must have read it, for in Book VI of his *Galatea*, in the "Song of Caliope," he refers to Camoëns as "You, the incomparable treasure of Lusus"[12] and pays tribute to Caldera for his genius in translating

[12] Miguel de Saavedra Cervantes, *Galatea*, "Song of Caliope," 35.

the epic. Many translations have since been made in French, Italian, German, Swedish, Dutch, Danish, and other languages.[18]

The earliest English translation, that of Richard Fanshawe, is dated 1655. In spite of its errors and evidence of haste and failure to correct and revise, this version still offers delightful reading in the 1940 reissue, with an introduction by Jeremiah D. M. Ford, whose annotated text of the original is of value for the English student of Portuguese.

From Fanshawe's time down to the present there have been nine complete English translations of *The Lusiads*, the most acceptable (at least to me) being J. J. Aubertin's (1878; revised in 1884), with the Portuguese text facing the English. The latest translations are those of Leonard Bacon in verse (The Hispanic Society of America, New York, 1950) and the very pleasant prose translation of William C. Atkinson (Penguin Books, 1952). These last English translations—two within two years—together with several recent biographies of Camoëns in Swedish, Dutch, and other languages, are ample evidence that he and his works are of continuing interest in world literature.

The first edition (incomplete) of the comedies of Camoëns appeared in 1587. Neither they nor the letters have ever (except for isolated paragraphs of the latter) been translated into English.

VII

THE SPANISH OCCUPATION of Portugal lasted for sixty years. In many ways it cut short the nation's political life, for the administration of the Spanish viceroys was not like that of the Portuguese sovereigns. Though Philip II had promised a continuation of the local government in both the motherland and the colonies and that the occupation would be simply a union of the two crowns, all of his pledges and those of his successors were quickly broken, Portu-

[18] In 1956, I found a modern Slovenian paraphrase of *The Lusiads* in Karlovac, Yugoslavia.

gal becoming an impotent satellite of Madrid—even being reduced later to the status of an unimportant Spanish province. The colonies lost ground quickly. English and Dutch raids and rivalry soon took over much of the trade, for Spain was far more interested in her American dominions than in Asia. Meanwhile the Spanish crown used Portuguese taxes for its own ends, and both the men and the resources of the country were employed unsparingly and callously for Spain's foreign ventures and wars, including the Armada.

Finally, after threescore years of Spanish misrule, the nobles and landed gentry of Portugal, who had gradually been stripped of their privileges and property, decided that the time had come to throw off the foreign yoke. That Spain was exhausted by her imperialism, that France, with Richelieu at the helm, was at war with her, and that Catalonia, as well as Holland, was in revolt against the Spanish king—all created a favorable opportunity for Portugal to rise against her masters. A leader was at hand in the person of the Duke of Bragança,[14] a direct descendant of an illegitimate son of John I. A weak and indolent man, he was dominated by his wife, D. Luisa de Guzman, who, though Spanish by birth, after her marriage became more Portuguese than the Portuguese themselves. Ambitious and thoroughly imbued with the belief that her husband had every right to the crown, as well as clinging to a childhood prophecy that she would some day be queen, she devoted all of her energies to scheming and plotting toward this end.

On December 1, 1640, the conspirators struck a sudden blow in Lisbon. The Spanish, taken unaware, were swept off their feet, and on the fifteenth of the same month the Duke was crowned, as John IV, in the Cathedral of Lisbon. Everywhere the people rose against the Spanish and hailed John as the rightful heir of King Manuel. Foreign nations quickly recognized the new regime, and

14 He was the eighth duke of Bragança.

soon thereafter the various Portuguese colonies declared for John Though plot and counterplot occupied the stage for some years, the victory of the Portuguese over the Spanish at Montijo on May 26, 1642, and the successful revolt of Brazil against the Dutch, who had occupied it,[15] marked the end of the struggle and Portuguese independence became a *fait accompli*.

[15] See C. R. Boxer, *The Dutch in Brazil, 1624–1654.*

Appendix I

POEMS TO WHICH REFERENCES
ARE MADE IN THE TEXT

I. SONETO

O gesto puro, emfim e transparente
Her every movement,
Graceful as rhythm of pure light,
Robbed beauty and its praises
Of all significance,
And the tender glances of her eyes
Held my spirit in suspense.
This was the cup by Heaven sent,
That I eagerly did drain—
And its magic draught bewitched my heart
For all the years to come.

2. REDONDILHA

Verdes são os campos
Green is the sward
As lemon leaves,
Or my beloved's eyes.

Sheep that graze on the verdant lea,
Your fare is herbage of the Spring.
And mine? Long thoughts of her I love.
Flocks that in contentment feed,
Wot ye not your pastures sweet
Are but the faint reflections
Of my beloved's eyes?

3. REDONDILHA

De dentro tengo mi mal [in Spanish]
  Within my breast
  Is locked my grief,
  Though it give no outward sign.

This sweet new strife of love
That rends my frame
Is hid from mortal eye;
My own flesh knows the secret not,
Though it pierce my very soul,
For as the living spark dwells in the flint,
So lurks this dull ache in my heart.

4. SONETO

Quando da bela vista e doce riso
  When with hungry eyes I look upon
  Thy beauty and thy grace,
  My soul is so exalted
  That this earth is Paradise.
  My burning ecstasy makes all
  That men call bliss seem vain,
  And reason is forgotten,
  Seeing thee.
  Thy face and form defy all words
  To sing thy loveliness,
  And so far above our world art thou
  That to behold thee is to know forthwith
  Who created sky and stars.

5. SONETO

Num bosque que das ninfas se habitava

Deep in a wood where dwell the nymphs
Sibela, fairest of them all,
Did stray one day
To pluck a yellow flower from the topmost bough.
Cupid, who often sought
The tree's cool shade,
Had hung his bow and quiver on a branch
And was sunk in sweet repose.
The nymph, since time and place were opportune,
Did not delay,
But seized the arms
And fled the angry god.

Now she bears the love-shafts in her eyes;
Unerring is her aim.
So flee, ye shepherds, ere she slay you all.
As for me, I lie already slain
—And therefore do I live!

6. SONETO

Este amor que vos tenho, limpo e puro

This love of mine, so pure, so chaste,
Where no unworthy thought dare dwell,
This love, firm, steadfast through the years,
I bring to thee; thou holdst my heart and soul.
It is a love untouched by taint of change,
A love secure from Fate's assaults,
A love serene in all the hours that are
Between the rising and the setting of each sun.
The daisy fades; all blossoms swiftly die.
Winter and summer strew their petals on the earth,
But for this great love I bring to thee
It is the eternal month of May.

Alas, the love thou once didst give to me

Is dead,
And that ingratitude which cast me off
Has strewn my dreams and hopes
Upon the earth
In saddest disarray.

7. ECLOGA

Cantando por um vale docemente [excerpt]

Eyes that have beheld thy beauty,
Life sustained by sight of thee,
Will, e'er bent to meet thy wishes,
Soul that lives but in thy soul
And to it, as to body, wed,
Now I am by thee rejected.
My torments thou must surely see,
Far worse than eyes by blindness stricken,
Far worse than soul from body fled,
Since I have lost all I hold dearest,
Take from me, too, this life forlorn.

8. SONETO

Alegres campos, verdes arvoredos

O smiling fields and forest green,
Reflected in the limpid stream
Winding from the gorge above,
O tree-clad hills and steep bare cliffs
Reared high in jagged peaks,
Never again as in days gone by
Can you comfort my downcast soul.
All unknowing have I wrought this ill
—And the world has changed for me!
Now, fresh green fields
And happy stream,
You bring no joy to my aching heart,
And from the seeds I sowed of love and faith
There spring but withered hopes.

9. CANÇÃO

Vão as serenas águas [excerpt]
The placid waters of Mondego
Wind slowly to the sea,
Ceasing not their gentle murmur
'Til they mingle with its waves.
Alas, 'twas here I learned of sorrow
Which endureth evermore.
Here, where now I look my last on life,
I first beheld that brow of snow,
Those golden locks, that queenly grace,
All so deeply 'graved upon my heart.

. . .

Thou, my song, wilt e'er sojourn
By these fields and waters clear;
Thou shalt be my lamentation,
Recounting these, my endless torments,
For which my tears now flow.

10. REDONDILHA

Sobolos rios que vão [excerpt]
The wayfarer in the forest
Shortens his weary way with song,
And singing calms the fearsome heart
In the watches of the night.
The convict's cares are eased with song;
He forgets his clanking chains;
The reaper's song rings blithe in the fields,
And song lightens the laborer's load.

11. SONETO

A violeta mais bela que amanhece
The sweetest violet in the vale,
Whose modest beauty opens to the dawn,

Bedeckt in garb of green,
Bows to thee, my Violante,
E'en more lovely than is she.
Thou wouldst know why?
Because in thee alone
Her name and purity are seen,
And she would learn from thy fair face
What beauty at its best may mean.
O velvet-petaled flower, sun most fair,
Thou captor of my heart,
Let not love so niggard be!
O sharpest shaft of Cupid,
What seekest thou?
That I repay thee and become
Aeneas to this Dido?

12. SONETO

Num jardim adornado de verdura

In a garden, verdure-clad,
Where varicolored blossoms wove a carpet underfoot,
There came one day the Queen of Love,
And with her walked
The goddess of the forest and the chase.
Diana plucked a rose of purest white
And Venus a crimson lily from its stem
(Though the modest violet on the bank
Rivaled both in beauty and in grace).
They asked of Cupid, who stood near,
Which of the flowers he himself would choose.
He smiled and said:
"They are both fair indeed,
But for me
The violet far excels
The lily and the rose."

233

13. REDONDILHA

Falso cavaliero ingrato

Mote: "False knight, ungrateful one,
You've deceived me by design,
You declare your heart is broken,
When you have broken mine."

Voltas: Deceits ensnare the guileless,
Smug pity hides your scorn,
I love you, oh, I love you,
And you've left me all forlorn,
Yet you say your heart is broken
—When your love you have forsworn.

Now bring this folly to an end
—Enough of this sad game—
Let justice call her herald,
And the simple truth proclaim.
Retract the lying slander!
Acknowledge humble shame!
Say your dear heart is not broken
—And of mine I'll say the same!

14. SONETO

Orfeu enamorado que tañía

Orpheus sang of his great love
And his longing for Eurydice,
Held captive in Death's realm.
So stirring were both harp and voice
That Ixion's wheel did cease to turn;
Stilled were the moanings of the damned
And soothed the tortured souls.
His music swayed with such a potent spell
That the kings of Hell,
In recompense and pity for his plight,
Bade him with his belov'd depart.

But ill-starred was his fate, alas!
Poor luckless wight! He turned to look
But once on her he so adored
—And both were lost.

15. SONETO

Aquela que, de pura castidade
   To defend her innocence
She cruel vengeance on herself did wreak,
For the violence to her body done
Had besmirched her station and her name.
She valued virtue more than life—
And vanished were her hopes and dreams.
The memory of her fortitude may teach
What love and truth and faith can dare.
Forgetful of herself and of the world
She plunged the dagger in her breast
And purged the tyrant's bloody deed.
O matchless spirit, wondrous act!
Now eternal fame is hers.

16. ECLOGA

As doces cantilenas que cantavam [excerpt]
   On Mount Parnassus' rocky peak,
Deep in a hidden glade,
Bubbles a pure and crystal spring
Whence flows a rippling stream.
It murmurs gently o'er its stones
In accents soft and low,
Inviting birds, who with their song
Soothe all to sweetest drowsiness.
So clear the waters wend their way
Each pebble gleams in its sandy bed.
No trace of feral beast is seen
Or footprints e'en of shepherd lad,

For they are banished from the height
And from the encircling wood.
No herb grows there of sad or noxious breed;
Sweet marjoram and fragrant mint embalm the air
And crimson lilies with the snow-white rose
And iris, symbol of a yearning love.
The twining myrtle burgeons, too:
Fair Venus' shield from prying faun.
No winter's chill or summer's drought
Can wither these or harm in aught.
Thus the winding stream flows on and on
Where man ne'er sets intruding foot.
Parnassus sleeps in leafy shade.

17. SONETO

De quantas graças tinha a Natureza

What graces from her treasury
Did Nature pour with lavish hand
What time with rubies, roses, snow and gold
She shaped thy angel form!
Reddest rubies on thy lips she laid
And with roses gently brushed thy cheeks
—For which I'd gladly die.
She touched thy locks with shining gold
And whitest snow to that fair breast
That sets my heart aflame.
But of all the gifts she granted thee,
None is as precious as thine eyes;
She made of them a sun
More radiant than clearest day at noon.
My lady,
Nature reached perfection's self
When she created thee
Of roses, rubies, gold and snow
And purest light.

18. SONETO

Quem pode ser livre, gentil Senhora
  Gentle lady,
  Who that once has looked upon thy beauty
  Can ever more be free?
  For the boyish god, blind Cupid,
  Dwells in thine eyes, enthroned,
  And summons all imperiously to love.
  Those eyes, that finely moulded face and form,
  Cause all to idolize and worship thee,
  And who sees the roses of thy snow-white cheeks,
  Thy coilèd tresses aureate,
  If he be not blinded by the sight,
  Beholds thy radiance incarnate,
  Which, as the sun dispels the murk,
  Pierces every doubting heart.

19. SONETO

Um mover de olhos, brando e piedoso
  A certain movement of thine eyes,
  So gentle and benign,
  Thy smile both modest and restrained,
  Thy manner sweet and shy,
  Thy radiant beauty unadorned—
  Pure loveliness of soul—
  A fear lest thou cause some hurt,
  Thine air serene,
  Patience with whate'er life may bring
  —This enchantment, Heaven sent,
  Circe's draught,
  Transforming life and love.

20. SONETO

Um admiravel erva se conhece
  There grows a plant, a wondrous plant,
  Whose gaze each hour

Is fixed upon the sun.
When her sovereign in the east appears
She stirs and wakes;
Unfolds her petals to the day
As he to the zenith climbs.
But when his golden chariot
Descends into the sea
Her color fades, her beauty dies,
And she withers in the dusk.

My daystar, when you light my world
Your radiance brings new life;
My soul unfolds its fairest flower:
My love for you.
But it grows sad when you depart;
It fades, its petals close;
My love rejoices in your love
And grieves, bereft of you.

21.   SONETO

Senhora já desta alma, perdoai

My lady, sovereign of my soul,
Forgive this madness;
Look with gentle eyes upon
This passion which glows within my breast.
Behold my faith,
Sure proof of my great love,
Then, if you must, reject me.
Let not this flame which burns within my heart
—A heart so filled with love for you—
Forever cause me grief.
Beware, my lady, lest it be said
That e'en in one as lovely as are you
There dwells ingratitude.

238

22. SONETO

Está o lascivo e doce passarinho
    The happy little bird swung on a bough
    And preened his feathers with his tiny bill,
    Singing the while his carefree lilting melody.
    But see! The hidden fowler with stealthy step
    Draws taut his bow.
    The deadly arrow wings its way,
    And the songster falls to earth.
    Just so my heart,
    Which once was free,
    When least it dreamed was smitten sore,
    For the blind archer lay in ambush,
    Hidden in your lovely eyes,
    And smote me unawares.

23. REDONDILHA

Se Helena apartar
    Mote: If from the meadow
                 Helen doth her eyes avert,
                 Straightway sharp thorns spring up.

    Voltas: O flocks that graze,
                 To Helen's eyes
                 You owe that tender grass.
                 The sharp wind dies
                 And thorns to blossoms turn
                 At the glance of Helen's eyes.

                 If the hillsides
                 Are with flowers strewn
                 And brooks like crystal flow,
                 What happens to our lives,
                 Tossed in the wind
                 Like bits of straw,
                 In the light of Helen's eyes?

Hearts of men she steals
With savage glee;
Love himself
Has lost the fight,
And humbly he on bended knee
Gazes into Helen's eyes.

24. REDONDILHA

Ferro, fogo, frio e calma

Mote: Iron, fire, cold or heat
May deal this earth a fatal blow,
But never can they tear thee
From out my heart, dear love.

Voltas: No tower, fortress, craft or snare
Can keep thee from me when I come;
The more they guard and watch o'er thee,
The more thou art my dearest love.
Cold or heat may hold their sway o'er life
But not o'er thee, my own.

25. SONETO

Na metade do Céu subido ardia

The sun stood blazing in mid-sky;
The herd had wandered from its pastures green
And sought the shadows by the cooling stream.
The birds had fled the burning rays
To the leafy branches of the trees;
Stilled was their lilting melody,
And only the chirp of crickets
Broke the hush.
With aching heart and tear-stained cheek
The shepherd Liso sought in vain
The fair cruel nymph, Natércia.
"Ah," moaned he,

"Why dost thou flee from him
Who would give the world for thee
To him who loves thee not?"
Only the echo answers:
"Loves thee not!"

26. CANÇÃO

Formosa e gentil Dama quando vejo [excerpt]
Love took the arch of your curvèd brow
To make his deadly bow,
And wove its string most cunningly
From the tresses of your hair.
Because in all things you did please the god,
He seized the glances of your eyes
And from them fashioned shafts
(Those eyes so fair that their potent light
Might heal or mar a soul).
But if perchance the arrow
From Love's quiver finds its mark,
The dying victim owes to death
A debt of gratitude.

27. ECLOGA

A quem darei queixumes namorados [excerpt]
To whom shall I address my lovelorn lamentations?
Who will receive them as they deserve?
Only you, excellent and famous sir,
Outstanding in good will among all others.
I sought upon this earth a star
To guide my verses rude
(One with whom was holy piety,
Pure and clear as noonday sun),
To give light unto my graceless art,
And, great sir, in your perfection is it found,
While within me grows a spirit new

That with voice as sweet as swan's
May in song astonish all the world.

. . .

May you with indulgence fair
Look upon the childish strife
Of two who love most tenderly.
Timid truths
That my soul breathes forth
With deep and oft-repeated sighs
Are in your generous hands now laid
That they may live
To move all souls to piety
Who mourn the age-old cruelty of maid to man.

28. SONETO

Qual tem a borboleta por costume

E'en as Nature's law compels the moth
To flutter round the burning candle's light,
Wheeling a thousand times about the flame
'Til in the end its flight brings blazing death,
So do I soar to meet the living light
That shines in fair Aonia's eyes,
And though the wiser part of me
Does warn of dire fate,
I am consumed.
I know how far my vision dares to fare,
How high my thoughts and dreams aspire;
Though I now perceive that life to death I give,
And that Love demands obedience to its laws,
My soul resists it not,
And I, despite my torment great,
In this greater glory am content to live.

29. SONETO

Diversos dões reparte o Céu benino

Various gifts does kindly Heaven grant,

But wills that one alone may each possess.
To the moon it gave a bosom pure,
The light which floods this earth by night,
To Venus every grace and loveliness
(Who sees in thee her beauty quite outshone).
To Pallas learning (in truth lesser than thine own)
And to Juno every queenly charm.
But in thee are all these gifts conjoined
(Though the least of those the Creator does possess).
Unwilling Luna gave her bosom pure,
Venus all her loveliness,
Pallas her great wisdom and her wit,
And Juno her nobility of soul.

30. SONETO

Olhos formosos, em quem quis Natura

Ah, lovely eyes,
Wherein all Nature's grace does lie,
If your magic charm you would discern,
Then turn to me, your creature,
Look steadfast in my eyes,
And you will find yourself and all my passion
Limned therein,
Together with the torments that I suffer, undeserved.
For myself I crave one simple gift,
To be all yours, forever yours,
And that upon my brow you set your seal,
The empery of your love.
When I look into your eyes,
I forget myself and all the world beside.
In deepest faith and truth do I confess
That you, and thoughts of you,
Make up my world.

31. CANÇÃO

Se este meu pensamento [excerpt]
I would paint thy glorious eyes—
Those eyes where dwells the god of love,
Now blinded in their light.
Thy locks of gold
In fillet of duller gold confined,
Before which pales the sun;
Thy shapely head
By Nature in perfection cast,
Thy profile, cameo-chiseled,
Thy lips, so gracious
That praise grows weak in lauding them.
Thou art a treasure-trove withal,
For pearls are thy lovely teeth
And all thy words pure gold.
My lady,
In you is seen
How the mother of all nature
Has excelled herself.

32. REDONDILHA

Mas porem a que cuidados [excerpt]
Mote: And indeed, why such grief?

Glosas: If this heartache
Which Love now lays on me
Has such a gentle source,
I have no cause to fear.
What are mine own woes to me
—Or e'en a thousand more—
If only in those lovely eyes
I see the light of joy?
But if I find in them a saddened state
Then indeed am I afraid.
Behold! Thence comes my grief.

33. SONETO
Dizei, Senhora, da Beleza ideia

I sing of you, my lady,
Beauty's own ideal.
Whence comes the glistening gold
Of which your locks are spun,
Tell me, from what dark mine or vein of ore?
How won you Apollo's sunny glance,
And stateliness imperial?
Was it with the wisdom of the gods
Or the witch Medea's wiles?
In what shells hidden in the sea
Found you those precious orient pearls,
Revealed by your gently smiling lips
When you do speak?
Since thus you are shaped to heart's desire,
Beware! Keep vigil constantly,
And remembering poor Narcissus' fate,
Gaze not in fount or mirror bright.

34. SONETO
Se a ninguém tratais com desamor

If thou meetest no man with aversion
And greetest each with equal smile,
If thou treatest all with like endearment
And acceptest courtship from them all,
Then, I pray, grant thy disfavor;
Heap upon me scorn and discontent
From this day forth.
If thou be thus kind to other suitors,
Then he who hath thy disdain hath won,
But if thy heart hath place for any other,
I truly disbelieve that thou art mine.
Love must be given entire to the lover,
And he can share with none.

35. SONETO

Que esperais, esperança? Desespero

Ah, Hope, what canst thou hope? For naught.
And what the cause? Inconstancy.
How farest thou O life? Bereft of hope.
What sayest thou, my heart? I truly love.
And thou, my soul? That love is cruel.
How then livest thou? I know not how.
And what sustaineth thee? A memory.
Hast thou no other hope? Nay, only this.
Where takest thou thy stand? Here where I am.
And where is that? At the end of life.
Then thou holdest death a boon? Love wills it so.
Who condemneth thee to this? My heart and soul.
Who then art thou? One shorn of all.
To whom dost thou then yield? To her I love.

36. SONETO

Quem vê, Senhora, claro e manifesto

Who beholds, my lady, at its best
The light in those your lovely eyes
And loses not his sight thereat
Pays your beauty less than its just due.
The price seems small to me,
Who give my all for love of you.
Thus my life and soul and all my hopes
Are yours,
And there abides with me but love of you.
Withal it is a blessed thing
To give you all I have and am,
Yet the more I give,
The more I still do owe.

37. SONETO

Crescei, desejo meu, pois que a Ventura
Grow ever stronger, O thou love of mine,
Since new good fortune
Doth uplift thee in her arms,
And the fair cause which gave thee birth
Holds promise of a happy end.
If to greater heights thou dost aspire,
Fear not the sun;
Thine is but the eagle's way,
Who the higher he doth soar the purer is.
Courage, O my heart!
Thy worth no longer in the balance weighed,
Grow thou from strength to strength
And know full well
That fortune ever smiles upon the bold.

38. SONETO

Criou a Natureza damas belas
Nature has created women fair,
Whose charms in deathless verse were sung,
But of each she took the fairest part
When she fashioned you, my own.
They are pale stars compared to you,
And fade into eclipse,
Yet if perchance they have your presence
As their sun,
How happy they!
In perfection, grace and gentleness
To mortal eye you are most rare,
Excelling all in loveliness.
Would that I might share divinity
And have merit in your eyes,
For, if purest love means aught to you,
Then in truth I've won your heart.

39. SONETO

Se me vem tanta glória só de olhar-te

If sight of thee doth give me greatest joy,
To see thee not brings sharpest pain.
If I think to praise thee with my verse,
I pay dearly for vain hopes of winning thee.
If I seek to sing thy graces as thou art,
I know that I offend thee, being who I am.
But e'en though I do chide myself for loving thee,
What greater prize can life afford me than thy heart?
O thou priceless treasure and great glory of this earth,
Happy the man who risketh death for thee!
Thou art forever on the tablets of my heart inscribed;
For thee would I fain live or gladly die,
Since at the struggle's end there standeth victory.

40. REDONDILHA

Amor loco, amor loco [*Mote* only; in Spanish]

Oh mad love, oh love insane,
That I love you, and you another.

41. SONETO

Sempre, cruel Senhora, receei

Watching your mistrust with eye perplexed,
Seeing inconstancy to cold indifference turn,
Ever, my lady, did I fear
Lest all hope die,
Since you longed to win another's love.
So clear to me is now your fickleness,
That all which I have given I conceal.
I gave my soul, my spirit and my life;
I gave you power over all I have and am;
You promised love, and that love promised, you deny.
Now I find myself forlorn;
I know not whither wend my steps.

But the day will come
When heavy on your soul will weigh
The injustice you have done.

42. SONETO

Se pena por amar-vos se merece

If to love you
Condemns to punishment,
Who shall escape or go unscathed?
Lives there spirit or heart, however bold,
That can behold you and not adore?
What greater glory has life to give
Than to dwell ever at your side?
For all the griefs and torments of a soul
Are vanished, forgotten, and as naught
At sight of you.
Yet, if you would destroy
The one who seeks your love,
Then all who live within this world
Must die,
For they are yours.
My lady, take me first,
For my eyes must surely tell you
That no one loves you dearly
As do I!

43. SONETO

Quando se vir com água o fogo arder

When water burns with lambent flame,
When day with midnight mates,
When low earth rises to the skies,
When love with logic walks,
When all men share a common lot,
Will thy beauty lose its lure,
And I shall cease to love thee

When my eyes no longer see.
But since such change has never been
(Nor can it ever be),
My love remains my love.
It sufficeth me to live in hope;
I reck not of my life or soul
If thou art by my side.

44. SONETO

Como quando do mar tempestuoso
As the weak and weary mariner,
Escaping from the sinking wreck
And from the ocean's greedy jaws,
First trembles at the name of "sea"
And swears that though its waves be calm
They never more can tempt him from his peaceful fireside,
Then, the horror and the fright forgot,
Sails away once more for gain,
So I, my lady,
Escaping from the tempest stirred by love of you,
First fly to seek safe haven,
Swearing nevermore to find myself
In such sad plight.
Then, with spirit haunted by your face and form,
I return where I had shipwrecked been,
In the hope of winning you.

45. SONETO

Que modo tão subtil da Natureza
How strange and how portentous life,
That she would flee this world
With its deceits,
And in her tender years thus hide her loveliness
Beneath the coarse drab garment of a nun!

Even this cannot conceal her noble mien,
Nor the grave sweet light that shines in her clear eyes,
Whose radiance blinds.
Whoever does bear her image in his heart
Yet seeks freedom from his earthly grief
Is sore deceived;
He lives henceforth a prisoned wight
Since love ordained
That she should conquer him.

46. SONETO

Eu cantei já, e agora vou chorando
I weep to think that once
In days gone by
In fullest faith I sang.
And now it seems despite my songs
My cheeks were wet with tears.
Yes, I sang. But if you ask me, "Why?"
I cannot say, for e'en in this was I deceived.
So melancholy is my present state
That I hold the past most happy to have been.
With cunning did they bid me sing.
Contented? No, but with a trusting heart,
Though even then methought
I heard the clank of chains.
Since life is all a lie,
Why cast the blame on hope?
Fortune's self did sin far worse than I.

47. SONETO

Já é tempo, já, que minha confiança
'Tis time, 'tis time my cherished dreams
Descend to earth.
But alas, since love was ne'er by reason ruled,
Can I surrender hope?

My life, ah yes, for cruel change decrees
That a heart in love should not endure too long.
I should in death alone my solace find,
But since he who longs for death oft finds it not,
Perforce I live—and hope.
Ah, love's harsh law will grant no peace
To souls which it in bondage holds.
If then I am thus doomed to live,
Why seek a fleeting joy
In unsubstantial dreams?

48. SONETO

Apolo e as nove Musas, descantando

Apollo plucked his golden lyre
And sang in chorus with the Muses nine.
Rapt in sweetest harmony
I seized my pen and thus began:
"Happy the day and blest the hour
When those gentle eyes first looked on me.
Ecstasy and rapture seized my frame
And I behold my heart's desire."
Here my song, half-sung, was broken off,
For Love's hand did touch the wheel of fate;
My day was turned to night
And hope was lost.
Now naught remains but greater griefs
—If such can be.

49. ELÉGIA

O Sulmonense Ovidio, desterrado [excerpt]

What time rose-tinted morn in loveliness bedeckt
To the sun flings wide her gates,
When the grass with dew is wet
And the nightingale sobs out her lamentation
.   .   .

252

I look out on Tagus' waters
Flowing smooth and clear,
The hollow ships borne on its breast,
Faring each upon its way.
Some skim the waves in the gentle breeze,
Others with flashing oar
Now cleave the crystal tide.
I speak to the insensate stream
Which cannot know
What sorrow fills my soul
—This soul is stained with tears.
"O waves that flow so swiftly, stay!
Since you cannot bear me off
With you,
Take these, my bitter tears, I pray,
Tears which will never cease to flow
Until that happy day
When I, too, can follow where you go,
With a heart that is free from care."

50. SONETO
Vos que de olhos suaves e serenos

You, who hold my heart imprisoned
With eyes so lovely and serene,
Have caused all other thoughts to vanish
As without meaning, base and vain.
If your dear lips have never tasted
The potent, fiery draught of love,
You have still to learn life's precious secret,
That love but deepens with the loving,
Though that love be not returned.
No flaws are found in my beloved,
Nor does perfect love in any wise decrease.
Its stature grows, yea doubles, rather,
And the yearning and the torment are the same.

The tender heart forgives with gentle patience,
And love like ours, so pure, so true,
Becomes but greater for each hindrance
In its path.

51. SONETO

Quem diz que Amor é falso ou enganoso

Who calls love false or frivolous,
Ungrateful, vain or hard of heart,
Deserves his fate
If love to him be cruel.
Love is tenderhearted, gentle, sweet beyond compare.
Whoe'er denies, weigh not his words;
He is blind, by gods and men despised.
If love now seems unkind to me,
'Tis but to prove it rules the destinies of man,
For e'en in wrath is love suffused with love;
Its evils turn to good,
And this great good I hold more dear
Than all the world beside.

52. SONETO

Todo o animal da calma repousava

All living things were resting
In the noonday calm.
Liso, alone, recked not the heat,
For peace to his soul could only come
From the nymph he sought in vain.
The very mountains echoed
With the sound of his lament,
But nothing moved the heart of her
Who loved him not.
Weary at last of wandering in the wood,
On the bole of a great beech
He 'graved these words:

254

"Let none put trust in woman's heart,
Constant in naught save in inconstancy."

53. SONETO

Doce contentamento já passado

O sweet content wherein I found all happiness,
Why have you left me exiled and alone?
During those brief hours of light and youth
When fickle fortune led me to believe
False love and joy were real,
Who could dream to find me as I am?
Fate, grim and cruel, has struck me down.
Let no mortal creature be deceived;
None can escape the lot his star ordains.

54. ENDECHAS

Vai o bem fugindo [excerpt]

The good always flies;
Evil grows with the years
And with time
Comes disillusion in all things.
Love and joy
Bide awhile;
Alas for him
Who seeks more,
For nothing is stable,
All subject to change,
Too certain the heartache
When memory calls.

. . .

Ah! happy lived I once
But now in distress.
All the day my soul weeps,
And sheds tears through the night.
I repent of illusion

Which once filled my thoughts;
Though it lasted for long,
'Twas gone in a flash.

. . .

Ah, world, I could tell you
The weight of my woe,
But so great is its burden
I dare not begin.
In the saddest of thoughts
My poor life lingers on,
Cares never ceasing,
Life without joy.
No one would believe
What now is my lot,
For pleasure did blind me
To the sorrow to come.
Ah, happy good fortune,
Why am I denied
My one—my sole treasure?
Why stolen so soon?

. . .

In this life filled with darkness
Now nothing remains;
Though at first joy did beckon
In a moment 'twas gone;
Like wind ever vanishes
Each hope as it comes.

. . .

Ah, love, blind illusion,
Only sorrow you bring,
Ill to him who resists you,
And to him who obeys.[1]

[1] This *endechas* (*redondilha*) is included in Alvaro J. da Costa Pimpão's edition of Camoëns' *Rimas*.

55. SONETO

Em prisões baixas fui um tempo atado
>Once I lay in a dungeon vile,
>Doing penance for my faults,
>And even now I drag my chains
>Until death shall set me free.
>I offered life upon the altar of my youth,
>Deeming love not satisfied
>With sacrifice of lambs.
>Today are grief and exile mine,
>As was from old ordained.
>I would be content with little here,
>For I have learned, with shame,
>The price one pays for passion's sake
>And for a life without an aim.
>Now my dark Star, blind Death, uncertain Fate,
>Have opened wide my eyes;
>I fear and shun all joys
>Or hope of happiness.

56. ELÉGIA

O poeta Simónides, falando [excerpt]
>And if our fate be cruel,
>We must endure
>With spirit brave and ever present cheerfulness.
>What serves it to remember
>What is past,
>Since all passes soon or late,
>And to brood brings but great heartache
>In its train?
>   . . .
>In ever present memory of the past,
>I gaze out upon the tranquil sea

With eyes from which tears unceasing flow,
For these happy days still live
In memory clear,
Until it seems
As though time could bring no change.

57. OS LUSÍADAS, I, 58

Now did the moon pour down its purest rays
Until the waves of Neptune were in silver drenched,
And Heaven with its attendant starry host
Was as a meadow all bedeckt with daisies fair.
Though the wild winds were sleeping for the nonce
In darkest caverns on the far-off shores,
A night-long vigil on the ship was kept,
As has been the custom of the sea
From days of yore.

58. OS LUSÍADAS, VI, 40

Said one:
"How can we best pass the time away
That now hangs heavy on our hands
Than by the telling of some hearty tale,
And thus drive slumber from our eyes?"
Then Leonardo,
He who carried love e'er deep within his breast,
Spoke up:
"How can we better while away the hours
Than by telling tales of love?"

59. SONETO

Gentil Senhora, se a Fortuna imiga

Gentle lady,
If cruel Fate, with which all Heaven conspires,
Should take from these, mine eyes, the sight of yours,

258

That it may deal me even sorer blows,
I shall within me hold a spirit brave.
Though doomed
To meet the wrath of fire and sea,
I dedicate to you a heart that yearns
To join with yours in one eternal bond.
In this immortal soul of mine
—Which ill-fortune doth assail in vain—
You are held in such a warm embrace,
No cold nor want nor mortal fear
Can loose my hold.
With this faint and weary voice
I call to you,
And the magic of your name, so well belov'd,
Will drive away and rout both storm and foe.

60. SONETO

Do están los claros ojos que colgada

Where are those eyes
Which hold my soul in thrall?
Where those cheeks whose blush
Doth shame the fragrant rose?
Where the warm red mouth
With smile of pearl,
The locks which make pure gold seem dull?
Where are they—and where that gentle hand?
O lovely one, where art thou now,
Why hidden from my sight?
My very soul is by my grief consumed,
And each hour threatens death.
Thou heedest not my frenzied plea,
Though thy image is ever in my heart enshrined.
Speak! Tell me,
Where dost thou conceal thyself?

61. SONETO

Oh! Como se me alonga de ano em ano

Oh! How from year to year
This weary pilgrimage of mine drags on!
The seasons of life's span grow short,
And ills increase
—For the balm that once did heal me
Is now lost.
If life could but reveal to us our destinies
Then would we learn that hopes are oft deceits,
The good that I pursue
Eludes me ever,
And, though but midway, I know the race is lost.
I stumble; a thousand times I fall;
My hope grows dim,
And happiness, when just within my grasp,
Escapes.

62. SONETO

Esfôrço grande, igual ão pensamento

Strong will wed to keenest mind,
Thought proved in act,
Not close-locked in coward breast
Or dissolved in wind and rain;
Soul not abased by greed for gold,
Deserving of the highest good.
Scourge of Malabar
—Late conquered by our arms—
Of stalwart form and noble mien;
Pure in life and continent;
Noble son of nature's lineage
These virtues, seldom seen—and more besides—
Worthy of Homeric eloquence,
Are at rest beneath this stone.

63. CANÇÃO

Junto de um seco, fero e estéril monte [excerpt]

Here by an arid, harsh and sterile mount,
Bare and treeless, without form,
In all things abhorred by Nature's self,
Where no bird e'er wings its way or wild beast sleeps,
Or river flows or cool spring bubbles forth,
Or e'en green branch gladdens the weary eye
(Whose name is "Felix"—blessèd—
So called by the world, because unblessed).

. . .

Here, in the sea that seeks in haste
To rush headlong through its narrow strait
—Here has cruel Fate transported me,
And here she holds me for a term.
In this distant corner of the world,
Where all is fierce and raw
She seeks to take my life
—A life so short (a span of days)—
For she wills that my life be torn,
Its pieces scattered to far corners of the earth.
Here did I pass sad lonely days
In evil and enforcèd solitude,
Days of travail, suffering, full of rage
And 'gainst me ranged e'en life itself—
Not only life, but broiling sun and waters chill
With the climate's fetid, burning air,
And, more than all, my thoughts,
Which seem to mock the very nature of my soul.
They, too, against me turned
And in memory brought
The brief and fleeting glory that is past,
In that world where once I lived
—When I did live—
Only to double the ills that now I bear,

Only to prove that there were once
In this life full many a happy hour for me.
Here with these saddened thoughts
Did I abide,
Wasting both time and life,
For on wings did they lift me to the heights,
Only to cast me down,
And look ye! Was that flight so free
From visions and vain dreaming of content?
So now I despair of e'en one day of joy.
Here did illusions turn to sudden tears
And long-heaved sighs which rend the air.
Here was my prisoned soul all pierced and torn,
Wounded in every part,
Encompassed about with sorrows and with pain,
Abandoned and laid bare to hostile Fortune's shafts—
Fortune, cruel, inexorable and harsh.
Nowhere was there refuge offered me,
Nor hope where my head, so weary now,
Might for a space repose.
All was sorrow, all a cause of heartache and of grief,
Yet not enough to kill,
But to let me live, to suffer more,
Did ill-fortune stay its hand.
Oh, how with my cries I still the angry sea,
And with my lamentations seem to curb these mighty
    winds!
Only stern Heaven's self,
The stars and Fate, forever cruel,
Make merry o'er my eternal grief,
Venting both their ire and might
On me, a tiny worm, offspring of vilest dust.
But if from out this travail great
I could but know—be sure—
That for a single hour

I am remembered by those dear eyes I once beheld,
If this sad voice, this cry from out my heart,
Could reach those ears angelic that are hers
—Hers by whose gentle smile I erst did live—
If just once in thought she would recall
Those times, now past,
Of my innocent though erring love,
Or those sweet sad days and stormy ones
Wherein I sought and suffered for her dear sake alone,
If, turning (though if now so late), in pitying wise
She shows some touch of grace
And confess herself the smallest bit too harsh,
If only this and no more could I know,
'Twould be a healing balm for what of life remains
And bring peace to this my aching heart.
Lady, oh how rich thou art, my lady,
That even here, so far from thee,
Thou sustaineth me with this phantom joy!
For when thy sweet image takes possession of my
    thought,
Straightway flee all my sorrow and my pain.
I have but to turn my heart to thee
And I am secure and strong;
E'en though I face the grim mask of Death himself,
Hope then to me returns.
It raises my bowed head, my brow's serene;
It turns my torments, howe'er grave they be,
To sweet sad reveries and visions dear.

64. SONETO

Ilustre e dino ramo dos Menezes

Illustrious scion of Menezes' line
To whom just Heaven's generous hand
Has given as your portion
To smite and break the Moslem host,

263

Go forth where Fate does lead!
Set the great Eritrean Sea aflame
And bring new laurels unto Portugal.
With unflinching breast and mighty sword,
Crush the insolent roving pirates of the main.
Make Ceylon tremble and Gedrosia shrink,
Give new tincture to the Arab straits
—Let the Red Sea true to its color be,
Dyed with the blood of the hated Turk.

65. REDONDILHA

Olhos em que estão mil flores

Mote:　There are roses and daisies
In your eyes,
And grace in your every glance.
And the gods of love of a verity dwell
Where'er you bide.

Volta:　In those eyes like stars
Die a thousand souls,
And I—I sigh and moan,
And these sighs and moans
Once more aver
That where'er you dwell
Bide the gods of love.

66. SONETO

Doces lembranças da passada glória

Sweet memories of years gone by,
Which thou, despoiling Fate, hast snatched from me!
Oh, may I rest and find an hour of peace,
Since conquest of me
Thou surely must count as little gain.
On my soul is graved a long, long tale
Of happy days which never should have been
—Or, had they been, they never should have fled,

Leaving me bereft of all, save memories.
I dwell in reveries of the past,
Yet I am dead to her
In whose heart I should ever live.
Oh, that I might be born once more!
Then should I know
The happiness that I have lost
And learn to bear the ills that now are mine.

67. SONETO

Foi já num tempo doce cousa amar

Love was passing sweet in days gone by,
What time my heart in fullest trust
Surrendered to deceits.
Oh, brittle, vain and feeble hopes,
How at last have life's changes undeceived me!
The more good fortune seems to smile,
The less does one dare believe it can endure.
He who deems the world is at his feet
Forthwith does find himself in deepest misery,
But whosoe'er has faced life's bitter trials
Is troubled not by threats or fears,
Nor finds he strange the evils of this world.

68. SONETO

O cisne quando sente ser chegada

When the dying swan feels his hour nigh
He lifts his voice in sweetest melody
Alone, on a desert shore.
He mourns, for life is dear to him,
And in sadness sees the twilight fall.
So, my lady,
When I contemplate the fruitless end of life,
And that it seems to hang but by a single thread,
In gentler and in sweeter verse

I sing
Your faith forsworn, my love betrayed.

69. SONETO

Grão tempo há já que soube da Ventura
'Twas long ago I learned what Fortune held for me,
For the sad experience of my past
Was sure forecast of days to come.
O cruel and savage Love, O hidden Fate,
Right well have ye tried your strength on me
—Strength no mortal can resist.
So come! Lay waste! Destroy!
Wreak vengeance on the years that still are mine!
Let naught of good abide!
Love taught that Fate would nothing grant,
And, that I might the better know what failure means,
Sent visions of deceit,
Dreams, none of which could e'er come true.
But even though mine be an evil star,
Thou abidest ever in my heart;
There Fate can naught undo.

70. SONETO

Quando o Sol encoberto vai mostrando
When the sun sinks slowly in the west,
Casting its pallid, fading light
Upon the world,
Along the peaceful shore I walk
—And dream of you.
Here you braided the long tresses
Of your hair,
And there you leaned your cheek
Upon your slender hand;
Here you spoke with happy voice,
And there you were silent,
Lost in thought.

71. SONETO

Árvore, cujo pomo, belo e brando
        Thou tree, whose smooth and noble fruit
        Did Nature tint with creamy white
        And crimson hue of blood,
        Like unto a blushing maiden's cheek,
        Never will the angry winds
        Which wreak fell havoc in their path
        Do harm to thee,
        Nor will noxious vapors ever pale
        The colors which thy fruitage grace.
        And, since thou dost lend thy welcome shade
        And shed the sweetest of perfumes
        On her whom I so love,
        If now I fail to sing full measure of thy praise,
        Know that thy memory ever will be dear to me
        When days of sadness come.

72. SONETO

Cara minha inimiga, em cuja mão
        Ah, dear beloved enemy
        Within whose little hand
        Fate chose to lay my happiness,
        Even the solace that thou hast an earthly tomb
        Cannot be mine,
        For the waters hold thy beauty
        In their chill embrace.
        But while this dreary life of mine on earth shall last,
        Thou livest ever on the altar of my heart.
        If aught of power is given a poet's pen,
        Then shalt thou have a shrine eternal in my verse,
        And, long as man's memory on this earth endures,
        That love of thine, so pure, so true, shall live.

73. OS LUSÍADAS, X, 126–27

Thou seest in this region broad
A thousand nations never named before:
The Laos, in both lands and numbers strong,
Avas, Burmans, dwellers in the hills about,
And in mountain fastnesses remote
Those called Gueos, a savage race,
Who eat men's flesh and sear their own
With irons hot, a custom cruel.

See, the Mekong through Cambodia flows,
Who the name "The Lord of Waters" bears,
Which in summer from its tribute streams
Swells mighty 'til it o'erflows the land
And alarms the vasty plains about,
Flooding them as the chilly Nile itself.
Its foolish folk believe, in truth,
That after death to beasts of every kind
They are in punishment or glory turned.

74. REDONDILHA

Aquela cativa

This captive maid
Whose thrall I am,
Since I live in her,
Wills not that I live.
Never a rose in garden set
More lovely was,
To my eyes entranced,
Nor bird in the field
Nor a star in the sky
Is as radiant for me
As is she I love.
Features that have rivals none,
Eyes in which I find repose—
Black and languid are those eyes,

268

Which seek not death to deal.
A living light doth dwell therein,
Making her my sovereign, me her slave.
Her hair so black and lovely is
That common folk can no more hold
Golden locks to be more fair.
Though dark indeed is she I love,
So comely is her graceful form
That e'en the snow itself might seek
To change its color for her own.
Gentle in all ways is she,
And with sweet reason well-endowed.
To some, exotic she may appear,
But of barbarous lineage—no!

Presence calm and serene has she,
Taming all tempests of the breast,
And in my loved one at the last
My heavy griefs find rest.
This the captive
Who holds me in thrall,
E'en must I live in her
—For she is my all![2]

75.   REDONDILHA

Nos livros doutos se trata
          In the learned volumes we are told
          That great Achilles in his rage
          Slew noble Hector, champion of beleaguered Troy.
          But now and here stark Hunger slays
          Our Hector, knight of Portugal.
          She by herself can put an end to him
          —And will,
          Unless Your Grace's boundless liberality
          Brings their fatal quarrel to a close
          —And stays his appetite.

[2] To Barbara, the slave girl.

269

76. SONETO

Que poderei de mundo já querer
What can I hope for in this world,
Whose love but received disfavor and disdain?
And now—death! What more remains,
Since life holds naught,
And grief itself will not destroy?
If there yet be sorrow it will come to me;
Death has brought full proof
What evil can befall,
For by this loss have I now learned
What loss can mean.
In life abides but sadness,
And in death but dire grief.
It seems, alas, it was for this alone
That I was born.

77. SONETO

Lembranças, que lembrais meu bem passado
Memories of past happiness
Make heartache but the worse today.
Let me, I pray you, live in peace,
That I die not in dire discontent.
If in fine we are but playthings of the fates,
I would depart this life of infelicity,
For what of good to me did come,
Came by fortune's merest chance,
But all my ills have been premeditate.
Far better then, to lose my life
And with it these fond memories
That so corrode my soul,
For he can lose no more
Who once has lost the hopes and dreams
Of what might be
—The thoughts which erstwhile calmed his sad and
   troubled heart.

78. SONETO

Mudam-se os tempos, mudam-se as vontades

Time changes for us all
And changes all for us.
The whole world is naught but change,
Assuming ever some new guise.
With time come changes in ourselves;
Our hopes, our visions and our dreams
Outlive the memory of our griefs,
But all joy turns to yearning in the end.
Time clothes the meadows with green grass,
Where erstwhile stretched broad snowy plains.
Alas!
The change of time for me doth mute
My joyful songs to sobs and tears.
Thus each day that passes brings its change,
Until the Terror comes at last
—That change, after which no change can come,
No change, forever more.

79. SONETO

Que me quereis, perpétuas saudades?

What would you, O endless longings,
With what false hopes deceive me now?
Time once run out returns no more,
Or, if it does, our youth has flown.
'Tis well that you are no more, my hopes,
For the joys you brought were brief,
The portions oft unequal
And contrary to my will.
So changed my friends,
I know them not.
The days have blighted happiness,
Nor do Time and Fortune
Give promise for the years to come;
They are but spies on my content.

271

80. SONETO

Pensamentos que agora novamente

Thoughts that now awake in me
Vain dreams of love long dead,
Is it not enough that you hold me fast
In this present discontent?
What phantoms raise you thus
Each hour before my eyes?
Why tempt me with these dreams
—One who never was content with dreams?
Why have you changed your ways, O thoughts,
What sly enticements do you thus conceal?
Deny me not an answer to my prayer, I beg,
For if in wrath you turn from me,
Even I myself will lend you aid to take my life.

81. SONETO

Memória de meu bem, cortado em flores

Memories of happy days slain in their prime
By decree of my sad and weary lot,
Grant me now surcease of sorrow and of care,
Release from this disquietude of soul.
Does not the present ill suffice,
Which bodes of still more evil yet to come?
Must the shade of a once cherished love
Now challenge my repose with bitter thoughts?
In a single hour did I lose my all,
All I had treasured through the passing years.
Begone, ye vain, glorious, shattered dreams,
For in this desert must I end my days,
And, because of these memories that pursue,
Must I die a thousand deaths
Instead of one!

82. SONETO

Quem quiser ver de Amor uma excelência

If you would know love's excellence,
Its tenderness and gentle ways,
Behold what it has brought to me
—And learn.
When long-drawn absence blots out memories
On ocean's wave or far-off battle front,
Grief and longing take their heavy toll,
And patience meets a fearful test.
Though hostile fate bring bitter bane
Or sorest hurt or loss—or even death—
Though fortune bring me all success
And raise me to a high estate—
As long as life remains to me
The world will find one name alone
Upon my lips,
One love within my heart.

83. ODE

Já a calma nos deixou [excerpt]

But come what may,
Though all nature 'gainst me turn,
Though love die in inconstancy,
Though fate be constant in inconstancy,
Though all that can be changed
Does change,
That which I have once begun
I shall maintain.

84. SONETO

Na ribeira do Eufrates assentado

By broad Euphrates' stream I sat,
Lost in sweet memories of the past

273

—Alas, so short! when I in blessèd Zion dwelt.
Communing thus within myself,
Seeking to learn my suff'ring's cause,
Methought I heard a voice that asked:
"Why singest thou not of thy youthful past,
And of the vict'ry thou hast won
O'er all thy ills?
Knowest thou not that he who sings
Forgets his wounds, however deep?
Sing then thy songs,
And cease to weep and wail."
"Alas," sighed I,
"When sadness thus is on sadness heaped,
Pity cannot heal by song,
Pity can but let me die."

85. SONETO
Cantando estava um dia bem seguro

I was singing one day with lightest heart,
When Silvio came
—Silvio, the shepherd, who foretold men's doom
From the cries and songs of birds.
He spoke, and warned:
"When unseen Fate decides to strike,
Two wolves in a single day will come.
You will lose forthwith both voice and song,
And sweet melody will cease!"
They came!
One tore the throats of the flock that grazed
And thus I lost all hope of worldly wealth.
Alas, far worse befell!
The other slew my gentle lamb,
The little one I loved so well
—And my soul grieves unto death.

86. SONETO

Chorai, Ninfas, os Fados poderosos

Weep, ye nymphs,
For inexorable Fate
Has robbed us of her matchless grace!
Have they vanished in the tomb,
Those glorious eyes, with their regal light?
O vain, false values of this world!
Must I then believe
That all thy loveliness of face and form,
Those lustrous flowing locks
Lie cold and stark in death?
If this can come to her,
Whose beauty did obscure the sun,
What hope may others have?
She was too pure for this world of ours,
So did not tarry long;
She has ascended to the skies,
To her appointed home.

87. SONETO

Julga-me a gente toda por perdido

This poor world misjudges me as lost,
For it sees me enwrapped in love of you,
Keeping myself from men apart
—Their ills, their vanities and strife.
I know the vulgar crowd full well;
I look with scorn upon its guile,
And hold him but a base, blind fool
Who has not tasted love.
O earth, O sea, O restless winds,
Speed on in your unceasing course!
Let others strive for gold and fame,
The elements, fire and war defy.

I am content to live alone,
Your image within my heart enshrined
Through all eternity.

88. ODE

Já a calma nos deixou [excerpt]
'Tis Nature's law
That fleeting time does thus change all.
Spring's loveliness makes way
For Summer's fruit;
Then follows Winter's cold.
So in their appointed time
Return the days of Spring,
The Summer's sun, the Autumn's yield,
The Winter's snow.
All is changed,
All that the warm sun looks down upon
And floods with golden light.
Nor is any man secure from change,
However blest or happy be his day,
For his fortunes change as change the years,
His hopes and fears,
For good or ill.

89. SONETO

Quem jaz no grão sepulcro, que descreve
Who lies within this lordly tomb,
Beneath this sculptured shield and noble coat of arms?
One who is naught,
For to this end come all.
Yet he was all, did all
That in mortal power lay.
Was he then a king?
He did all a king might do.
—In peace upheld the olive branch,

276

In war the naked blade—
But heavy as his hand lay on the Moor,
So, cold earth, rest lightly thou on him.
Is it imperial Alexander? No!
This man strove to rule his kingdom fair;
No dreams of conquest spurred him on.
Is it Hadrian, ruler of the Roman world?
Nay! This one upheld the law of God.
Is it Numa? No, but John the King,
Portugal's third,
But second he to none.

90. ODE

A quem darão de Pindo as moradoras [excerpt]
You as my Maecenas do I hold,
And celebrate your name.

. . .

As long as sounding lyre
With its learned and jocund melodies
Has honor in this world,
As long as Tagus
And the Douro do give birth
To sons dear to crisp-haired Mars
And Apollo of the golden curls,
Immortal glory shall be thine,
Dom Manuel of Portugal.

Appendix II

91. SONETO

Ai, imiga cruel! Que apartamento?
Unkind you are, and cruel!
Why leave you thus your native land?
What drives you from the home you love,
O glory of my eyes, center of every thought?
Does uncertain fortune tempt you
To brave the raging seas,
Their deeps and shoals, their high-heaped waves,
And the storm-wind's greedy claws?
May Heaven bless your faring,
Though you bid me no good-by.
Hear this one truth before you go:
You leave more saddened hearts to mourn
Than prayers for your safe return.[1]

[1] Written when D. Francisca da Aragão and her husband, who was an ambassador of Philip II of Spain, left Portugal for Germany.

92. SONETO

Conversação doméstica afeiçoa

Converse with those dear to us
Has many many moods.
Now it speaks with frank and right good will,
Again with warm affection, deepest love,
Where each is held above suspicion
By the other,
But if, alas, strife enters in,
Then straightway gentle love,
That selfsame love which pardons all,
Condemns the true as false.
This is not hearsay that I write
Where thought takes outward shape in empty words
To fill books with pretty phrase.
I do upon my conscience swear
That what I write is solemn truth,
In life's encounters learned.

93. SONETO

De vós me aparto, ó Vida, em tal mudança

I leave you, Life, and in departing
I feel a sense of death in life.
I know not why man seeks content,
For he who does the more receive, the more must lose.
But to you this firm assurance do I give,
That though my torments may this transient body kill,
Beyond the waters of forgetfulness,
In memory secure, the past will live.
Better that my eyes shed tears, bereft of you,
Than rejoice in other scenes;
Better that you forget, though I cannot.
Rather let memories bring sharp pain
Than that I prove unworthy in forgetting those
Of love's glory, e'en though it heartbreak caused.

279

94. SONETO

Ditoso seja aquele que sòmente

Happy is he whose only grief
Is over love's transient, insubstantial trials,
For these do not destroy his hope
To find content at last.
Happy is he who far from home
Bewails but happy memories,
For though change may come,
The things he fears are known.
Happy is he indeed in any plight
If deceit, disdain or love's reserve alone
Torment his heart.
But alas for him who has regret
For acts for which no pardon lies
And whose conscience bears no stain of his offense.

95. SONETO

Está-se a Primavera trasladando

Spring looks upon thy features fair
And strives to emulate
The lilies and the roses of thy cheek.
Dame Nature finds herself bewitched
By thy entrancing grace,
And mountain, field and river
Pay thee court.
But if thou dost refuse the love
These fragrant blossoms hide,
Cease henceforth all pretense of love.
The loveliness that Love itself
Hath all around thee sown
Availeth nought
If the fruit thereof
Doth prove but thorns.

96. ODE

Já a calma nos deixou [excerpt]

Before the onset of summer's fiery sun
The flowers have fled
In wild dismay.
Vanished are the lilies white
And the roses, blushing red.
The birds have ceased their cheery song
And seek the shelter of their nest.
In the forest trees
A vagrant breeze
Lazily stirs among the leaves,
And a murmuring spring
Plashes o'er its stones,
Empearling the grassy mead.

97. CANÇÃO

Junto de um sêco, duro, estéril monte [excerpt]

My lady,
How rich in all kindness you must be
That even here, so far from happiness,
You send alluring visions of yourself.
I have but to see you in my thoughts;
Straightway grief and pain are healed.
To recall your face
Gives strength and courage to my heart,
And with calm I look upon
The cold forbidding mask of Death.
I am possessed again of hope,
My tortured brow is smoothed,
And sweet reveries have caused to flee
All worry and torment.

98. CANÇÃO

Junto de um sêco, duro, estéril monte [excerpt]

Here in reverie I ask
Of the breezes wafting love
And of the birds that wing their way
From where you dwell,
If they have seen you,
What words are uttered by your lips,
How and where you fare, with whom,
And what you do each day, each hour.
There at your side alone does life seem kind,
And with you I find new strength
For conquest both of fortune and of toil.
Oh, once more to see you,
Once more to love you and to serve!
Time gives pledge to grant this boon forthwith
But love, impatient, flings off all restraint
Reopens scars, old wounds of discontent,
—And so I live.

99. SONETO

Não vás ao monte, Nise, com teu gado

Nise,
Go not upon the mountain with thy flock,
For Cupid seeks thee everywhere,
He asks of all where thou may'st be,
And he has anger in his eye.
He claims that thou hast robbed him
Of his quiver's sharpest darts,
And swears to pierce thy tender breast
With blazing bolt.
Fly far from disadventure,
For if his wrath hath been incurred by thee,
Without mercy he'll pursue.
Alas! My fears do counsel thee in vain

If at thy heart
He launch his fiery shaft.

100. SONETO

No mundo poucos anos, e cansados

But few years were granted me
—And those years weary ones
Of suffering and grief,
Days eclipsed in darkest night
Ere my winters numbered five times five.
I crossed great seas and far off lands
To seek healing for my ills,
But fortune willed not to grant its gift,
And neither toil nor risk availed.
Beloved Portugal gave me birth,
And fair green Alenquer was my home,
But that black humor which did lurk
Within this earthly tenement
Hath cast me into thee, brute sea,
To feed thy monsters,
Thou, sea, whose wild waves beat
'Gainst Abyssinia's shores,
Far, far from my native land.[2]

101. SONETO

No mundo quis o Tempo que se achasse

Time decrees that each accept
What certainty or chance may bring;
In learning this have I been Fortune's toy.
All my hopes have proved but vain,
My dreams have come to naught.
I e'en entrusted life to shattered wood[3]
To learn if Fate might change.

[2] To Pero Moniz, who died at sea at Monte Felix.
[3] This line refers to Camoëns' shipwreck on the Indo-Chinese coast.

But Heaven has pronounced its stern command,
And failure marks my days.

102. SONETO

Nunca em amor danou o atrevimento

Never in Love were the brave condemned,
And Fortune ever favors him who dares.
Thought once freed from shrinking fear
Can soar to heights sublime to meet its star,
For what we prize most is substanceless,
Elusive as the wind.
To dare to live is fitting, not blind madness,
And each must venture forth with courage high,
Once Fate has shown the way.
If happiness is offered, full of promise,
Fears must forthwith be cast aside,
Lest heart's desire flee our grasp forever,
And, desolate, have we ourselves to blame.

103. ODE

Nunca manhã suave [excerpt]

Never did flush of early dawn,
Casting its beams o'er the waking world,
Rejoice a vessel, tempest-tossed
All the long night on a raging sea,
As do your eyes, radiant as the sun.
Their glory floods the world with light,
The flowers and meadows nod and smile.
When brooding sadness seizes me,
Their beauty cheers my downcast heart
And clouds are scattered far.
My breast, beloved, wherein you dwell,
Is but narrow lodging for your soul;
As the moth is drawn to the searing flame,
So turn my eyes to you.

284

104. ELÉGIA

O poeta Simónides, falando [excerpt]

For him who fares to far-off lands
To seek that calm repose
Which you, cruel Fate, with unkind hand deny,
For him who learns that life, however harsh,
Must be endured
With courage and undaunted soul,
What purpose can it serve
To call to mind
That which is past since all does pass—
Unless it be
To bring heartache and despond?

105. ELÉGIA

O poeta Simónides, falando [excerpt]

Oh! blessed tillers of the soil!
Could they but know their happy lot,
Dwelling in their peaceful fields!
To them the kindly earth grants sustenance,
The cool spring bubbles crystal clear,
And their ewes give ample yield.
They never see the tossing waves, the darkened sky,
As they who seek the precious orient store,
Nor need they face the fury of cruel war.
Each lives content beneath his vine,
Where no greed for gleaming gold
Disturbs his dreams.
It recks them not that they may lack
Fine clothes that reek of strong perfume,
Garments that Assyrian hands have dyed,
Or Atalic lacy garb,
Nor do they yearn for Corinth's joys,
For Parian marble carved with craft,
Or for garnet, jacinth and emerald rare.

And if their homes are not with gold adorned,
Their fields are with countless flowers strewn,
Where graze and sport their joysome kids.
Their meadows with the changing season's hues are
tinged,
And boughs bend low with weight of ripened fruit.

106. ECLOGA

Que grande variedade vão fazendo [excerpt]

Sing now, O shepherd, as thy peaceful flock
Grazes on the dew-drenched grass,
For in the shadowed hills where he doth find his source,
Sacred Tagus lies
With cheek on palm, eyes fixed upon the plain,
And hath stayed his course to hearken
While in silent sadness stand the nymphs about.

107. SONETO

Que levas, cruel Morte? Um claro dia

What didst thou carry off, O Death? A perfect day.
At what hour didst thou seize it? At day's dawning.
Dost thou know whom thou hast taken? I wot not.
Who willed this deed? He who willed it.
Who now finds joy in her? The cold damp earth.
What abides of her life's light? The brooding dark.
Has Portugal yet spoken? Benumbed, she speaks.
What are her words? "She deserved not this."
And what says Love? He dare not speak.
Wherefore has he no word? By my command.
What is left at court? But grief and tears.
What now remains? An empty world.
What glory hath departed? Her loveliness.[4]

4 Written at the death of D. Maria de Távora, daughter of Luis Alvaro de Távora.

108. SONETO

Quem pudera julgar de vós, Senhora?

> Who could believe, my lady,
> That my faith was all in vain?
> E'en though my love may cause displeasure,
> At no hour are you absent from my thoughts.
> Will you scorn him who loves you and adores you
> And turn to one who values not your heart?
> But I have been, alas, unworthy,
> And my blindness now I know.
> Never could I understand your whims or fancies
> Or convince you that my love was true,
> Yet to all the world 'twas manifest
> —Nor can it alter while I live.
> Though I plead my suit to no avail,
> The more you spurn, the greater grows my love.

109. REDONDILHA

Querendo escrever, um dia [excerpt]

> There stands a tree that mourns
> When all else in nature does rejoice.
> Her blossoms to the night unfold,
> But at dawn they droop and fall.
> At sight of you
> My poor heart leaps with joy,
> Then straightway mourns,
> For undeserving though I be,
> Melancholy is my lot.

110. REDONDILHA

Querendo escrever, um dia [excerpt]

> A tale is told of swallows;
> If the nestling's eyes are blind,
> The mother quickly seeks an herb
> That heals her little ones.

When I behold your eyes,
Luminous, so like the stars,
I am blinded by their loveliness,
But when their radiance touches me,
Straightway am I healed.

III. SONETO

Se a Fortuna, inquieta e mal olhada

If Fortune, fickle and of evil eye
(Who in herself does Heaven's law defame),
Would grant me what she most abhors,
A quiet, peaceful, honest life,
It might well be that my beloved Muse,
Aroused by more inspired and ardent flame,
Would sing with cherished, tuneful lyre
And lull to sleep fair Tagus
In our fatherland.
But since my stormy destiny
Casts darkness on my weak and feeble Muse
And denies consent to such great praise,
Your tribute, undeserved,
Should for another be,
One more famous,
Like yourself, to whom the world pays court.

112. SONETO

Tal mostra de si ád vossa figura

The light of this rounded world
In all its force and power
Doth glow the more in brightness
For thy beauty, my Sibela.
Who can gaze on such allure
And not surrender?
For all resistance is in sooth but vain
To escape thy scorn so great.

288

I sought to bend all reason to my purpose;
My senses fail,
I, too, ensnared.
But if in this my boldness hath offended,
Take further vengeance
And seize what e'er of life
May still remain.

113. CANÇÃO

Vinde cá, meu tão certo secretário [excerpt]

Thus was life changed against my will
By decree of cruel, unloving Fate,
An exile from my fatherland
Have I braved the broad and raging seas.
I have felt the war god's fiery wrath,
I have seen and touched his bitter fruit,
I have wandered through the whole wide world,
I have seen strange lands and customs weird,
Heard barbarous tongues 'neath alien skies,
Driven ever forth by Destiny,
Who devours man's years before his time.
High hope, which gleams like diamond bright,
Eludes my grasp, it falls and breaks.
Alas! 'Tis but common glass.

114. SONETO

Ditosa pena, como a mão que a guia

Pen, happy as the hand that guides
With such perfection and subtle artistry,
When with good reason I would praise thee,
I lose the words which fancy seeks.
But Love, creator of such lofty thoughts,
Now bids me sing of thee in all thy ways
—Not with the warlike wand of Mars,
But in sweet and gentle melody.

Thy name, Emanuel, soars from pole to pole,
Extolling thee and spreading thy renown,
Where but now were none to know.
Thou art immortal,
For behold! Apollo grants the floral crown
Which he has held in trust for thee
These many years.[5]

115. SONETO

Ditosas almas, que ambas juntamente

O happy pair
Whose souls together did ascend
Unto those skies where love and beauty reign!
There through all eternity you share the joys
That were so fleeting here;
There that content
Whose briefness was your sole lament on earth
Is peaceful bliss,
Which through succeeding years will but increase.
Sad am I, who have my life begirt
With love's entanglements—
A love whose glory as it grows
Brings naught but discontent;
Sad, for my grief knows no respite,
And love, to injure me the more,
Prolongs my life.

[5] Camoëns' authorship of this sonnet is questionable.

Appendix III

1502 Valentim Fernandes' volume of Portuguese translations of Marco Polo, Book IV of Poggio Bracciolini's *De Varietate Fortunae* (containing Nicolò de' Conti), and Girolamo da Santo Stefano.

1521 *Carta das nouas . . . do descobrimento do preste Joham.*

1537 Pedro Nunes, *Tratado da sphera.*

1540 Francisco Álvares, *Verdadera* [sic] *informaçam das terras do Preste Joam.*

1545 Garcia de Resende, chronicle of João II.

1551 Fernão Lopes de Castanheda, Book I.

1552 (January 20) Castanheda, Book II.

1552 (June 28) João de Barros, Decade I.

1552 (October 12) Castanheda, Book III.

1553 (March 24) Barros, Decade II. The *São Bento* sailed March 24!

1553 (October 15) Castanheda, Books IV and V (in same volume).

1554 (February 3) Castanheda, Book VI.

1554 (no day indicated) Castanheda, Book VII.

1554 (end of May) Resende, second edition of chronicle of João II.

1554 (July 20) Castanheda, second edition of Book I.
1554 *Relaçaõ da muy notavel perda do Galeaõ Grande S. Joaõ . . . a 24. de Junho de 1552.* James Duffy, *Shipwreck & Empire,* p. 175, on the basis of internal evidence, doubts the existence of an edition this early. The first extant edition is 1594.
1555 Jesuit letters received in 1555. Translated from Portuguese into Spanish.
1556 Lopo de Sousa Coutinho, *Liuro primeyro do cerco de Diu, que os Turcos poseram á fortaleza de Diu.* Also Book II in same volume.
1557 (January 19) *Commentarios de Afonso Dalboquerque.*
1557 (February 10) Fidalgo de Elvas, *Relaçam verdadeira . . . da prouincia da Frolida.*
1560 António Tenreiro, *Itinerario . . . em que se contem como da India veo por terra a estes Reynos de Portugal.*
1561 Castanheda, Book VIII (posthumous). The first thirty-one chapters of Book IX were only published in the twentieth century.
1562 Jesuit letters. Translated from Portuguese into Spanish.
1563 (August 18) Barros, Decade III. Decade IV was posthumously published in 1615.
1563 (December 15) António Galvão, *Tratado* on the discoveries.
1564 (June 27) Miguel de Castanhoso, *Historia das cousas que o muy esforçado capitão Dom Christouão da Gama fez nos Reynos do Preste Ioão.*
1564 (day ?) Manuel de Mesquita Perestrelo, *Naufragio da Nao S. Bento sendo Capitão Fernão Alvares Cabral, que se perdeo a 22 de Abril de 1554 . . . .*
1565 (colophon says 1564!) Jesuit letters from 1548 to 1563. Translated from Portuguese into Spanish.
1565 (June 20) João Bermudes, *Breue relação da embaixada que o Patriarcha dom Ioão Bermudez trouxe do Emperador da Ethiopia.*
1565 (September 20) Tenreiro, second edition of *Itinerario.*
1566 *Naufragio da viagem que fez a Nao Sancta Maria da barca,*

deste Reyno pera a India . . . No anno. M D L. VII. The ship was wrecked in 1559.

1566–67   Damião de Góis, chronicle of Manuel I, four parts.

1567   Damião de Góis, chronicle of Prince João (later João II).

1569   (colophon says February 20, 1570) Gaspar da Cruz, O.P., *Tractado . . . da China.*

1570   (July) Jesuit letters from 1549 to 1566.

1570   (August 31) Jesuit letters from 1549 to 1566. (These are two different editions by the same printer.)

1571   Jerónimo Osório, history of Manuel I (in Latin).

Appendix IV

GENEALOGY OF THE HOUSE OF AVIZ

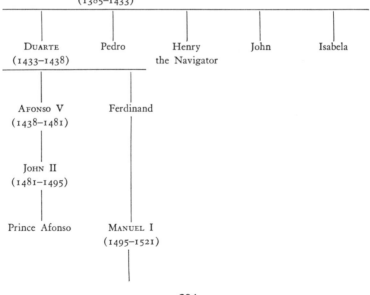

JOHN I (Aviz) m. Philippa, d. of John of Gaunt.
(1385–1433)

DUARTE   Pedro   Henry   John   Isabela
(1433–1438)   the Navigator

AFONSO V   Ferdinand
(1438–1481)

JOHN II
(1481–1495)

Prince Afonso   MANUEL I
(1495–1521)

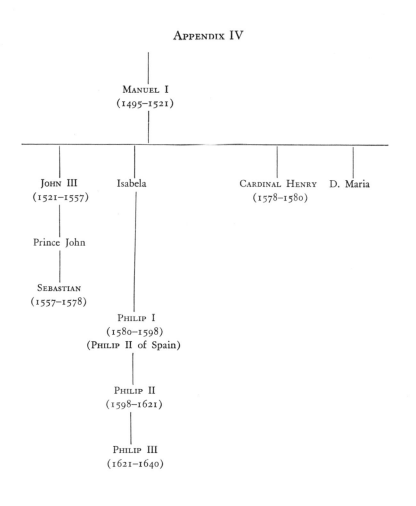

MANUEL I
(1495–1521)

JOHN III   Isabela   CARDINAL HENRY   D. Maria
(1521–1557)   (1578–1580)

Prince John

SEBASTIAN
(1557–1578)

PHILIP I
(1580–1598)
(PHILIP II of Spain)

PHILIP II
(1598–1621)

PHILIP III
(1621–1640)

Bibliography

THE WORKS OF LUIS DE CAMOËNS

Collected Works

Obra Monumental de Luis de Camões. Ed. by Pedro Wenceslau de
Brito Aranha. 2 vols. Lisboa, 1886.
Obras Completas. Vol. V, *Parnaso.* Porto, 1873.
————. In *Biblioteca de Actualidade.* Porto, 1873.
————. Ed. by Hernani Cidade. 5 vols. Lisboa, 1946–47.
Obras de Luiz de Camões. Ed. by Visconde de Juromenha. 6 vols.
Lisboa, 1860–69.

Lyrics

Camões Lirico. Ed. by Agostinho de Campos. 5 vols. Lisboa, 1925–38.
Lirica. Ed. by José Maria Rodrigues and A. L. Vieira. Coimbra, 1932.
Lyricas. Com Traduccões Francezas e Castelanas de José Benoliel.
Lisboa, 1896.
The Lyrics. English trans. by Richard F. Burton. 2 vols. London, 1884.
Poesias Lyricas. Rio de Janeiro, 1880.
Rimas. Third ed. Lisboa, 1607.
————. Ed. by Alvaro J. da Costa Pimpão. Coimbra, 1953.
70 Sonnets of Camoës. English trans. by J. J. Aubertin. London, 1881.

I Sonetti. Italian trans. by T. Cannizzaro. Bari, 1913.
Les Sonnets. French trans. by F. D'Azevedo. Lisbonne, 1913.

The Epic

The Lusiad. English trans. by Richard Fanshawe. London, 1655.
———. English trans. by William Julius Mickle. First ed., Oxford, 1776. Fifth ed., London, 1950.
———. English trans. by Thomas Moore Musgrave. London, 1826.
———. Books I–V. English trans. by Edward Quillinan. London, 1853.
———. English trans. by Robert Ffrench Duff. Lisbon, 1880.
———. English trans. by Richard Fanshawe; ed. by Jeremiah D. M. Ford. Cambridge, Mass., 1940.
Os Lusíadas. Ed. by Manuel Correa. Lisboa, 1613.
———. Avinhão, 1818.
———. Ed. by José Maria de Sousa-Botelho. Paris, 1836.
———. Ed. by José de Fonseca. Paris, 1846.
———. Ed. by Carl von Reinhardstoettner. Strassburg, 1874.
———. Lisboa, 1875.
———. Ed. by Francisco Gomez de Amoriam. Lisboa, 1889.
———. Ed. by F. de Salles Lancastre. Lisboa, 1892.
———. Ed. by Mendes dos Remedios. Second ed. Coimbra, 1903.
———. Commentados por Augusto Epiphanio de Silva Dias. 2 vols. Porto, 1910.
———. Ed. by José Maria Rodrigues. Lisboa, 1921.
———. Edição Nacional. Lisboa, 1931.
———. Ed. by H. Guedes de Oliveira. Porto, 1938.
———. French trans. by Charles Magnin. Paris, 1941.
———. Ed. by Jeremiah D. M. Ford. Cambridge, Mass., 1946.
———. Ed. by Claudio Basto. Third ed. Porto, n.d.
La Lusiade de Camoens. French trans. by M. Duperron de Castera. 3 vols. Paris, 1768.
Die Lusiaden. German trans. by A. E. Wollheim da Fonseca. Leipzig, 1879.
———. German trans. by Otto Freiherr von Taube. Freiburg, 1949.
———. German trans. by Karl Eitner. Leipzig, n.d.

Lusiaderne. Swedish trans. by Nils Lovĕn. London, 1852.

Les Lusiades. French trans. by J.-B.-J. Millié. Paris, 1841.

Les Lusiades de Luis de Camões. French trans. by Roger Bismut. Lisbonne, 1954.

I Lusiadi. Italian trans. by Antonio Nervi. Second ed. Milan, 1821.

————. Italian trans. by Adriano Bonaretti. Firenze, 1925.

————. Italian trans. by Briccolani. Parigi, 1926.

————. Italian trans. by Silvio Pellegrini. Torino, 1945.

The Lusiads. English trans. by Leonard Bacon. New York, 1950.

————. English trans. by William C. Atkinson. London, 1952.

Luzitanci. By Luiza de Camõesa. Zagreb, 1952.

Miscellaneous

"Carta Inedita," *Lusitania,* Fasciculo Camoniano, V and VI. Lisboa, 1905.

El-Rei Seleuco. Ed. by Vieira de Almeida. Lisboa, 1944.

Episodio da Ilha de Venus. French trans. by Cournand. Braga, 1880.

————. French trans. by Pereira Caldas. Braga, 1880.

Parnaso de Luis de Camões. Ed. by Theophilo Braga. 3 vols. Porto, 1880.

Poesias Castellanes y Autos. Ed. by Marques Braga. Lisboa, 1929.

Redondilhas de Amor. Lisboa, 1925.

Rimas Varias. Commentada por Manuel de Paria Sousa. 4 vols. Lisboa, 1685.

"Uma Carta Inedita de Camões," ed. by Xavier da Cunha, *Boletim das Bibliotecas e Archivas Nacionaes.* Coimbra, 1904.

OTHER REFERENCES

Abrégé ... de l'Histoire ... de Portugal. 2 vols. Paris, 1765.

Academia Brasileira de Letras. *Arquivo Camoniano.* Rio de Janeiro, 1943.

Adamson, John. *Memoirs of the Life and Writings of Luis de Camoens.* 2 vols. London, 1820. *See also* Southey, Robert.

Adler, Elkan Nathan (ed.). "David Reubeni." In *Jewish Travelers.* London, 1930.

BIBLIOGRAPHY

Agostinho, José. *A Chave dos Lusiadas.* Sixth ed. Porto, n.d.

Alciati, Andrea. *Emblemata.* n.p., 1522.

Allan, J., *et al. The Cambridge Shorter History of India.* Cambridge, 1934.

Almeida-Garrett, João Baptista. *Camões.* Seventh ed. Porto and Braga, 1880.

———. *Camões.* French trans. by Henri Faure. Paris, 1880.

Altamira, Rafael. *A History of Spain from the Beginnings to the Present Day.* New York, 1949.

Andrade, Francisco de. *Cronica do Muyto Alto e Poderoso Rey Destes Reynos de Portugal Dom João o III Deste Nome.* Lisboa, 1613.

Andrade, Miranda de. *A Lição de Camões.* Braga, 1951.

Aquino, Thomas Joseph de. *A Vida de Camões.* Porto, 1900.

Araujo, Norberto de. *Peregrinacões em Lisboa.* 3 vols. Lisboa, n.d.

Atkinson, William C. *Spain: A Brief History.* London, 1934.

Axelson, Eric. *South-East Africa.* London, 1940.

Azevedo, Pedro A. de. "Os Escravos." In *Archivo Historico Portuguez,* Vol. I. Lisboa, 1903.

Azurara, Gomes Eannes de. *Chronicle of the Discovery and Conquest of Guinea.* English trans. by C. Raymond Beazley and Edgar Prestage. 2 vols. London, 1896.

Baião, Antonio. "Un Manuel Lira, un dos Mais Antigos Impressadores dos Lusíadas," *Lusitania,* Fasciculo VII. Lisboa, 1923.

———, *et al. Historia da Expansão Portuguesa no Mundo.* 3 vols. Lisboa, 1937–40.

Barata, A. F. *A Luiz de Camões: Homenagem.* Evora, 1880.

Barbosa, Duarte. *The Book of Duarte Barbosa.* English trans. by Mansel Longworth Dames. 2 vols. London, 1918.

———. *Livro de Duarte Barbosa.* In *Collecção de Noticias para a Historia e Geografia das Nações Ultramarinas,* Vol. II Lisboa, 1813.

Barros, João de, and Diogo do Couto. *Da Asia: Decadas.* 24 vols. Lisboa, 1778–88.

Bearn, Pierre. *La Conquête de la Mer.* Paris, 1956.

Beckford, William. *The Journal of William Beckford in Portugal and Spain.* Ed. by Boyd Alexander. London, 1954.

————. *Recollections of an Excursion to the Monasteries of Alcobaça and Batalha.* London, 1835.

Beirão, Caetano. *Historia Breve de Portugal.* Lisboa, n.d.

Bell, Aubrey F. G. *Cervantes.* Norman, 1947.

————. *Diogo do Couto.* Oxford, 1924.

————. *Fernam Lopez.* Oxford, 1921.

————. *Gaspar Correa.* Oxford, 1924.

————. *Gil Vicente.* Oxford, 1921.

————. *In Portugal.* London, 1912.

————. *Luis de Camões.* Oxford, 1923.

————. *The Oxford Book of Portuguese Verse.* Second ed. Oxford, 1952.

————. *Poems from the Portuguese.* Oxford, 1913.

————. *Portugal of the Portuguese.* New York, 1916.

————. *Portuguese Bibliography.* Oxford, 1922.

————. *Portuguese Portraits.* Oxford, 1917.

————. *Studies in Portuguese Literature.* Oxford, 1914.

Bellermann, Fr. Christ. *Alten Lieder Bücher der Portugiesen.* Berlin, 1840.

Bertrand, Louis, and Charles Petrie. *The History of Spain.* Second ed., revised. London, 1952.

Birot, Pierre. *Le Portugal.* Paris, 1951.

Botelho, Bernardo de Brito. *Historia Breve de Coimbra.* Lisboa, 1873.

Bottineau, Yves. *Portugal.* London, 1957.

Bouchot, Auguste. *Histoire du Portugal et de ses Colonies.* Paris, 1854.

Bouterwek, Friedrich. *Geschichte der Poesie und Beredsamkeit.* Vols. IV, V, and VII. Göttingen, 1805–1809.

————. *History of Spanish and Portuguese Literature.* English trans. by Thomasina Ross. 2 vols. London, 1823.

Bovill, E. W. *The Battle of Alcazar.* London, 1952.

Bowles, William Lisle. *The Poetical Works of William Lisle Bowles.* Edinburgh, 1895.

Bowra, C. U. *From Vergil to Milton.* London, 1945.

Boxer, C. R. *The Dutch in Brazil, 1624–1654.* Oxford, 1957.

————. *Fidalgos in the Far East, 1550–1570.* The Hague, 1948.

————. *South China in the Sixteenth Century.* London, 1953.

BIBLIOGRAPHY

————. "Was Camoens Ever in Macau?" *Tien Hsia Monthly,* Vol. X, No. 4 (April, 1940). Shanghai, 1940.

Brady, Cyrus Townsend, Jr. *Commerce and Conquest in East Africa.* Salem, 1950.

Braga, Theophilo. *Os Amores de Camões.* Porto, n.d.

————. *Camões e o Sentimento Nacional.* Porto, 1891.

————. *Camões, Epoca e Vida.* Porto, 1907.

————. *Camões, A Obra Lyrica e Epica.* Porto, 1911.

————. *Historia de Camões.* 2 vols. Porto, 1873.

————. *Historia da Litteratura Portugueza—Introducção.* Porto, 1870.

————. *Historia da Litteratura Portuguesa.* Vol. II. Porto, 1914.

————. *Povo Portuguez nos Seus Costumes.* 2 vols. Lisboa, 1885.

————. *Primeira Poesia Impressa de Luiz de Camões.* Lisboa, 1887.

Banco, Camillo Castello. *Luiz de Camões.* Porto and Braga, 1880.

————. "Estudo Sobre Camões." Biographical note in João Baptista Almeida-Garrett, *Camões.*

Brandão, Mario. "Duas Cartas de Nicolau Clenardo," *Biblos,* Vol. XII. Coimbra, 1936.

Brazão, Eduardo. *Apontamentos para a história das relações diplomáticas de Portugal com a China, 1516–1753.* Lisboa, 1949.

Brenan, Gerald. *The Literature of the Spanish People.* Cambridge, 1951.

Breton, M. *Spanien och Portugal.* Stockholm, 1819.

Bridge, Ann, and Susan Lowndes. *The Selective Traveller in Portugal.* London, 1949.

Brito, Bernardo Gomes de (ed.). *Historia Tragico-Maritima.* 6 vols. Porto, 1942.

Brochado, Costa. *Sebastião o Desejado.* Lisboa, 1941.

Browning, Elizabeth Barrett. "Catarina to Camoëns." In *The Complete Poems of Elizabeth Barrett Browning.* 2 vols. London, n.d.

————. "A Vision of Poets." In *The Complete Poems of Elizabeth Barrett Browning.*

Bryden, H. A. *History of South Africa.* Edinburgh, 1904.

Bueno, Silveira. "As Mulheres Que Camões Amou." In *Arquivo Camoniano.*

Burguete, Adriano. *Luis de Camões em Constancia.* Lisboa, 1942.

Burton, Richard F. *Camoens: Life and Lusiads and Lyrics.* 6 vols. London, 1887–94.

——. *Goa and the Blue Mountains.* London, 1851.

Busk, M. M. *The History of Spain and Portugal.* London, 1832.

Byron, George Gordon, Lord. *Childe Harold's Pilgrimage.* In *Poetical Works.* London, 1928.

Calahan, Harold Augustin. *The Sky and the Sailor.* New York, 1952.

Calmon, Pedro. "Camões, Poeta Politico e Social." In *Arquivo Camoniano.*

——. *O Estado e o Direito Nos Lusíadas.* Rio de Janeiro and Lisboa, 1945.

Caminha, Pedro de Andrade. *Poesias.* Lisboa, 1791.

Campbell, Thomas. *Life of Petrarch.* Philadelphia, 1841.

Campos, Antonio de, Jr. *Luis de Camões.* 3 vols. Lisboa, 1954.

Cardin, Luiz. *Projecção de Camões nas Letras Inglesas.* Lisboa, 1940.

Cardosa, Nuno Catharino. *Cintra.* Porto, 1930.

——. *Dicionario Camoniano.* Lisboa, 1950.

Carvalho, Joaquim de. "Estudos sobre as Leituras Filosoficas de Camões," *Lusitania,* Fasciculo Camoniano, V and VI.

Castilho, Julio de. *Lisboa Antiga.* Second ed. 2 vols. Lisboa, 1902.

Castro, João de. *Roteiro de Lisboa a Goa.* Annotated by João Andrade Corvo. Lisboa, 1882.

Castro e Almeida, Virginia. *Vie de Camoëns.* Paris, 1934.

Catanzaro, Carlo. *Dom Luis de Camoens.* Firenze, 1881.

Cavalheiro, Rodrigues, and Eduardo Dias. *Memorias de Forasteiros Aquem e Além-Mar.* Lisboa, 1945.

Caverel, Philippe de. *Ambassade en Espagne et en Portugal de . . . D. Jean Sarrazim.* Paris, 1582.

Celso, Affonso. "Quarto Centenario de Camões," Academia Brasileira de Letras, *Revista,* Vol. XVII. Rio de Janeiro, 1925.

Cervantes, Miguel de Saavedra. *El Ingenioso Hidalgo Don Quijote de la Mancha.* Ed. by M. Aguilar. Madrid, 1939.

——. *The Ingenious Gentleman Don Quixote de la Mancha.* English trans. by Samuel Putnam. 2 vols. New York, 1949.

——. *Trabajos de Persiles y Sigismunda.* In *Obras de Miguel de Cervantes Saavedra.* Third ed. Madrid, 1864.

Chang T'ien-tse. *Sino-Portuguese Trade from 1514 to 1644.* Leyden, 1934.

Charignon, A. J. H. *A Propos des Voyages Aventureux de Fernand Mendez Pinto.* Pékin, 1935.

Chaucer, Geoffrey. *Canterbury Tales.* Ed. by Arthur Burrell. London, 1910.

Cidade, Hernani. *Lições de Culture e Literatura Portuguesa.* Third ed. 2 vols. Coimbra, 1951.

———. *Luis de Camões.* Lisboa, n.d.

———. *Luis de Camões, A Vida e a Obra Lirica.* Lisboa, 1943.

———. *Luis de Camões. II, O Épico.* Lisboa, 1950.

Circourt, Adolphe. *Fragments d'une Vie Inédite de Camoens.*

Clenardus, Nicolaus. *Epistolarum Libri Duo.* Antwerpiae, 1561.

Coelho, J. M. Latino. *Luis de Camões.* Lisboa, 1880.

Coleridge, Henry James. *Life and Letters of St. Francis Xavier.* 2 vols. London, 1882.

Collis, Maurice. *The Grand Peregrination.* London, 1949.

Correa, Gaspar. *Lendas da India.* 8 vols. Lisboa, 1838–64.

Correia, Alberto C. Germano da Silva. *La Vieille . . . Goa.* Bastora, 1931.

Correia, Vergilio. *Batalha.* 2 vols. Porto, 1922.

———. *A Arte em Coimbra e Arredores.* Coimbra, 1949.

———, and Noqueira Gonçalves. *Inventário Artístico da Cidade de Coimbra,* Lisboa, 1947.

Corte Real, Jeronimo. *Naufragio . . . de Sepulveda.* Lisboa, 1783.

Cortesão, Jaime. *O que o Povo Canta em Portugal.* Rio de Janeiro, 1942.

———. "Camoes e o Descobrimento do Mundo." In *Arquivo Camoniano.*

Cossio, José Maria de (trans.). *El Soneto Portugues.* Madrid, 1943.

Costa, Fernandes. "Camões Exemplar e Modelo de Modernos Sonetistas," Academia das Sciencias de Lisboa, *Boletim da Segunda Classe,* Vol. XI. Coimbra, 1918.

Costa, J. da Providencia. "O Trocadilho em Camões," *Biblos,* Vol. III. Coimbra, 1927.

Costigan, Arthur William. *Sketches of Society and Manners in Portugal.* 2 vols. London, 1937.

Coutinho, B. Xavier. *Camões e as Artes Plasticas.* Porto, 1946.

———. *Ensaios.* Porto, 1941.

Coutinho, Gago. "A Rota de Vasco da Gama, n'Os Lusiadas." In *Arquivo Camoniano.*

Couto, Diogo do. *Decadas. See* Barros, João de.

———. *Observações sobre as Principaes Causas da Decadencia dos Portugueses na Asia.* Lisboa, 1790.

———. *O Soldado Pratico.* Lisboa, 1937.

———. *Vida de D. Paulo de Lima Pereira. Lisboa,* 1903.

Cruz, Fr. Bernardo da. *Chronica de Elrei D. Sebastião.* Ed. by Alexandre Herculano and A. C. Paiva. Lisboa, 1837.

Cruz, Gaspar da. *A Treatise in which the things of China are related in South China in the Sixteenth Century.* English trans. by C. R. Boxer. London, 1953.

———. *A Treatise of China.* In *Purchas, His Pilgrimes,* Vol. XI. Glasgow, 1906.

Cunha, Arlindo Ribeiro da. *A Lingua e a Literatura Portuguesa.* Braga, 1941.

Cunha, V. de Bragança. *Eight Centuries of Portuguese Monarchy.* London, 1911.

D'Antas, Miguel. *Les Faux Don Sébastian.* Paris. 1866.

Dantas, Julio. *O Heroismo, a Elegancia, o Amor.* Lisboa, 1923.

Dantas, Olavo. "Camões, Poeta do Mar." In *Arquivo Camoniano.*

Daux, A. A. *Le Portugal de Camões.* Paris, 1890.

Day, Clive. *A History of Commerce.* New York, 1926.

Day, Francis. *The Land of the Premauls, or Cochin, Its Past and Its Present.* Madras, 1863.

D'Ayalla, Frederico Dinaz. *Goa Antiga e Moderna.* Lisboa, 1888.

D'Azavedo, J. Lucio. "Noticias de Portugal de 1578–1580, Segundo Cartes de uma Casa Commercial Noerlandesa," *Lusitania,* Vol. I, Fasciculo II. Lisboa, 1924.

D'Eça, Almeida. *Luis de Camões, Marinheiro.* Lisboa, 1880.

Dellon, Charles. *Dellon's Account of the Inquisition at Goa.* Trans. from the French. Hull, 1812.

———. *Nouvelle Relation d'un Voyage Fait aux Indes Orientales.* Amsterdam, 1699.

———. *Relation de l'Inquisition de Goa.* Amsterdam, 1719.

Denis, Ferdinand. *Portugal.* Paris, 1846.
———. "Vie de Camões." In *Camoens Dans l'Almanac des Muses.* Paris, 1891.
Dornellas, Affonso de. "Luis de Camões," *Elucidario Nobiliarchico,* Vol. I, No. 4. Rio de Janeiro, 1928.
Duckworth, George E. (ed.) *The Complete Roman Drama.* 2 vols. New York, 1942.
Duffy, James. *Shipwreck & Empire.* Cambridge, 1955.
Durdent, J. R. *Beautés de l'Histoire de Portugal.* Paris, 1816.
Eduarte, Dom. *Leal Conselheiro.* Lisboa, 1942.
Eldridge, F. B. *The Background of Eastern Sea Power.* London, 1948.
Encyclopedia Pela Imagem. *Coimbra.* Porto, n.d.
———. *Lisboa.* Porto, n.d.
———. *Palacios e Solares Portugueses.* Porto, n.d.
Encyclopédie de la Pléiade. *Historie des Littératures.* 2 vols. Paris, 1956.
Entwistle, William J. "The 'Lusiads,' da Gama and Modern Criticism," *Lusitania,* Vol. X, Lisboa, 1921.
Estaço, Gaspar. *Varias Antiguidades do Portugal.* Lisboa, 1625.
Faculdade de Letras da Universidade de Lisboa. *Livro Comemorativo da Fundação de Cadeira de Estudos Camonianos.* Coimbra, 1937.
Falcão, Luis de Figueiredo. *Livro em que Se Contem Toda a Fazenda.* Lisboa, 1859.
Faria, Manuel Severim de. *Discursos Varios Politicos.* Evora, 1624.
Faria y Sousa, Manuel de. *Asia Portuguesa.* Trans. by Manuel B. de Aguilar. 6 vols. Lisboa, n.d.
———. "Cintra." In Thomas Joseph de Aquino, *A Vida de Camões.*
———. *Europa Portuguesa.* Second ed. 3 vols. Lisboa, 1678.
Faure, Francisco G. J. *Amor e Genio.* Leiria, 1880.
Federici, Caesar. *The voyage and travell of M. Caesar Fredericke.* English trans. by M. Thomas Hickocke. In Hakluyt's *Voyages,* Maclehose Reprint, Vol. V. Glasgow, 1904. *See also* Frederick, Caesar.
Felner. "Letter to an Abbot of Beira," *Bibliophilo* (April-August, 1849). Lisboa, 1849.
Fernandes, Roberto de M. *Camões: Poet of a New Era.* Rio de Janeiro, n.d.

Ferrarin, A. R. *Storia de Portogallo.* Milano, 1940.

Ficalho, Conde de. *Flora dos Lusíadas.* Lisboa, 1880.

———. *Garcia da Orta e o Seu Tempo.* Lisboa, 1886.

Figueiredo, Antero de. *D. Sebastião, Rei de Portugal.* Sixth ed. Lisboa, 1925.

———. *Camoens.* Spanish trans. by Marques de Lozoya. Madrid, 1928.

Figueiredo, Fidelino de. "Camões: Epica Portuguesa do Seculo XVI." In *Arquivo Camoniano.*

———. *Historia de la Literatura Portuguesa.* Barcelona, 1921.

———. *Literatura Portuguesa.* Rio de Janeiro, 1940.

Figueiredo, José de. "A Iconografia de Camões," *Lusitania,* Fasciculo Camoniano, V and VI. Lisboa, 1925.

Fitzmaurice-Kelly, James. *A History of Spanish Literature.* New York, 1918.

Fonseca, José Nicolau da. *An Historical and Archaeological Sketch of the City of Goa.* Bombay, 1878.

Ford, Jeremiah D. M. (ed.). *Letters of John III, King of Portugal.*

———. *Letters of the Court of John III, King of Portugal.* Cambridge, 1933.

Foster, William. *Early Travels in India.* Oxford, 1921.

Frederick, Caesar. *Extracts of His Eighteene Yeeres Indian Observations.* In *Purchas, His Pilgrimes,* Vol. X. Glasgow, 1905. See also Federici, Caesar.

Freitas, Jordão de. *Camões em Macau.* Lisboa, 1911.

———. *Dom Bento de Camões e o Principe dos Poetas Lusitanos.* Lisboa, 1917.

———. *Morte e Enterramento de Camões.* Lisboa, 1925.

———. *Naufragio de Camões e dos Lusíadas.* Lisboa, 1915.

Freyre, Gilberto. *Casa Grande e Senzala.* English trans., *The Masters and the Slaves,* by Samuel Putnam. New York, 1946.

Fryer, John. *A New Account of East India and Persia.* London, 1698.

The Fugger News-Letters. Ed. by Victor von Klarwill. New York, 1926.

Galippe, V. *Hérédité des Stigmates de Dégénérescence.* Paris, 1905.

Gandavo, Pero Macalhães de. *Dialogo Em Defesa Da Lingua Portuguesa.* Lisboa, 1574.

BIBLIOGRAPHY

———. *Historia da Provincia Sancta Cruz.* Lisboa, 1576.

Garnett, Richard. *Dante, Petrarch, Camoens, CXXIV Sonnets.* London and Boston, 1896.

Gazeta de Noticias. *Luiz de Camões: Homenagem.* Rio de Janeiro, 1880.

Gentil, Georges le. *La Littérature Portugaise.* Paris, 1935.

Girão, A. de Amorim, *et al. Coimbra.* Second ed. Coimbra, 1942.

Goes, Damião de. *Chronica d'El-Rei D. Manuel.* 6 vols. Lisboa, 1910–11.

Goldberg, Isaac. *Brazilian Literature.* New York, 1922.

———. *Camoens: Central Figure of Portuguese Literature.* Girard, Kan., 1924.

Gonçalves, Luis da Cunha. *Camões não Esteve em Macau.* Coimbra, 1928.

——— (ed.). *Estudos Camonianos.* Porto, 1947.

Gonçalves, Rebelo. *Dissertações Camonianas.* São Paulo, 1937.

Gonzalez-Bianco, Pedro. *Vida y Tribulaciones de Luis de Camoens.* Mexico City, 1946.

Grande Enciclopédia Portuguesa e Brasileira. "Camões." Lisbon, n.d.

Grant, Cyril F. and L. *The African Shores of the Mediterranean.* New York, 1912.

Grave, João. "Soneto Inedito de Camões," Academia das Sciencias de Lisboa, *Boletim da Segunda Classe,* Vol. XI. Coimbra, 1918.

Gribble, Francis. *The Royal House of Portugal.* London, 1915.

Gubernatis, Angelo de. *Storia dei Viaggistori Italiani nelle Indie Orientali.* Livorno, 1875.

Guimãres, Ribeiro. *Summario de Varia Historia.* 5 vols. Lisboa, 1872.

Hakluyt, Richard. *Principal Navigations . . . of the English Nation.* Maclehose Reprint. 12 vols. Glasgow, 1905.

Hardung, Victor Eugenio (comp.). *Romanceiro Portuguez.* Vol. I. Leipzig, 1877.

Hart, Henry H. *Sea Road to the Indies.* New York, 1950, and London, 1952.

———. *Venetian Adventurer.* Stanford, 1942.

Hawks, Ellison. *Pioneers of Plant Study.* London, 1928.

Hemans, Felicia D. *Translations from Camoens and Other Poets.* Oxford, 1818.

Herculano, Alexandre. *History of the Origin and Establishment of the Inquisition in Portugal.* English trans. by John C. Branner. Stanford, 1926.

Herrmann, Paul. *Conquest by Man.* New York, 1904.

Highet, Gilbert. *The Classical Tradition.* New York, 1949.

Histoire des Inquisitions. 2 vols. Cologne, 1769.

Humboldt, Alexander von. *Kosmos.* 2 vols. Stuttgart, 1847.

Hume, Martin A. S. *Philip II of Spain.* London, 1911.

Hutson, Arthur E., and Patricia McCoy. *Epics of the Western World.* Philadelphia, 1954.

Inchbold, A. C. *Lisbon and Cintra.* New York, 1908.

Instituto de Coimbra. *Sarau em Commemoração do Tri-Centenario de Luis de Camões.* Coimbra, 1880.

Izon, John. *Sir Thomas Stucley.* London, 1956.

Jacobs, Joseph. "David Reubeni." In *The Jewish Encyclopedia,* Vol. X. New York, 1905.

Jayne, K. C. *Vasco da Gama and His Successors.* London, 1910.

Jerrold, Maud F. *Francesco Petrarca.* London, 1909.

Kammerer, Albert. "Découverte de la Chine par les Portugais au XVIᴵᵉᵐᵉ Siècle," *T'oung Pao,* Vol. XXXIX. Leiden, 1944.

Kelly, Marie Noele. *This Delicious Land, Portugal.* London, 1956.

Keltie, J. Scott. *The Partition of Africa.* London, 1893.

Kendrick, T. D. *The Lisbon Earthquake.* London, 1956.

Kloguen, Denis L. Cottineau de. *An Historical Sketch of Goa.* Madras, 1831.

Lacerda, Hugo de. *Macau e Seu Futuro Porto,* Macau. 1922.

Laclède, M. de la *Histoire Générale de Portugal.* Paris, 1735.

Lamarre, Clovis. *Camões et les Lusiades.* French trans. of *The Lusiads* by J.-B.-J. Millié. Paris, 1890.

Lampridius, Aelius. *Antoninus Elagabalus.* In *Scriptores Historiae Augustae* (Loeb), Vol. II. London, 1925.

Lane-Poole, Stanley. *Mediaeval India.* London, 1925.

Le Blanc, Vincent. *Les Voyages Fameux.* Paris, 1658.

Legrand, Théodoric. *Histoire du Portugal.* Paris, 1926.

Leite, Duarte. *Coisas de Varia Historia.* Seara Nova, 1941.

Leite, Serafim. "Camõcs, Poeta da Expansão da Fe." In *Arquivo Camoniano*.

Leithauser, Joachim C. *Worlds Beyond the Horizon*. New York, 1955.

Lemos, Miguel. *Luis de Camoëns*. Paris, 1880.

Leoni, Francisco Evaristo. *Camões e os Lusíadas*. Lisboa, 1892.

Ley, Charles David (ed.). *Portuguese Voyages, 1498–1663*. London, 1947.

Lichnowsky, Prince. *Portugal: Recordaçoes do Anno de 1842*. Trans. from the German. Lisboa, 1844.

Linschoten, Jan Huygen van. *Voyage to the East Indies*. 2 vols. London, 1885.

Liske, Javier. *Viajes de Extranjeros por Espana y Portugal en Los Siglos XV, XVI*. Trans. by F. Rozanski. Madrid, 1879.

Livermore, H. V. *A History of Portugal*. Cambridge, 1947.

———. *Portugal and Brazil*. Oxford, 1953.

Lobo, D. Francisco A. (Bispo de Vizeu). *Obras*. Vol. I. Lisboa, 1848.

Loiseau, A. *Histoire de la Littérature Portugaise*. Second. ed. Paris, 1887.

Lopes, Fernão. *Cronica de D. João I*. 2 vols. Porto, 1945.

Louture, Robert de. *Navigation à Travers les Ages*. Paris, 1952.

Lucus, C. P. *Historical Geography of the British Colonies*. Vol. IV. Oxford, 1897.

Lusitania. Revista de Estudos Portugueses. Fasciculo Camoniano. Lisboa, 1928.

Macedo, Joaquim Antonio de. *A Guide to Lisbon*. London, 1874.

Macedo, José Tavares de. *Relatorio Feito em Nome da Commissão . . . para Buscar os Ossos de Camões (1854)*. Lisboa, 1880.

McMurdo, Edward. *History of Portugal*. London, 1888.

Mamede, São. *Don Sébastien e Philippe II*. Paris, 1884.

Manrique, Sebastien. *Travels*. English trans. by C. Eckford Luard. 2 vols. Oxford, 1926–27.

Manuel II, King D. (1889–1932). *Livros Antigos Portugueses, 1489–1600*. 3 vols. London, 1929–35.

Marquard, Leo. *The Story of South Africa*. London, 1955.

Marryat, Frederick (Captain). *The Phantom Ship*. London, n.d.

Martino, Christiano. *Camões: Tomas e Motivos da Obra Lirica.* Rio de Janeiro, n.d.

Martins, José F. Ferreria. *Vice-Reis da India, Os 1505–1917.* Lisboa, 1935.

Matos, Antonio de Oliveira. *Vida de Luis de Camões.* Lisboa, 1943.

Mattosa, Antonio G. *Historia de Portugal.* 2 vols. Lisboa, 1939.

Maugham, R. F. C. *Portuguese East Africa.* New York, 1906.

Mendes, A. Lopes. *A India Portuguesa.* 2 vols. Lisboa, 1886.

Mendonça e Costa, L. de. *Manuel do Viajante em Portugal.* Lisboa, 1907.

Menon, K. N. *Portuguese Pockets in India.* New Delhi, 1953.

Mercadal, J. Garcia. *Viajes de Estranjeros por Espana y Portugal.* Madrid, 1952.

Moçambique Directory. Lourenço Marques, 1950.

Mocquet, Jean. *Voyages en Afrique, Asie, Indes Orientales & Occidentales.* Rouen, 1645.

Múrias, Manuel. *A Short History of Portuguese Colonization.* Lisbon, 1940.

Murphy, James. *Travels in Portugal.* London, 1795.

Nabuco, Joaquim. *Camões.* Rio de Janeiro, 1880.

———. *Camões e os Lusíadas.* Rio de Janeiro, 1872.

———. *The Place of Camoens in Literature.* New Haven, 1908.

Nash, Roy. *The Conquest of Brazil.* New York, 1926.

Natividade, V. Viera. *O Mosteiro de Alcobaça.* Second ed. Porto, 1937.

Noronha, Tito de. "Camões, Rimas de 1607," *Annuario da Sociedade Nacional Camoneana,* Vol. I, Porto, 1881.

Nowell, Charles E. *A History of Portugal.* New York, 1952.

———. "Vasco da Gama—First Count of Vidigueira," *Hispanic American Historical Review,* Vol. XX, No. 3 (1940).

Nunes, Leonardo. *Crónica de Dom João de Castro.* Ed. by Jeremiah D. M. Ford. Cambridge, Mass., 1936.

Oaten, Edward F. *European Travellers in India.* London, 1909.

Ogrizek, Doré (ed.). *Le Portugal.* Paris, 1950.

Oliveira, Eduardo Freire. *Elementos Para A Historia Do Municipio De Lisboa.* Part I. Lisboa, 1882.

Oliveira Martins, J. P. *O Brazil e as Colonias Portuguesas.* Fifth ed. Lisboa, 1920.

———. *Camões, os Lusíadas e a Renascença em Portugal.* Porto, 1891.

———. *Os Filhos de D. João I.* Lisboa, 1947.

———. *The Golden Age of Prince Henry the Navigator.* London, 1914.

———. *Historia de Portugal.* Eighth ed. Lisboa, 1913.

———. *A History of Iberian Civilization.* English trans. by Aubrey F. G. Bell. Oxford, 1930.

———. "Marinha Portugueza na Era das Conquistas," *Annuario da Sociedade Nacional Camoneana,* Vol. I. Porto, 1881.

———. *Portugal Nos Mares.* Third ed. 2 vols. Lisboa, 1924.

Oliveyra, Frey Nicolao di. *Livro das Grandezas de Lisboa.* Lisboa, 1620.

Orica, Osvaldo. *Camões y Cervantes.* Santiago de Chile, 1945.

Orta, Garcia da. *Colloquies on the Simples & Drugs of India.* English trans. by Clements Markham. London, 1913.

———. *Coloquios dos Simples e Drogas da India.* Ed. by Conde de Ficalho. 2 vols. Lisboa, 1891.

Osório, Jerónimo. *History of the Portuguese During the Reign of Emmanuel.* English trans. by James Gibbs. 2 vols. London, 1752.

———. *Da Vida e Feitos de El-Réi D. Manuel.* 2 vols. Lisboa, n.d.

Pachecho, Miguel. *Vida de la Serenissima Infanta Dona Maria, Hija del Rey D. Manuel.* Lisboa, 1675.

Palmer, Katharine Ward. Review of José Maria Rodrigues, *Camões e a Infanta D. Maria, The Romantic Review,* Vol. VII, No. 4. New York, 1916.

Paxeco, Francisco. *The Intellectual Relations between Portugal and Great Britain.* Lisbon, 1937.

Pedroso, Sebastião José. *Resumo Historico Acerca da Antica India Portugueza.* Lisboa, 1884.

Peixoto, Afranio. "Brancas Flores," *Lusitania,* Fasciculo Camoniano, V and VI. Lisboa, 1925.

———. "Camões e Dinamene," *Revista da Academia Brasileira de Letras* (April, 1925). Rio de Janeiro, 1925.

———. "Camões, Poeta Escolar." In *Arquivo Camoniano.*

———. *Dinamene: Alma Minha Gentil.* Lisboa, 1926.

———. *Ensaios Camonianos.* Coimbra, 1932.

———. "A Paixão de Camões." In *Arquivo Camoniano.*

———. " 'Parnaso' de Camões, Fonte d 'Os Lusíadas,' " *O Instituto,* Vol. LXXIII. Coimbra, 1932.

———. "Quatro Centenario de Camões," *Revista da Academia Brasileira de Letras* (January, 1925). Rio de Janeiro, 1925.

———, and Pedro A. Pinto. *Dicionario dos Lusíadas.* Rio de Janeiro, 1924.

Pennafort, Onestaldo de. *Shakespeare e Camões.* Rio de Janeiro, 1941.

Pereira, Leonis. *Historia da Provincia Santa Cruz.* Lisboa, 1858.

Pessanha, Camillo, and Wenceslav de Moraes. *Camões nas Paregens Orientais.* Porto, n.d.

Pessanha, José. *Sintra.* Porto, 1932.

Petrarca, Francesco. *Rime, Trionfi e Poesie Latine.* Milano, n.d.

———. *Sonnets and Songs.* New York, 1946.

Pinto, Américo Cortez. *Da Famosa Arte de Impressão.* Lisboa, 1948.

Pinto, Loureiro J. "Novos Subsidios Para a Biografia de Camões," *O Instituto,* Vols. LXXXIX–XC. Coimbra, 1935–36.

Pires, Tomé. *The Suma Oriental.* 2 vols. London, 1944.

Post, H. Houwens. *Het Heroicke Leven van Luis Vaz de Camoens.* Amsterdam, 1944.

Prawdin, Michael. *The Mad Queen of Spain.* Boston, 1939.

Prestage, Edgar. *D. Francisco Manuel De Mello.* Oxford, 1922.

———. *Minor Works of Camões (not hitherto made English).* London, 1924.

———. "Portugal." In *The Catholic Encyclopedia.* New York, 1911.

———. *Portuguese Literature to the End of the 18th Century.* London, 1909.

———. "Two Elegies of Luis de Camões," *The Tablet,* April 26, 1924. London, 1924.

Primor e Honra da Vida Soldadesca no Estado da India. Lisboa, 1630.

Putnam, Samuel. *Marvelous Journey.* New York, 1948.

Pyrard, Francisco de Laval. *Viagem.* 2 vols. Porto, n.d.

———. *The Voyage of François Pyrard.* English trans. by Albert Gray. 3 vols. London, 1880–90.

Ramos, Fr. Jeronymo de. *Chronica dos Feytos ... do Infante Santo D. Fernando.* Lisboa, 1730.

Raynal, François. *Histoire Philosophique et Politique.* 7 vols. (with atlas). La Haye, 1774.

Reade, Brian. "Dominance of Spain." In *Costumes of the Western World; Fashions of the Renaissance.* New York, 1951.

Real Sociedade Geográfica. "Discursos Que Se Dijeron o Leyeron . . . para solemnizar el IV Centenario de Nacimiento de Luis de Camoens," *Boletim,* Vol. LXV. Madrid, 1925.

Recio, José. *As Mais Belas Liricas Portuguesas.* Lisboa, n.d.

———, and Alberto de Serpa. *Poesia de Amor.* Porto, 1945.

Reinhardstoettner, Carl von. *Luis de Camões, der Sänger der Lusiaden.* Leipzig, 1877.

———. *Luis de Camões, der Sänger der Lusiaden.* In *Aufsätze und Abhandlungen, Vornehmlich zur Litteraturgeschichte.* Berlin, 1887.

———. *Portuguesische Literaturgeschichte.* Leipzig, 1904.

Remedios, Mendes dos. "Camões," *Revista de Lingua Portuguesa,* Vol. I, No. 4. Rio de Janeiro, 1928.

———. *Historia de Literatura Portuguesa.* Sixth ed. Coimbra, 1930.

Remy. *Goa, Rome of the Orient.* London, 1957.

Renault, Gilbert. *Caravelles du Christ.* Paris, 1956.

Resende, Garcia de. *Cancioneiro Geral.* Reproduction of the original by Archer Huntington. New York, 1904.

Ribeiro, Aquilino. *Camões, Camilo, Eça e Alguns Mais.* Lisboa, 1949.

———. *"Edição Princeps" dos "Lusíadas."* Lisboa, n.d.

———. *Luis de Camões.* Third ed. 2 vols. Lisboa, n.d.

Richter, Elise. "Luis de Camões," *Germanisch-Romanische Monatschrift,* Vol. XIII. Heidelberg, 1925.

Roddis, Louis H. *James Lind: Founder of Nautical Medicine.* New York, 1950.

Rodrigues, Bernardo. *Anais de Arzila.* Ed. by David Lopes. 2 vols. Lisboa, 1915.

Rodrigues, José Maria. *Camões e a Infanta D. Maria,* Coimbra, 1910. See also Palmer, Katharine Ward.

———. "Comentario da Carta Inedita," *Lusitania,* Fasciculo Camoniano, V and VI. Lisboa, 1925.

―――. "D. Carolina Michaelis e os Estudos Camonianos," *Lusitania,* Fasciculo X. Lisboa, 1927.

―――. "Fontes dos Lusíadas," *O Instituto,* Vol. LI–LX. Coimbra, 1904–13.

―――. *A Tese da Infanta nas Liricas de Camões.* Coimbra, 1933.

Rosenkrantz, K. *Handbuch Einer Allgemeinen Geschichte der Poesie.* Dritte Theil. Halle, 1833.

Rossi, Giuseppe Carlo. *Storia della Letteratura Portoghese.* Firenze, 1953.

Rozmital, Leo of. *The Travels of Leo of Rozmital.* Cambridge, 1957.

Ruegg, August. *Luis de Camões und Portugals Glanzzeit im Spiegel Seines Nationalepos.* Basel, 1925.

Ruge, Sophus. *Geschichte des Zeitalters der Endeckungen.* Berlin, 1881.

Ruiz, Antonio Maldonado. *Cervantes, Su Vida y Sus Obras.* Barcelona, 1947.

Sá de Miranda, Francisco. *Obras Primas.* Lisboa, 1889.

Sabugosa, Conde de. *Donas de Tempos Idos.* Third ed. Lisboa, n.d.

Saint-Victor, G. de. *Portugal.* Paris, n.d.

Salcado, Antonio, Jr. "Camões e a Visão Humanistica de Geografia da Europa Quinhentos," *Ocidente,* Vol. XXXVI, No. 143. Lisboa, 1949.

Salisbury, W. A. *Portugal and Its People.* London, 1893.

Salter, Cedric. *Introducing Portugal.* London, 1956.

Sampaio, Albino Forjaz de (ed.). *Historia da Literatura Portuguesa.* 4 vols. Lisboa, n.d.

Sanceau, Elaine. *D. João de Castro.* Porto, 1946.

Sandberg, Graham. "A Recent Visit to Goa," *Murray's Magazine,* Vol. VIII. London, 1890.

Santarem, Visconde de. *Opusculos e Esparsos.* Vol. II. Lisboa, 1910.

Santiago y Gomez, José de. *Historia de Vigo y Su Comarca.* Madrid, 1896.

Santos, Luis Reis. *Monumentos do Portugal.* Lisboa, 1940.

Santos, Reynaldo. *O Mosteiro de Belem.* Porto, 1930.

Sarmento, Zeferino. *Santarem.* Porto, 1931.

Sassetti, Filippo. "Lettere a Francisco I de Medici." In Angelo de Gubernatis, *Storia dei Viaggiatori Italiani nelle Indie Orientali.*

Schäfer, Heinrich. *Geschichte von Portugal*. 5 vols. Hamburg, 1836.

———. *Histoire de Portugal*. Paris, 1945.

Schmidt, Augusto Frederico. "Discurso sobre Camões." In *Arquivo Camoniano*.

Schmidt, Max G. *Geschichte des Welthandels*. Leipzig, 1912.

Schneider, Reinhold. *Das Leiden des Camões*. Hellerau, 1930.

Schuchhardt, Hugo. "Camoens." In *Romanisches und Keltisches*. Berlin, 1886.

Schwerin, H. H. von. *Store Opdagelrejser*. N.p., 1905.

Selfridge, H. Gordon. *The Romance of Commerce*. Second ed. London, 1923.

Septenville, Édouard de. *Découvertes et Conquêtes du Portugal dans Les Deux Mondes*. Paris, 1863.

Seshadri, P. "Camoens and His Epic of India." In *Dr. S. Krishnaswami Aiyangan Commemorative Volume*. Madras, 1936.

Shepherd, William R. *Historical Atlas*. Sixth ed. New York, 1927.

Silva, L. R. Rebello da. *Invasion et Occupation du Royaume de Portugal*. Vol. I. Paris, 1864.

Silva, Luciano Pereira da. "Concepção Cosmologica nos Lusíadas," *Lusitania*, Fasciculo Camoniano, V and VI. Lisboa, 1925.

Silva, Pereira da. *A Astronomia dos Lusíadas*. Lisboa, 1918.

Silveira, Francisco Rodrigues. *Mémorias de um Soldado da India*. Ed. by A. de S. S. Costa Lobo. Lisboa, 1877.

Silveira, Joaquim da. "Sobre o Nome 'Camões,'" *Biblos*, Vol. III. Coimbra, 1927.

Sismondi, J. C. L. Simon de. *De la Littérature du Midi de l'Europe*. Vol. IV. Paris, 1813.

———. *Historical View of the Literature of Southern Europe*. 2 vols. London, 1903.

Sociedade Nacional Camoneana. *Annuario*. Vol. I. Porto, 1881.

Sousa, Antonio Sercio de. *Ensaios*. Vol. IV. Lisboa, 1934.

Sousa, Fr. Luis de *Anais de D. João III*. 2 vols. Lisboa, 1938.

Sousa, Luiz de. *Portugais et l'Afrique du Nord de 1521 à 1552*. French trans. by Robert Picard. Lisbonne, 1940.

Southey, Robert. Review of John Adamson. *Memoirs of the Life and*

Writings of Luis de Camoens, Quarterly Review, Vol. XXVII. London, 1822.

Staunton, Sir George. *An Authentic Account of an Embassy . . . to China.* 2 vols. (with atlas). London, 1797.

Stephens, H. Morse. *Albuquerque.* Oxford, 1892.

———. *Portugal.* New York and London, 1903.

Stevens, Thomas. "Letter from Goa." In Richard Hakluyt. *Principal Navigations . . . of the English Nation,* Vol. VI.

Storck, Wilhelm. *Hundert Altportugiesische Lieder.* Paderborn, 1885.

———. *Luis de Camoens Buch der Lieder und Briefe.* 5 vols. Paderborn, 1880.

———. *Luis de Camoens Leben.* Paderborn, 1890.

———. *Vida e Obras de Luis de Camões, Primeira Parte.* Portuguese trans. by Carolina Michaelis de Vasconcellos. Lisboa, 1897.

Strangford, Lord Viscount. *Poems from the Portuguese of Luis de Camoens.* Fourth ed. London, 1805.

Suttner-Erenwin, Hermann von. *Camões, Ein Philosophischer Dichter.* Wien, 1883.

Talegre, Mar. *Tres Poetas Europeus.* Lisboa, 1947.

Tavernier, Jean-Baptiste. *Travels in India.* English trans. by V. Ball. Second ed. 2 vols. Oxford, 1925.

Taylor, E. G. R. *The Haven-finding Art.* London, 1956.

Teixeira, Augusto Garcez. *Tomar.* Porto, 1929.

Teixeira, F. A. Garcez. *Familia Camões em Tomar.* Lisboa, 1925.

Teixeira, Pedro. *The Travels of Pedro Teixeira.* London, 1902.

Theal, George M. *The Beginning of South African History.* Cape Town, 1902.

Thomas, Henry. "English Translations of Portuguese Books before 1640," *The Library,* Fourth Series, Vol. VII. Oxford, 1927.

———. *Spanish and Portuguese Romances of Chivalry.* Cambridge, 1920.

Thomson, John Stuart. *The Chinese.* Indianapolis, 1909.

Thornton, Philip. *The Voice of Atlas.* London, 1936.

Torre Negra, Henrique Manuel da. *Maior Êrro de Todas as Edições de os Lusíadas.* Lisboa, 1938.

Towle, George M. *The Voyages and Adventures of Vasco da Gama.* Boston and New York, 1898.

Trend, J. B. *The Civilization of Spain.* London, 1944.

——. *The Language and History of Spain.* London, 1953.

T'Serstevens, A. *L'Itineraire Portugais.* Paris, 1940.

Tunis, Edwin. *Weapons.* Cleveland and New York, 1954.

Valle, Pietro della. *The Travels of Pietro della Valle in India.* 2 vols. London, 1892.

Varende, Jean de la. *La Navigation Sentimentale.* Paris, 1952.

Varthema, Ludovico di. *Itinerario.* Milano, 1929.

——. *The Itinerary of Ludovico di Varthema.* English trans. by John Winter Jones. London, 1928.

Vasconcellos, Carolina Michaelis de. *Biblioteca Romanica.* Vol. X, *Os Lusíadas.*

——. *O Cancioneiro do Padre Pedro Ribeiro.* Coimbra, 1924.

——. *Cancionciro de Fernandes Tomas.* Coimbra, 1922.

——. *Infanta D. Maria de Portugal (1521–1577).* Porto, 1902.

——. *Lições de Filologia Portuguesa.* Vol. I. Lisboa, 1912.

——. "Luis de Camoens' Sämmtliche Gedichte," *Zeitschrift für Romanische Philologie.* Vol. VII. Wien, 1883.

——. "Neus zum Buche der Kamonianischen Elegien," *Zeitschrift für Romanische Philologie,* Vol. VII. Halle, 1883.

——. "Olhos Verdes—Olhos de Alegria," *Revista da Lingua Portuguesa.* Rio de Janeiro, 1920.

——. "O Texto das Rimas de Camões (Poesias Apocryphas, Attriboadas a Camões)," *Revista da Sociedade de Instrucção do Porto,* Vol. II. Porto, 1882.

——, and Theophile Braga. *Geschichte der Portugiesischen Litteratur.* In Gustav Gröber, *Grundriss der Romanische Philologie,* Vol. II, Part 2. Berlin and Leipzig, 1933–37.

Vasconcellos, J. Leite de. *Ditados Topicos em Portugal.*

Vasconcellos, Jorge Ferreira de *Comedia Eufrosina.* Ed. by Aubrey F. G. Bell. Lisboa, 1919.

Vasconcelos, Antonio. *Ines de Castro.* Second ed. Barcelos, 1933.

Vega, Garcilaso de la. "Eclogues in Classicos Castellanos." In *Madrid Obras.* Second ed. Madrid, 1924.

Velloso, Queiroz. *D. Sebastião, 1554–1578.* Third, ed. Lisboa, 1945.

Ventura, Augusta F. S. "Subsidios para o Estudo da Flora Camoniana," *Biblos,* Vols. XI–XII. Coimbra, 1935–36.

Ventura, Faria G. V. "Fruta da Ilha dos Amores," *Biblos.* Vol. XII. Coimbra, 1936.

Verissimo, José. *Estudos de Literatura Brazileira.* Vol. IV. Rio de Janeiro and Paris, 1904.

Vertot, L'Abbé. *Révolutions de Portugal.* Fourth ed. Paris, 1737

Vicente, Gil. "Farsa Chamada 'Auto da India.' " In *Obras Completas,* Vol. V. Lisboa, 1944.

———. *Obras Completas.* Ed. by Marques Braga. 6 vols. Lisboa, 1943–44.

Victor, D. Marcarida. *Camões e as Mulheres Portuguezas.* Lisboa, 1880.

Villier, Alan. *Monsoon Seas.* New York, 1952.

Vising, Johan. *Camões, Portugals Nationalskeld.* Stockholm, 1920.

Vossler, Karl (trans.). *Romanische Dichter.* Wien, 1936.

Waley, Adolf. *A Pageant of India.* London, 1927.

Walter, Felix. *Littérature Portugaise en Angleterre à l'Epoque Romantique.* Paris, 1927.

Watts, Henry Edward. *Miguel de Cervantes: His Life and Works.* London, 1895.

Welch, Galbraith. *North African Prelude.* New York, 1949.

Welch, Sidney R. *South Africa under King Manuel 1495–1521.* Cape Town, 1946.

Welsh, Doris Varner. *A Catalogue of Portuguese History and Literature.* Chicago, 1953.

West, George. "Luis de Camões e a Romantismo Inglez," *Revista Portuguesa.* Lisboa, 1939.

Wiffen, Jeremiah H. *The Works of Garcilaso de la Vega.* London, 1823.

Williams, Edwin B. *From Latin to Portuguese.*

Winstedt, Richard O. *Malaya.* London, 1923.

——— (ed.). *Malaya and Its History.* London, n.d.

Wordsworth, William. "Scorn Not the Sonnet." In *The Poems of Wordsworth.* Oxford, 1926.

Wright, Arnold, and Thomas H. Reid. *The Malay Peninsula*. London, 1913.

Xavier, Alberto. "Perfis Gloriosos dalguns Portugueses da Epoca dos Descobrimentos," *Boletim da Sociedade de Geográfica de Lisboa* (November, 1951). Lisboa, 1951.

Young, George. *Portugal: An Anthology*. Oxford, 1916.

———. *Portugal: An Historical Study*. Oxford, 1916.

Younger, William and Elizabeth. *Blue Moon in Portugal*. London, 1956.

Yule, Henry, and A. C. Burnell. *Hobson-Jobson*. New ed. by William Crooke. London, 1903.

Zain Ed Din. *Tohfut-ul-Mujahideen*. English trans. by Lt. M. J. Rowlandson. London, 1833.

Ziervogel, Evald. *Portugals Geographie*. Uppsala, 1757.

Zimmern, Halen. *The Hansa Towns*. New York and London, 1880.

Index of First Lines of Poems in Portuguese

Index of First Lines of Poems in English

Index of First Lines of Poems Quoted in the Text

First Lines in English

General Index

Adamastor: 174, 193
Adamson, John: vii
Adler, Elkan Nathan: 38n.6
Albuquerque, Affonso de: 9, 10, 91n.
Alcácer Kebir: 207ff.
Alcobaça: 23
Alecheluby: 108ff.
Alighieri, Dante: 37
Aljubarrota: 23n.
Almeida, D. Francisco de: 57; Camoëns' letter to, 212
Almeida-Garrett, João Baptista: 215, 217n.6
Amphytrion: 50
Aragon, D. Francisca de: 46ff.
Assassination: 66n.
Ataide, Catherine de: 35ff., 55, 81, 97, 106, 120, 139; death of, 150; tomb of, 184, 220
Atkinson, William C.: viii, 225
Aubertin, J. J.: 226
"Auto da India": 79n.
Aviz, House of: 294–95

Bab-el-Mandeb: 104
Bacon, Leonard: viii, 225
Barbara, Luisa: 155

335

The text of *Luis de Camoëns and the Epic of the Lusiads* has been set on the Linotype machine in eleven-point Granjon with two points of leading between the lines. Selected for use here because of its beauty and readability, Granjon was designed in 1924 by the Englishman George W. Jones, who derived it from the elegant sixteenth-century French Garamond.

University of Oklahoma Press

NORMAN